Mastering ... The Official Guide

Mastering ICQ™:
The Official Guide

by Peter Weverka

ICQ Press

Dulles, VA

Mastering ICQ™: The Official Guide

Published by

ICQ Press

An imprint of IDG Books Worldwide, Inc.

An International Data Group Company

919 E. Hillsdale Blvd., Suite 300

Foster City, CA 94404

www.icq.com (ICQ Web site)

Library of Congress Control Number: 00-104777

ISBN: 0-7645-3519-6

Printed in the United States of America

10 9 8 7 6 5 4 3 2 1

1B/QY/RS/QQ/IN

Distributed in the United States by IDG Books Worldwide, Inc. and ICQ Inc.

For general information on IDG Books Worldwide's books in the U.S., please call our Consumer Customer Service department at 800-762-2974. For reseller information, including discounts and premium sales, please call our Reseller Customer Service department at 800-434-3422.

is a trademark of ICQ Inc.

is a registered trademark or trademark under exclusive license to IDG Books Worldwide, Inc. from International Data Group, Inc. in the United States and/or other countries.

Welcome to ICQ Press™

Mastering ICQ: The Official Guide is intended to you how to get the most out of ICQ's revolutionary and user-friendly software program. The guide shows you how to get connected and stay connected with your friends and colleagues wherever they may be. No longer will you search in vain on the Net. ICQ does the searching for you, alerting you in real time when they log on. With ICQ, you can chat, send messages, files and URL's, play games, or just hang out with your fellow 'Netters' while still surfing the Net.

ICQ Press is an exciting partnership between two companies at the forefront of the knowledge and communications revolution – ICQ and IDG Books Worldwide. ICQ is the developer of revolutionary Internet communications software, and IDG Books excels at helping people understand technology.

To meet our high-quality standards, all books are authored by experts with the full participation and exhaustive review of ICQ's own development, technical, managerial, and marketing staff. Together, ICQ and IDG Books have created Mastering ICQ to help you in every aspect of your online life.

We hope you enjoy reading Mastering ICQ: The Official Guide and find it useful. We welcome your feedback at icqbook@icq. com, so we can keep providing information the way you want it.

ICQ Press

Dedication

For Tenzig Norgay

Acknowledgments

This book owes a lot to many hard-working individuals. I would like to thank the acquisitions editors at IDG Books Worldwide, Inc. for giving me the opportunity to write it.

The heroes and heroines of the book creation process, with patience and forbearance, helped me keep abreast of changes to the ICQ software to make sure that this book is entirely up-to-date and accurate.

I would like to thank the editors at the offices of IDG in Indianapolis and the ICQ team in Israel who gave their all to making sure that the instructions in this book are indeed correct.

Finally, I would like to thank my family for putting up with the late nights and the occasional lost weekend.

Contents at a Glance

Table of Contents

Introduction

This book is for anyone who wants to get the most out of ICQ — or anyone who simply wants to learn how to use ICQ better. It is for ICQ users who want to get to the heart of ICQ and its many excellent features without having to spend a lot of time doing it.

This book covers all areas of ICQ. By reading this book, you will discover how to make the best use of a feature. Topics are presented in such a way that you can look up instructions in a hurry. You will find many numbered lists and labeled figures so you can find out exactly how to do a task or solve a problem. And this book is loaded with cross-references so you know where to go if one part of the book doesn't completely explain how to do a task or you need background information to undertake something new.

What You Need to Run ICQ

To run ICQ, you need to download the ICQ software from the Internet, install it on your computer, and register with ICQ (see Appendix A). The ICQ software occupies about 25 megabytes of disk space, so you need that much free space on your computer to run ICQ.

You also need an account with an Internet Service Provider (ISP). ICQ is the finest Internet tool that I know of, but it is no substitute for subscribing to an ISP. You need an ISP subscription to connect to the Internet.

ICQ runs on all popular operating systems. Versions of ICQ are available for Windows 95/98/2000/NT, Windows CE, PowerPC, and the Macintosh. This book focuses on the version of ICQ for Windows 95/98/2000/NT. However, the instructions that are presented in this book serve for running ICQ under other operating systems and platforms as well.

How This Book Is Organized

This book is organized to help you find the instructions you need quickly. Your best bet for finding instructions is to turn to the index or the table of contents, but you are also invited to turn the pages at leisure. Find a chapter whose topic interests you and thumb through its pages — you will discover tips and tricks you didn't know before.

This book is divided into four parts. What's more, two appendixes and a glossary appear at the back of the book to help you install and register ICQ, find your way around the PeopleSpace Directory, and learn ICQ terminology.

Part I: Getting to Know ICQ

Part I introduces you to ICQ and briefly explains the many things you can do with the program. It describes basic tasks such as starting and quitting the program and offers instructions for managing the ICQ window so you can use ICQ comfortably. You learn how to send different events to and receive different events from other ICQ users, as well as what "follow-me" phoning is and how to offer your photograph to other ICQ users.

Part II: Reaching Out to Others in ICQ

Part II starts by explaining everything you need to know about the Contact List, including how to manage names on the list and authorize your name for other people's Contact Lists. You also learn about chatting — how to handle the Chat window, find people to chat with, and chat on the IrCQ-Net. You will also find detailed instructions for making new friends in ICQ in the White Pages, ActiveLists, User Lists, Interest Groups, the Message Boards, and public chat rooms. Part II also describes all the ICQ e-mailing features; both the e-mailing features you get as an ICQ user, and ICQmail, the private e-mail service to which all ICQ users are entitled to subscribe for free.

Part III: Getting More Out of ICQ

Part III explains how to customize ICQ. You learn how to make special considerations for people on your Contact List — how to ignore them or broadcast your online status to one person, for example. You find out how to maintain your privacy in ICQ and still reach into every corner of the network. Part III also describes how to be a good citizen of the ICQ community by, for example, entering a thorough profile in the White Pages, creating your own Interest Group, and inviting others to join. You also discover how to use the ICQ Message Archive.

Part IV: Branching Out from ICQ

Part IV explains how to use ICQ in conjunction with the Internet and the World Wide Web. You discover ICQ Surf, a means of surfing the Internet along with other ICQ users, how to search the Internet without leaving ICQ, and how to bookmark Web pages in ICQ. You learn how to create and maintain your ICQ homepage and 2way Web Communication Page. You also learn how to find and connect with others in order to use telephony applications or play online games.

Conventions Used in This Book

To help you understand all the instructions in this book, I adopted a few simple conventions.

To show you how to give commands, I use the ⇨ symbol. For example, you can click the ICQ button and choose Add/Invite Users⇨ICQ White Pages to search the ICQ White Pages. The ⇨ is just a shorthand method of saying "Choose Add/Invite Users and then choose ICQ White Pages from the submenu that appears."

Where you see boldface letters in this book, it means to type the letters. For example, "Type **Let's make friends** in the text box" means to do exactly that: Type **Let's make friends**.

Every chapter in this book begins with a "Quick Look," a handful of brief descriptions that tell what you can learn in the chapter. Then you find a "chapter itinerary" that lists the main headings. At the end of each chapter is a "Coming Up Next" section that explains what the following chapter is all about.

You will find these icons and the accompanying headings in the margin:

Tips present a bit of advice that will make you a better user of ICQ.

Notes provide background or technical information of some kind.

Definitions define technical or ICQ terms.

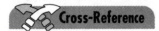

Cross-references tell you where in the book to turn to get further instruction.

Cautions tell you when and how to make a critical choice or decision.

Part

I

Getting to Know ICQ

Chapter

1

Introducing ICQ

Quick Look

Taking a Quick Look at ICQ
page 8
ICQ is a free program that offers ways to reach out to other people — your family, friends, and the new friends you will make on ICQ. As you make new friends in ICQ, you put their names on your Contact List. That way, you can tell which of your friends is connected to ICQ and be able to get in touch with your friends quickly.

Surveying the Different ICQ Features
page 10
In ICQ, you can chat, keep in touch with others in various ways, find new friends, send and receive events, search the Internet, cruise the Internet, and take advantage of different Web services.

Distinguishing between ICQ and ICQ.com
page 15
ICQ maintains a Web site called ICQ.com. The site is complimentary to ICQ. It offers many of the same commands as ICQ and also gives you the chance to keep in touch with others and use the Internet in exciting ways.

Chapter 1

Introducing ICQ

This short chapter gets you started with ICQ. It tells you what ICQ is and briefly describes all the different things you can do in ICQ. This chapter also explains the difference between ICQ and ICQ.com, the complementary Web site that ICQ maintains on the Internet.

What Is ICQ ("I Seek You")?

ICQ ("I Seek You") is the most comprehensive Internet tool that you will find anywhere — and it's free. ICQ is a community of friends, a way to stay in touch with your friends and family, a way to reach out to other people, a way to search the Internet, and most of all, a way to communicate easily and speedily with others.

To use ICQ, you download the program, install it, and register your name (see Appendix A). After you register, you can test the waters and explore the myriad features that are available in ICQ. Not only that, but you can find out who you know that is already an ICQ user (see Chapter 4). You will be pleasantly surprised to find out how many of your friends, family members, and associates already use ICQ.

When you find someone with whom you want to stay in touch, enter his or her name on your Contact List (see Chapters 4 and 5). The Contact List represents your roster of friends in ICQ. Then, by clicking a name on your Contact List and choosing an option from the pop-up menu, you can communicate with your friends in many different ways, as shown in Figure 1-1.

Note

ICQ is not a substitute for having an Internet Service Provider (ISP). You have to subscribe to an ISP to run ICQ.

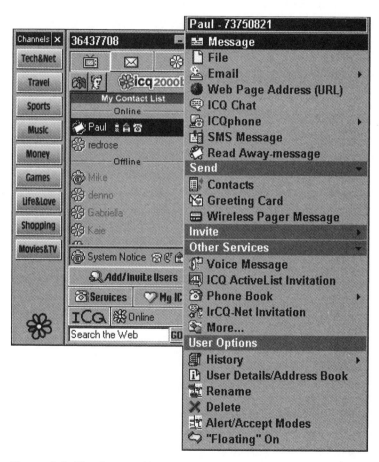

Figure 1-1. The Contact List is your roster of friends in ICQ.

Your name, meanwhile, appears on other peoples' Contact Lists when other people enter it there. They can tell when you are online and connected to ICQ (see Chapters 2 and 3). And when they see that you are connected, they can communicate with you.

The Many Things You Can Do in ICQ

Try clicking the ICQ button, the Services button, the My ICQ button, the Add/Invite Users button, and the Status button in the ICQ window to get an idea of all the different commands you can choose in ICQ.

Explore ICQ for as little as an hour or two, and you soon discover that ICQ is rich with possibilities. This book explores every nook and cranny of ICQ to help you get the most out of the program. Meanwhile, read on to get a taste of the many things you can do in ICQ.

Sending and Receiving Events

ICQ offers many different ways for ICQ users to communicate — by instant-message, by chatting, and by sending Web page addresses, for example. ICQ uses the term *event* to describe the items that users send to and receive from one another. Users can send and receive these events:

▼ **Instant messages:** A message similar to an e-mail message — except it arrives faster because you don't have to check for it. You don't have to spend any time addressing instant messages. And you can view the messages you've exchanged with someone right on the screen. Exchanging instant messages is like having a conversation with someone. (See Chapter 3.)

▼ **Files:** A data file. (See Chapter 3.)

▼ **E-mail:** An e-mail message received from or sent to a source outside ICQ. (See Chapter 8.)

▼ **Web page addresses (URLs):** A message listing a Web page worth visiting. The recipient can click a button in the Incoming Web Page Address dialog box to go straight to the Web page. You can book-mark Web page addresses as well. (See Chapter 13.)

▼ **Chats:** An ongoing chat, or exchange of messages. (See Chapter 6.)

▼ **ICQphone calls:** Telephone calls that travel over the Internet sidetrack the regular phone network and are therefore cheaper to make. As long as a microphone and sound card are installed on your computer, you can have real conversations with others in your own voice. (See Chapter 15.)

▼ **SMS messages:** SMS (short messaging service) text messages that you can send to and receive from cellular phone users. (See Chapter 15.)

▼ **Greeting cards:** A colorful message that you create with the Greeting Card plug-in, an ICQ program for creating greeting cards. (See Chapter 3.)

▼ **Wireless pager messages**: Wireless pager messages that you can send to wireless pager users. (See Chapter 15.)

▼ **Voice-messages:** A recorded voice file. (See Chapter 15.)

▼ **Birthday greetings:** A message wishing someone happy birthday. (See Chapter 11.)

▼ **Invitations to voice-chat, video-conference, or play an online game:** ICQ offers several useful commands for finding and connecting with others in order to use telephony applications or play online games. (See Chapter 15.)

ICQ keeps records of events you send to and receive from others in case you want to review them (see Chapter 3). If you download the Message Archive (see Chapter 12), you can play back chats and review events in other ways.

Finding and Keeping in Touch with Friends, Family, and Associates

As I mention earlier in this chapter, ICQ users know when their friends are online and connected to the ICQ network — they can tell by glancing at their Contact Lists. ICQ offers many ways to find (and stay in touch with) your friends:

▼ **Add/Invite Users command:** All you have to do is click the Add/Invite Users button to search the ICQ database for your friends, family members, and associates (see Chapter 4). After you have found someone you know, you can add him or her to your Contact List.

▼ **Invitations to join ICQ:** ICQ offers a bunch of different commands for inviting others to join and letting others know how to reach you in ICQ. (See Chapter 4.)

▼ **Phone Book:** A feature that permits you to place the telephone icon next to your name on others' Contact Lists when you are available for telephone calls. When others see the icon, they can click your name on their Contact Lists, choose User Details/ Address Book, and find out not only what your phone numbers are, but which number to call to reach you. (See Chapter 3.)

▼ **ActiveLists:** An *ActiveList* is a collection of people who share an interest in the same topic. ICQ users create and maintain ActiveLists. Being the member of an ActiveList puts you in touch with people who share your interests whenever you connect to ICQ. After you join an ActiveList, you can see its members' names on your Contact List. (See Chapter 7.)

▼ **Interest groups and user lists:** These are two more ways that ICQ users can associate with one another and find people who share their interests. (See Chapter 7.)

▼ **Message boards and the Chat Request page:** ICQ offers message boards where users can post or reply to messages. On the Chat Request page, users can engage others in a chat or post a topic they would like to chat about. (See Chapter 7.)

E-Mailing

ICQ may be integrated with your own e-mail account to send and check for e-mail via ICQ, and ICQ provides a free Web-based e-mail account for users, which may be used in conjunction with the ICQ program or independently (see Chapter 8). Every ICQ user can receive e-mail messages that were sent from private e-mail accounts such as AOL and Yahoo!. And ICQ users can send e-mail to addresses outside the ICQ network as well. You can also configure ICQ so that the program alerts you when e-mail has arrived in your private e-mail accounts.

If you sign up for ICQmail, the free ICQ e-mail service, you get a private account for sending and receiving e-mail. Not only that, but you can keep an address book in your private ICQmail account. You don't even have to be connected to ICQ to send e-mail from or receive e-mail in your ICQmail account. (See Chapter 8.)

Searching and Cruising the Internet

By clicking a button on the Channels bar, you can visit an area of the Web, maintained by ICQ, where you can get information and insights that pertain to different topics. (See Chapter 13.)

ICQ offers an exciting way to search the Internet alongside other ICQ users — ICQ Surf (see Chapter 13). While you are visiting the same Web page or domain as other ICQ surfers, you can chat with them. ICQ Surf is also a neat way to find out where other ICQ users are going on the Internet, as shown in Figure 1-2.

What's more, you can search the Internet without leaving ICQ, because ICQ offers search engines and search services for conducting Internet searches (see Chapter 13). You can even search the Internet for people you know and add their names to your Contact List. (See Chapter 4.)

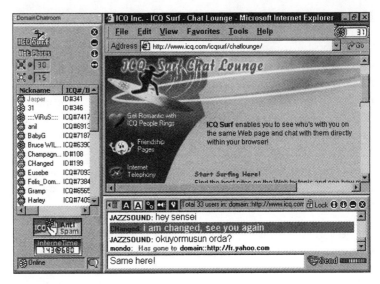

Figure 1-2. In ICQ Surf, you can tell where other ICQ users are surfing.

Promoting Your "Presence" on the Web

Every ICQ user gets or can take advantage of the following Web services:

> ▼ **Personal Communication Center:** Every ICQ user gets a Personal Communication Center, a page on the Web that others can visit (click the Services button and choose My Communication Center on the pop-up menu to visit yours). From the Personal Communication Center, others can contact you, learn more about you, chat with you, or send you a message. (See Chapter 14.)

> ▼ **Web Front:** This is a Web site hosted from your computer that others can visit while you are connected to ICQ. Other ICQ users download your Web Front right from your computer. ICQ offers tools for constructing a Web Front. (See Chapter 14.)

> ▼ **ICQ homepage:** ICQ members can post a Web page, called the ICQ homepage, on the Internet for free. ICQ offers templates and other tools for creating the ICQ homepage. (See Chapter 14.)

Maintaining Your Privacy

The makers of ICQ want you to be able to reach into
every corner of the network and still maintain your privacy.
In that spirit, ICQ offers many techniques for safeguarding
your privacy. For example, you can clamp a password on
ICQ, ignore certain ICQ users, and decide on a person-by-
person basis who gets to put your name on their Contact
Lists. (See Chapter 10.)

Caution

ICQ cannot completely guarantee any user's
privacy. To some degree,
all Internet applications
involve a risk to privacy.

ICQ and ICQ.com

ICQ maintains a Web site called ICQ.com at this address:
www.icq.com. The homepage of the ICQ Web site is
shown in Figure 1-3. Think of this Web site as a community
center for ICQ users. Visit there occasionally to discover
new ICQ features. Click on a few hyperlinks and see what
happens. Something good is always cooking at ICQ.com.

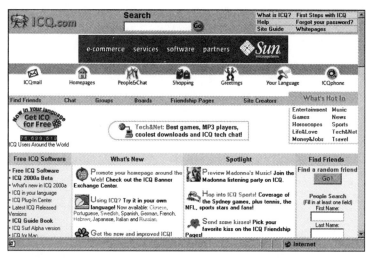

Figure 1-3. The ICQ Web site.

Coming Up Next

In the next chapter, you get up and running with ICQ.
You discover how to start and disconnect from ICQ, how
to manage the ICQ window to make the time you spend
in ICQ more comfortable, and how to switch between
Simple and Advanced mode so you can use ICQ to the
hilt. The chapter also explains how to choose your status
mode so that other ICQ users know whether you want to
receive events or not be disturbed.

Chapter

2

Finding Your Way Around ICQ

Quick Look

Chapter 2

Finding Your Way Around ICQ

In this chapter, you really get going with ICQ. You learn how to start the program, find your way around the ICQ window, and declare your online status to other ICQ users so they know whether you are up for a chat or message exchange. You also discover the difference between Simple and Advanced mode and explore the different ways to shut down ICQ.

Starting ICQ

ICQ is different from other computer programs in that it is designed to start automatically whenever you connect to the Internet. When you go online, ICQ starts, and all is well. However, not everyone wants ICQ to start automatically. Casual users of ICQ, the kind of people who use the program now and then to trade messages with their friends, prefer to start ICQ on their own. Read on to discover the conventional way of starting ICQ and strategies for starting ICQ automatically or manually.

Starting ICQ the Conventional Way

No matter what you are doing on your computer, you can always start ICQ the conventional way by following these steps:

1. Click the Start button.

2. Choose Programs⇨Icq⇨ICQ, as shown in Figure 2-1.

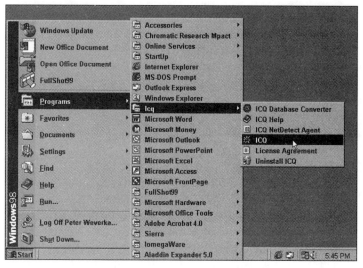

Figure 2-1. Starting ICQ the conventional way.

As soon as you start ICQ, you hear a foghorn (if your computer plays sounds), and the ICQ Welcome box appears. The box is designed to close in 60 seconds, but if the announcement arouses your interest, click the box to make it stay on-screen. The ICQ Welcome dialog box usually offers news from ICQ and descriptions of ICQ features.

Appendix A explains how to install the ICQ software and register with ICQ. You must register before you can run ICQ.

A quick way to start ICQ is to double-click the NetDetect Agent icon in the desktop tray, which is usually found in the lower-right corner of your computer screen. Later in this chapter, "Deciding How *You* Want to Start ICQ" describes the NetDetect Agent icon.

Sometimes you can't connect to ICQ because the network is down. To find out if the network is down, you can visit the ICQ Network Status Web page at this address: web.icq.com/ status.

2

Finding Your Way Around ICQ

Dealing with the ICQ Welcome Box

If you prefer not to see the ICQ Welcome box each time you start ICQ, you can keep it from getting in the way when you start the program. Follow these steps:

1. Click the ICQ button and choose Preferences. You see the Owner Preferences For dialog box.

2. On the left side of the dialog box, click Miscellaneous.

3. Uncheck the Show ICQ Announcements check box and then click the Apply button.

Repeat these steps, but check the Show ICQ Announcements check box this time, if you decide you want to see the Welcome box after all.

As long as you are connected to ICQ, you can display the ICQ Welcome box anytime, anywhere, by clicking the ICQ button and choosing Help⇨ICQ Welcome.

Deciding How *You* Want to Start ICQ

Definition

Tray: The area on the right side of the Taskbar, to the left of the clock, where icons such as the Volume icon are found.

When you installed ICQ, you also installed the ICQ NetDetect Agent. The NetDetect Agent starts ICQ automatically whenever you go online. If you look in the tray in the lower-right corner of your screen next to the clock when ICQ is not running, you will see the NetDetect Agent icon, a small yellow box with the letters ICQ.

Enthusiasts of ICQ like the NetDetect Agent to start ICQ automatically. They want to be available to their ICQ friends every moment that they are connected to the Internet. Others, however, prefer to disable the NetDetect Agent and start ICQ on their own.

Here are the strategies for starting ICQ:

▼ **ICQ Starts Automatically and You Go to the ICQ Homepage:** When you go on the Internet, ICQ starts automatically and your browser opens the ICQ homepage (`web.icq.com`).

▼ **ICQ Starts Automatically:** When you go on the Internet, ICQ starts automatically, but the ICQ homepage does not appear.

▼ **NetDetect Agent Disabled, You Start ICQ Manually:** The NetDetect Agent is disabled. When you go on the Internet, ICQ doesn't start, and you don't go to the ICQ home page. To start ICQ, you do so manually by clicking the Start button and choosing Programs⇨Icq⇨ICQ.

Follow these steps to decide how *you* want to start ICQ:

1. Click the ICQ button.

2. Choose Preferences.

The Owner Preferences For dialog box opens.

3. Click Connections on the left side of the dialog box. You see the General tab, as shown in Figure 2-2.

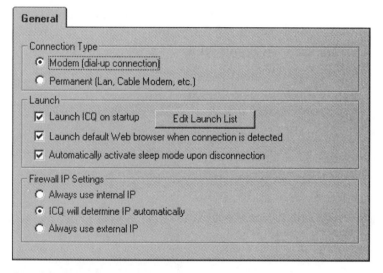

Figure 2-2. How ICQ starts depends on which Launch options you choose in the Owner Preferences For dialog box.

4. Under Launch, check or uncheck the Launch ICQ on Startup and Launch Default Web Browser When Connection Is Detected check boxes. What you check or don't check determines how ICQ starts:

▲ **ICQ Starts Automatically and You Go to the ICQ Homepage:** Make sure both check boxes are checked.

Note

The Launch ICQ on Startup and Launch Default Web Browser When Connection Is Detected options aren't available if you connect to the Internet through a network or cable modem.

    ▲ **ICQ Starts Automatically:** Check the Launch ICQ on Startup check box, but uncheck the Launch Default Web Browser When Connection Is Detected check box.

    ▲ **NetDetect Agent Disabled, You Start ICQ Manually:** Uncheck both check boxes.

5. Click the Apply button.

Switching Between Simple Mode and Advanced Mode

Figure 2-3 shows the ICQ window in Simple mode and Advanced mode. As the figure demonstrates, Advanced mode offers many more features and options. In fact, most of the instructions in this book are given on the premise that you are in Advanced mode.

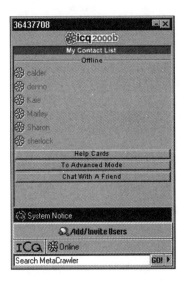 

Figure 2-3. The ICQ window in Simple mode (left) and Advanced mode (right).

The makers of ICQ want you to get off to a good start, so the ICQ window appears in Simple mode to begin with. But most people make the jump to Advanced mode sooner than later. Advanced mode isn't as advanced as all that. And many of the things that make ICQ fun are only available in Advanced mode.

Follow these instructions to switch from Simple mode to Advanced mode:

1. Either click the To Advanced Mode button (you will find it in the middle of the ICQ window) or click the ICQ button and choose To Advanced Mode on the pop-up menu. The Simple/Advanced Mode Selection dialog box appears.

2. Click the Switch to Advanced Mode button.

To go back to Simple mode, either click the To Simple Mode button (you'll find it where the To Advanced Mode button was) or click the ICQ button and then choose To Simple Mode. In the Simple/Advanced Mode Selection dialog box, click the Switch to Simple Mode button.

Managing the ICQ Window

In these days of inexpensive Internet connections and fast modems, people stay online for hours at a time. And many ICQ users stay connected to ICQ for long periods of time as well.

The trick to staying online and running ICQ for long periods of time is being able to handle the ICQ window. You want to be able to surf the Internet, run ICQ, word process, and work on a spreadsheet at the same time, right? This section explains how you can manage the ICQ window in such a way that you can be connected to ICQ and do a bunch of other things at once.

Minimizing and Maximizing the ICQ Window

The simplest way to take charge of the ICQ window is to minimize it. When the window gets in your way, click its Minimize button. You'll find it in the upper-right corner of the ICQ window next to the Close button (the X).

To maximize the ICQ window after you have minimized it, double-click the flower icon in the tray on the right side of the Windows Taskbar. ICQ isn't like other programs in that an ICQ button doesn't appear on the Taskbar. So instead of clicking a Taskbar button to maximize the ICQ window, you double-click the flower icon.

The ICQ window is like any other program window. To change its size, move the pointer over the perimeter of the window, wait until you see the double-headed arrow, and start dragging. As Figure 2-4 demonstrates, the outline of a window shows what size the window will be when you release the mouse button.

Minimizing the ICQ Window Automatically After a Certain Time Period

Here's a little trick: You can make the ICQ window disappear from the screen automatically after a certain amount of idle time has elapsed. This is a great way to get the ICQ window off the screen without lifting a finger when you are working in another program. The ICQ window just disappears on its own.

To minimize the ICQ window automatically after you have done nothing in ICQ for 30 seconds (the default value), follow these steps:

1. Click the ICQ button in Advanced mode.

2. Choose Contact List Options.

3. Check the Auto Hide command.

Is 30 seconds too short for you? You can change the idle-time interval by following these steps:

1. In Advanced mode, click the ICQ button.

2. Choose Preferences.

    You see the Owner Preferences For dialog box.

3. Click Contact List on the left side of the dialog box.

4. Under Auto Hide on the Options tab, check the Auto Hide Delay check box (if necessary) and enter a number in the Seconds box.

5. Click the Apply button.

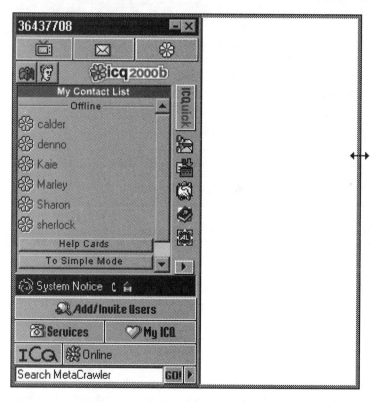

Figure 2-4. Drag a side of the ICQ window to change the window's size.

Fastening the ICQ Window to a Side of the Screen

Yet another way to handle the ICQ window is to fasten it to the left or right side of the screen, as shown in Figure 2-5. Normally the window floats, and it goes wherever you drag it. But you can follow these steps to attach it safely to a side of your computer screen:

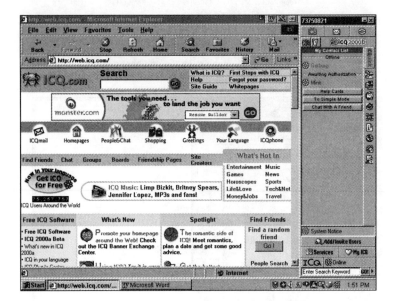

Figure 2-5. Attach the ICQ window to a side of the screen to get it out of the way.

1. In Advanced mode, click the ICQ button.

2. Choose Contact List Options⇨Contact List Position.

3. Choose Left or Right on the submenu.

To make the ICQ window float again, drag it by the title bar into the middle of the screen. Or else click the ICQ button and choose Contact List Options⇨Contact List Position⇨Floating.

Making the ICQ Window Appear When Someone Contacts You

Another way to handle the ICQ window is to minimize it, but make it leap on-screen whenever someone sends you a message, chat request, or other event. With this technique, the ICQ window springs to life on its own whenever one of your ICQ friends tries to reach you.

Follow these steps to make the ICQ window appear when someone contacts you:

1. In Advanced mode, click the ICQ button.

2. Choose Contact List Options⇨Contact List Popup.

For Experienced Users: Turning the ICQ Window into a Button

Experienced users of ICQ often work from the *flower button* instead of the ICQ window. As shown in Figure 2-6, you can click the flower button to see a short menu with essential ICQ commands. The button can be dragged to a corner of the screen while you are doing other work. When you want to see the ICQ window again, all you have to do is click the flower button and choose Open ICQ.

Follow these steps to work from the flower button:

1. In Advanced mode, click the ICQ button.

2. Choose Contact List Options⇨Status "Floating" On.

3. Click the Minimize button to minimize the ICQ window.

Now look closely on your computer screen for the flower button, a small button with the letters *ICQ* on it. You will find the button floating on its own somewhere. Drag the button to a corner of the screen where it won't be in the way.

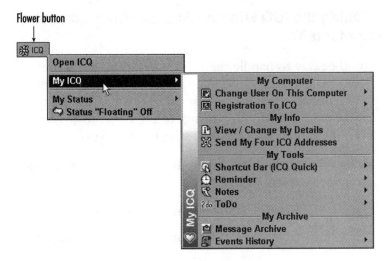

Figure 2-6. You can run ICQ from the flower button instead of the ICQ window.

When you want to work from the ICQ window again, do one of the following:

▼ Click the flower button and choose Open ICQ on the popup menu.

▼ Double-click the flower button.

When you want to remove the flower button from the screen, click it and choose Status "Floating" Off on the popup menu.

Enlarge the ICQ window if you don't see labels on some of the buttons. When the window has been shrunk, only icons appear on buttons.

Finding Your Way Around the ICQ Window

It takes a while to learn your way around ICQ. What are all those buttons for? Why, when you click a button, do you sometimes go to a page on the Internet? I explain what the different buttons in the ICQ window are for throughout this book. For now, all you need to know is the basics of the ICQ window. As you experiment with ICQ, you will soon learn your way around.

Read the descriptions in Table 2-1 to start getting ac-
quainted with the ICQ window.

Table 2-1. The ICQ Window

Button/Part of Window	Description
Channels*	Displays the Channels bar with its buttons that you can click to visit Web pages at icq.com (see Chapter 13)
ICQmail*	For sending e-mail to others by way of the ICQmail service (see Chapter 8)
Interests*	Opens the ICQ Interests box, which offers hyperlinks that you can click to access ICQ-related items
Online Mode*	Displays the names of people on the Contact List who are connected to ICQ (see Chapter 5)
Contact List Groups*	Organizes Contact List names by group instead one long list (see Chapter 5)
My Contact List	Lists the names of people on your Contact List (see Chapters 4 and 5)
How to Start	Accesses Help instructions
To Simple/Advanced Mode	Switches the ICQ window to Simple or Advanced mode (see this chapter)
Chat With A Friend	Allows you to chat at random with ICQ users (see Chapter 7)
Shortcut Bar (ICQuick)*	For performing ICQ tasks quickly (see Chapter 9)
System Notice	For reviewing messages from ICQ (see Chapter 3)

continued

Table 2-1. The ICQ Window *continued*

Button/Part of Window	Description
Add/Invite Users	For inviting others to join ICQ and learning about ICQ services (see Chapter 4)
Services*	For accessing commands that have to do with many ICQ services
My ICQ*	For accessing the Message Archive and registering with ICQ (see Chapter 12 and Appendix A)
ICQ	For changing system settings and searching for new friends on ICQ (see Chapters 4 and 10)
Flower	For changing your online status (see the next section in this chapter)
Search the Web	For searching the Internet (see Chapter 13)

* Only available in Advanced mode.

Handling the Message Boxes

The first time you choose most ICQ commands, you see message boxes like the ones shown here. The message boxes are designed to help you learn ICQ. After you have read one the first time, however, you probably get the idea and don't really need to be reminded about how a command works. If you want to prevent the message box from appearing again, click the Don't Show This Message Again check box and click OK.

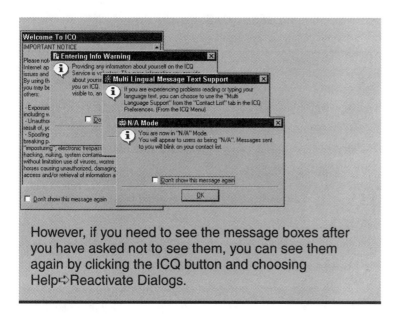

However, if you need to see the message boxes after you have asked not to see them, you can see them again by clicking the ICQ button and choosing Help⇨Reactivate Dialogs.

Broadcasting Your Online Status to Others

When you are connected to ICQ, people who have put your name on their Contact Lists see a status icon beside your name. You see status icons next to the names on your Contact List as well. These icons tell who is connected to ICQ and what peoples' *online status* is. By glancing at the icons, you can tell, for example, who is busy, is away from their desk, is available for instant–messaging, or does not want to be disturbed.

Table 2-2 describes the options on the Online Status popup menu for declaring your status to others. What others choose from this menu determines which icon appears beside their name on your Contact list.

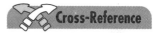

Cross-Reference

See Chapter 9 for more details about broadcasting your online status.

Tip

Want to know what your online status is? Glance at the status icon in the lower-right corner of the screen or at the flower button itself

Table 2-2. Online Status Options

Status Option	Status Icon	Description
🌸 Available/Connect	🌸 Sugar	You are connected to ICQ and available for exchanging events.
🌸 Free For Chat	🌸 Sugar	You are online and would like others to join you for a chat. Requests to join a chat are accepted automatically.*
🌸 Away	🌸 Sugar	You are temporarily away from the computer. (ICQ switches to Away status automatically after 20 minutes.)
🌸 N/A (Extended Away)	🌸 Sugar	You will be away from your desk for a long time (appears after 20 minutes of Away status).*
🌸 Occupied (Urgent Msgs)	🌸 Sugar	You are busy with something else but can be interrupted by messages marked "urgent."*
🌸 DND (Do not Disturb)	🌸 Sugar	You are connected to ICQ and want others to know it, but you don't want to be disturbed by incoming events.*
🌸 Privacy (Invisible)	🌸 Sugar	You are connected to ICQ, but others do not know it. On Contact Lists, it appears that you are not connected to ICQ.*
🌸 Offline/Disconnect	🌸 Sugar	You are not connected to ICQ.

Only available in Advanced mode.

Tip

You can also right-click the flower button in the tray, choose My Status, and choose a status option.

Follow these steps to change your online status:

1. Click the Status button.

2. Choose an Online Status option, as shown in Figure 2-7.

Refer to Table 2-2 for a description of the options.

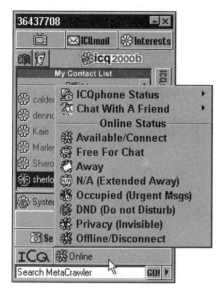

Figure 2-7. Changing your online status.

Disconnecting from ICQ

Closing ICQ is a bit like starting the program in that ICQ
offers more than one way to do it. How you close ICQ
depends on whether you want to shut down altogether or
remain connected but be invisible to other ICQ users.
Here are the three ways to quit using ICQ:

▼ **Quit ICQ altogether:** To close the ICQ window
    and sever your connection to the ICQ network as
    well, do either of the following:

      ▲ Click the Close button (the X) in the upper-
        right corner of the ICQ widow.

      ▲ Click the ICQ button and choose Shut
        Down.

▼ **Quit ICQ but standby to reconnect next time
    you go on the Internet:** Click the ICQ button
    and choose Standby. With this technique, the
    NetDetect Agent goes to work. The next time you
    connect to the Internet, ICQ starts automatically.

Earlier in this chapter, "Deciding How *You* Want to Start ICQ" describes the NetDetect Agent. (Only people who connect to the Internet by way of a modem can choose this option.)

▼ **Disconnect from ICQ but keep the window open:** Click the Status button and choose Offline/Disconnect on the popup menu.

Coming Up Next

The next chapter explains instant–messaging and a half–dozen other ways to communicate with people in ICQ. You'll find out how to trade data files and greeting cards with others. You'll also see how to make your photo or telephone number available to people whose names are on your Contact List.

Chapter
3
Communicating with Others over ICQ

Quick Look

No matter what you send or receive in ICQ, the procedures for sending and receiving are pretty much the same. You can send or forward events such as messages, files, and Web page addresses to more than one person at a time.

You can send and receive an instant-message almost immediately. ICQ offers two ways to trade instant messages — in Split Message mode or Single Message mode.

Greeting cards are colorful messages you can send to others. They are tailor-made for different occasions. When you send someone a greeting card, the recipient clicks a button and goes to a Web page where the card is on display.

Spreadsheets, graphic files, documents — any kind of file at all — can be exchanged over ICQ. The recipient is notified that the sender wants to send a file, at which point the recipient can download it.

With the "Follow Me" Phoning features, you can make a telephone icon appear next to your name on others' Contact Lists so they know to call you. You can tell others where to call you, and others can tell you where to call them. What's more, you can also send and receive telephone call requests.

You can make your photo available to others — and see someone else's photo as well. You decide who gets to see your photo on a person-by-person basis. Someone who has permission to see your photo can view it in the User Details dialog box.

Chapter 3

Communicating with Others over ICQ

IN THIS CHAPTER

▼ Understanding the basics of sending and receiving events

▼ Trading instant messages in ICQ

▼ Sending and receiving an ICQ greeting card

▼ Sending and receiving files

▼ Telling others where to get in touch with you with "Follow Me" Phoning commands

▼ View others' photos and letting others view yours

This chapter explains the basics of sending and receiving ICQ events. Read on to discover all the different ways you can communicate with others over ICQ, how to send one event to many different people, and how to forward events. You'll discover instant messaging, how to send files, and how to send a colorful greeting card to someone else. This chapter includes instructions for obtaining others' photos and for making your photo available to others. And you also learn how to alert everyone on your Contact List that you are accepting telephone calls, as well as request others to call you.

The Basics of Sending and Receiving

ICQ offers many different ways to communicate with other people, but no matter how you communicate, the procedures for sending and receiving are pretty much the same. Table 3-1 describes all the different ways to communicate in ICQ.

Table 3-1. Ways to Communicate in ICQ

Method	Icon	Description
Instant Message		Sending and receiving instant messages. See "Instant Messaging in ICQ" in this chapter.
File		Sending and receiving files such as documents and graphic files. See "Sending and Receiving Files" in this chapter.
E-mail		A notice that e-mail has arrived at your Internet Service Provider. See Chapter 8.
Web Page Address		Sending and receiving Web page addresses (URLs) so that others can visit Web pages. See Chapter 13.
Chat		Chatting with others in real time. See Chapter 6.
ICQphone		Sending and receiving requests to engage in PC-to-PC, PC-to-Phone, and Phone-to-PC telephone calls with ICQphone. See Chapter 15.
SMS Message		Exchanging short messages service (SMS) messages with cellular phone users. See Chapter 15.
Contacts		Sending names and ICQ numbers on your Contact List to others or receiving names or numbers on others' Contact Lists. See Chapter 5.
Greeting Card		Sending and receiving ICQ greeting cards, the colorful messages you can create with the Greeting Card plug-in. See "Sending and Receiving Greeting Cards" in this chapter.

continued

3

Communicating with
Others over ICQ

Table 3-1. Ways to Communicate in ICQ *continued*

Method	Icon	Description
Wireless Pager		Send messages to wireless Messagepager users. See Chapter 15.
Other		Sending or receiving a request to a video telephony application. See Chapter 15.
Other IP Phones/		Sending or receiving a request Voice Chat to chat with an IP phone or voice chat application. See Chapter 15.
Games		Sending or receiving a request to play a game. See Chapter 15.
Voice-Message		Sending or receiving voice-messages or WAV sound files. See Chapter 15.
ICQ ActiveList		Sending or receiving invitations Invitation to join ActiveLists, a list of people who share an interest in the same topic. See Chapter 7.
ActiveList Message		Sending or receiving a message to or from other members of an ActiveList that you belong to. See Chapter 7.
ActiveList URL		Sending or receiving a Web page address to or from other members of an ActiveList that you belong to. See Chapter 7.
Phone Call Request		Receiving a request to speak by telephone, or a dialog box for authorizing someone to see your phone numbers. See "'Follow Me Phoning: Fast Ways to Tell Others Where to Reach You" in this chapter.

Method	Icon	Description
Photo Request		Receiving a dialog box for authorizing someone to view your photo. See "Viewing Others' Photos (And Letting Them View Yours)""in this chapter.
IrCQ-Net Invitation		An invitation to engage in a chat on the IrCQ-Net, the network of chat rooms that users and non-users of ICQ can visit. See Chapter 6.
Email Express Message		Receiving notification via ICQ of incoming e-mail messages. See Chapter 8.
ICQmail Message		Receiving an e-mail message sent by ICQmail, the free e-mail service that all ICQ users can subscribe to and use. See Chapter 8.
WWPager Message		Receiving a message sent from someone who visited your Personal Communication Center and sent the message by way of your WWPager. See Chapter 14.
Birthday Message		Receiving "happy birthday" wishes. See Chapter 11.
Unknown Message		Receiving a request to communicate with an unknown telephony application. See Chapter 15.
System		Receiving a message from ICQ Announcement or a notice that your name has been placed on someone's Contact List. See "System Announcements and System Messages" in this chapter.
System Message		Receiving a request to place your name on someone's Contact List. See the "System Messages" sidebar in this chapter.

The following pages explain the details of sending and receiving events over ICQ. You can send events right away or postpone sending them. You can even send the same event to many different people at once. To start with, here are the basics of sending and receiving events:

▼ **Sending an event:** Click a name on your Contact List and make a choice from the pop-up menu.

▼ **Receiving an event:** You can tell when someone has sent you an event because ICQ alerts you with a sound, and a blinking icon appears in the desktop tray and on your Contact List next to the sender's name. (Table 3-1 explains what the icons mean.) To receive the event, either double-click the icon or click it and choose Receive from the pop-up menu that appears. You see a dialog box for fielding the event.

Receiving Events That Someone Sent to You

When someone sends you an event, an icon starts blinking in the tray and on your Contact List, as shown in Figure 3-1. (Earlier in this chapter, Table 3-1 explains the icons). The icon appears beside a Contact List name if the event was sent from someone whose name is on your Contact List. When someone whose name is *not* on the list sends you an event, the icon appears in the ICQ window under the Not In List heading.

To receive an event, do one of the following:

▼ Double-click the icon in the tray.

▼ Double-click the icon in the ICQ window.

▼ Click the icon and choose Receive from the pop-up menu that appears.

▼ Right-click the icon in the tray and choose Receive on the pop-up menu.

An Incoming dialog box appears on-screen so you can see what was sent you and perhaps reply.

To find out who sent you an event when the ICQ window is minimized, move the pointer over the icon in the tray. You see the sender's name along with a couple of words that describe what that person sent.

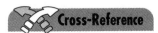

Chapter 2 explains how you can minimize ICQ and make the window open automatically whenever you receive an incoming event.

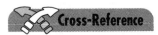

Chapter 9 explains how you can receive items right away, without having to negotiate an Incoming dialog box.

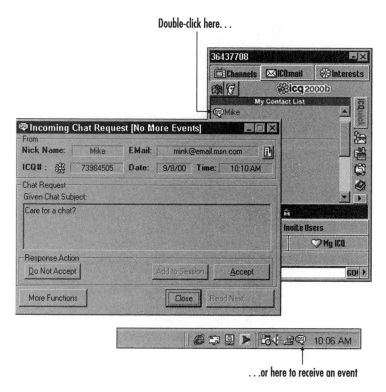

Double-click here. . .

. . .or here to receive an event

Figure 3-1. Receiving an event.

When more than one event from the same person arrives at the same time, the Incoming dialog box includes a Read Next button. The button tells you how many events have arrived. To dismiss the event in the dialog box and go straight to the next event that you received, click the Read Next button.

Sending Events to Others (Now or Later)

To send an event, click a name on the Contact List, select the kind of event you want to send from the pop-up menu that appears, fill in the relevant fields, and click the Send button, as shown in Figure 3-2. That's all there is to it if the recipient is online and so are you.

Note

To send some kinds of events, both parties must be online and connected to ICQ.

System Messages

You receive a system message under these circumstances:

▼ When your name is put on someone's Contact List (you receive a "You Were Added" message)

▼ When someone authorizes your request to be on a Contact List (you receive an "Authorization" Request Accepted message)

▼ When you receive a request from someone to put your name on his or her Contact List (you receive a Request for Authorization message)

▼ When ICQ sends you a message (you receive a System Request message)

ICQ keeps a copy of all the system messages you receive. To review a message, double-click the System Notice button (or click it and choose History and OutBox). You see the History of Events dialog box. Double-click a message to read it. By examining messages in the dialog box, you can tell who put your name on their Contact List.

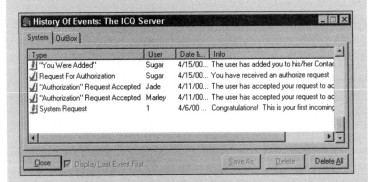

By the way, ICQ sends all its messages to users in the form of system messages. ICQ will never, for example, send you an e-mail that asks for your password or other personal details.

Things are not always so simple, however. Perhaps you
want to postpone sending an event. Maybe you're not connected to the Internet when you send an event. The following list describes the different situations that may crop
up when you send an event:

▼ **You're connected to ICQ and the other party
is too:** The event is sent right away.

▼ **You want to postpone sending the event:** Click
the More button in the lower-left corner of the
Send dialog box. As shown in Figure 3-3, a new set
of options appears on the bottom of the dialog box.
You can tell ICQ to deliver the event the next time
the recipient connects to ICQ or the next time he
or she connects to ICQ while you are online.
Perhaps you want to postpone sending the message
because you want to be connected to ICQ when
the other party replies.

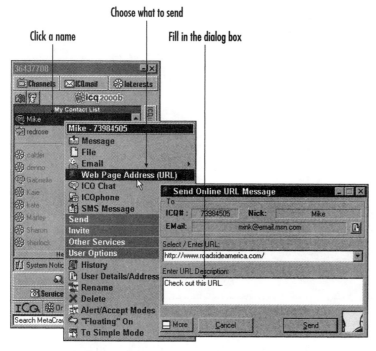

Figure 3-2. Click a name on the Contact List to send an event.

Click the More button and check the Email a Copy check box to send a copy of the event by e-mail. If the recipient's e-mail address is on file in the White Pages, the event is sent to that address. If the address isn't on file, you are given the chance to enter an e-mail address in the ICQ Email dialog box after you click the Send button.

The More options are only available in Single Message mode. If you are sending a message and you don't see the More button, click the Msg Mode button and switch to Single Message mode.

Click the More button and then check the Send Later, When Recipient(s) check box. Choose one of these options to send to tell ICQ when to deliver the event:

▲ **Offline or Online:** If you are not connected to ICQ, the message is sent the next time you connect. If you are connected but the recipient is not, the message is delivered when the recipient connects.

▲ **Online Only:** The event is delivered the next time the recipient connects to ICQ while you are also connected. With this technique, you can write a message when you're not connected to ICQ and send it when both you and the recipient are online.

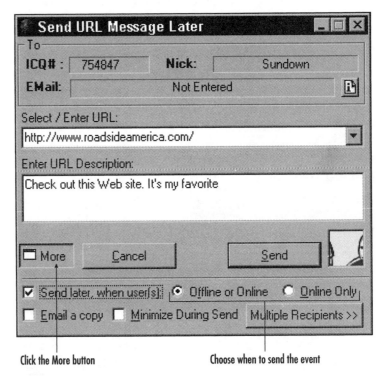

Click the More button   Choose when to send the event

Figure 3-3. Click the More button to postpone sending an event.

▼ **You're connected to ICQ but the other party isn't:** The event is delivered when the other party connects to ICQ.

▼ **You're not connected to ICQ:** The event is sent the next time you connect to ICQ. It is delivered, after that, when the other party connects to ICQ.

Events that you postponed sending or that can't be sent because you are not connected to ICQ are kept in the OutBox. Suppose you change your mind about sending an event or you want to review the outgoing events. Follow these steps to open the OutBox, review outgoing events, and perhaps delete one:

1. Either double-click the System Notice button or click it and choose History and OutBox on the pop-up menu. The History of Events dialog box appears.

2. Click the OutBox tab. You see a list of outgoing events.

3. Review, delete, or send the events:

▲ **Review an event:** Double-click an event to open and be able to examine it in a dialog box.

▲ **Delete an event:** Click an event to select it and then click the Delete button. You can click the Delete All button to delete all the events in the OutBox.

▲ **Send events you have postponed sending:** Click the Send Messages Now button.

4. Click the Close button.

3

Communicating with
Others over ICQ

Reviewing Events You Sent and Received

ICQ keeps copies of events you send and receive. The message you sent or received last week can be opened and read again. The URL message whose Web address you forgot to bookmark can be retrieved and bookmarked. Follow these steps to review and reopen events you sent and received:

1. Starting in Advanced mode, click the name of the person on your Contact List to whom you sent or from whom you received the event.

2. Choose History⇨View Messages History. You see the History Events Of dialog box.

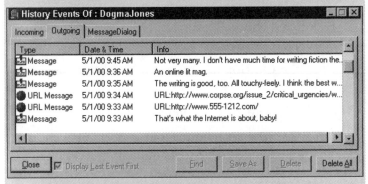

3. Click one of these tabs:

   ▲ **Incoming:** Lists events the other person sent to you.

   ▲ **Outgoing:** Lists events you sent to the other person.

   ▲ **MessageDialog:** Shows all the instant messages and SMS messages you sent and received from the other person.

4. Double-click an event to open it in the Event Details dialog box and examine it.

By clicking the Previous and Next buttons in the lower-right corner of the Event Details dialog box, you can go from event to event without returning to the History Events Of dialog box.

Sending the Same Event to Several Different People

With ICQ, you always have the option of sending people messages, Web page addresses, greeting cards, Contact List names, or ActiveList invitations. Instead of writing a message four different times, however, you may want to write it once and send it to four people, as shown in Figure 3-4. Being able to send the same event to different people saves time and trouble.

Follow these steps to send the same event to several different people:

1. On your Contact List, click the name of one person to whom you want to send the event.

2. Click the event you want to send from the pop-up menu — a message, Web page address, greeting card, Contact List name, or ActiveList invitation.

3. Fill in the Send dialog box as you normally do.

4. Click the More button (refer to Figure 3-4). After you click the button, more options appear in the bottom of the dialog box.

5. Click the Multiple Recipients button. You see a checklist with the names of the people on your Contact List (refer to Figure 3-4).

6. Under Select Recipients, select the check box beside the name of each person to whom you want to send the event.

7. Click the Send button.

Cross-Reference

Chapter 5 explains how to send the same event to all the people in a Contact List group. Hint: With group names displayed on the Contact List, click a group name, choose a Send command, and choose Entire Group.

Tip

When sending a message, the More button doesn't appear unless you are in Single Message mode. If you don't see the More button, click the Msg Mode button to switch modes.

3

Communicating with Others over ICQ

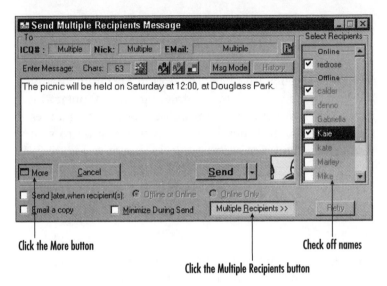

Click the More button   Check off names

Click the Multiple Recipients button

Figure 3-4. Sending the same event to more than one person.

Forwarding an Event to Others

Suppose you get a Web page address or message that you want to share with others. ICQ makes forwarding events very easy — as long as the people to whom you want to forward an event are on your Contact List.

Follow these instructions to forward an event to others so they can read it:

Earlier in this chapter, "Reviewing Events You Sent and Received" explains the History of Events dialog box.

▼ **If you just received the event:** Click the Forward button in the Incoming dialog box. You see the Send Multiple Recipients dialog box (refer to Figure 3-4). In the text box, write a few words of your own beside the words that are already there. Under Select Recipients, select the names of the persons to whom you want to forward the event and then click the Send button.

▼ **If you received the event some time ago:** On your Contact List, click the name of the person from whom you received the event, choose History, and choose View Messages History. Then, on the

Incoming tab of the History Events Of dialog box, double-click the event you want to forward. (You can also right-click the event and choose Forward.) Next, in the Event Details dialog box, click the Forward button. Then follow the instructions for forwarding an event you just received.

Declining an Event

Occasionally in ICQ, you have to decline to accept an event. As shown in Figure 3-5, ICQ offers the Do Not Accept button so you can choose how to decline. After you click the button, you can choose from these Decline options:

▼ **Decline — Without Giving a Reason:** The other party sees a message box that states, "User has declined your request — no reason given."

▼ **Decline — "Sorry I'm busy right now, and cannot respond to your request":** The other party sees a message box with this message.

▼ **Decline — "Sorry I'm busy right now — but I'll be able to respond to you later":** The other party sees a message box with this message.

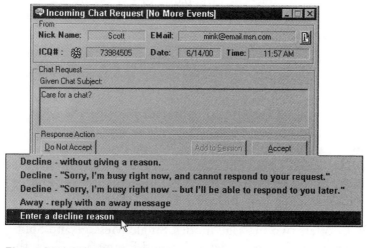

Figure 3-5. Click the Do Not Accept button and choose how you want to decline an event.

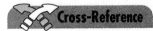

Chapter 2 describes the
Away status icon and the
other status icons.

▼ **Decline — Reply with an Away Message:** The
   Away status icon appears next to your name on the
   other party's Contact List to let the other party
   know that you plan to be away from your computer
   very soon.

▼ **Decline — Enter a Decline Reason:** The
   Decline User Request dialog box appears so you
   can explain why you don't care to accept that event.
   Enter a reason and click the OK button. The other
   party sees a message box with the reason you entered.

Instant Messaging in ICQ

In ICQ, messages can be sent back and forth instantly
when both parties are online. And if one of the parties isn't
online, ICQ will hold the message on its computers until
the message can be delivered. ICQ pioneered instant
messaging and does it better and faster than anyone else.

The fastest way to open a dialog box to send an instant
message is to double-click a
name on your Contact List.

You will find many opportunities in ICQ to send instant
messages. To send an instant message to someone whose
name is on your Contact List, follow these steps:

1. Either double-click the name or click it and choose
   Message on the pop-up menu. You see a dialog box
   for sending a message.

2. Enter your message in the text box.

3. Click the Send button.

At the beginning of this
chapter, "The Basics of
Sending and Receiving" explains how to open and read
a message when it arrives.

When someone sends you an instant message, the Message
icon appears in the tray and beside the sender's name on
your Contact List if the message came from someone
whose name is on your Contact List. Open the message,
click on the Reply button, type your reply in the Send
Message dialog box, and then click the Send button.

ICQ offers two message modes, Single Message and Split
Message, as shown in Figure 3-6 and Figure 3-7. Click the
Msg Mode button to switch between modes. Both modes
have advantages and disadvantages:

▼ **Split Message mode:** Much like a Chat window, you can read messages and replies in the top of the dialog box. (Click the Show/Hide Timestamp button to see precisely when messages were sent.) By clicking the User Menu button, you can bring up the same menu you get when you click a name on the Contact List. Click the User Details button to get White Pages information about the person who sent you a message.

▼ **Single Message mode:** Messages are sent back and forth one at a time. You can click the More button to postpone sending a message or send a message to more than one person. Except by clicking the History button, which doesn't display many messages, you can't view messages you sent or received from the other party. Click the down arrow beside the Send button and choose Send As Email to send an e-mail message to the other party.

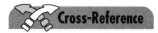 **Cross-Reference**

Earlier in this chapter, "Sending Events to Others (Now or Later)" explains how to use the More button to postpone sending a message. "Forwarding an Event to Others" describes how to send a message to more than one person by clicking the More button.

Messages exchanged

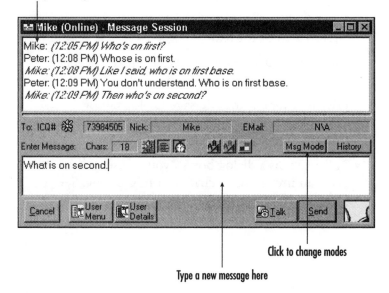

Click to change modes

Type a new message here

Figure 3-6. Instant messaging in Split Message mode.

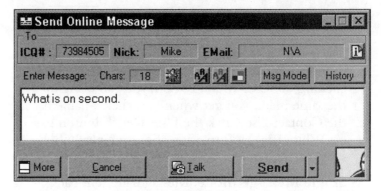

Figure 3-7. Instant messaging in Single Message mode.

In the Single Message and Split Message mode, you can take advantage of these handy buttons:

- ▼ **Sound On/Off:** Turns on or off the old-fashioned typewriter noises the ICQ software plays when you type messages.

- ▼ **Font:** Opens the Font dialog box so you can choose a new font for text.

- ▼ **Font Color:** Opens a drop-down menu so you can choose a color for text.

- ▼ **Background Color:** Opens a drop-down menu so you can choose a background color.

- ▼ **History:** Opens the Message Dialog tab of the History Events Of dialog box so you can review past message you exchanged.

- ▼ **Talk:** Opens a dialog box so you can send the other party an invitation to chat with ICQphone. See Chapter 15.

Sending and Receiving Greeting Cards

An ICQ *greeting card* is a colorful message that you can send to others — and that others can send to you. Figure 3-8 shows a greeting card. Notice that the greeting card appears in a browser window, not an ICQ dialog box. When you receive a greeting card, the Incoming Greeting Card dialog box tells you to "Click here to see the card in your Web browser." When you click, you go to a Web page at `icq.americangreetings.com` like the one shown in Figure 3-8. A greeting card is actually a self-generating Web page, and a colorful one at that.

You already know how to receive a greeting card. Follow these steps to send one:

1. On your Contact List, click the name of the person to whom you want to send a greeting card.

2. Choose Greeting Card on the pop-up menu. You see the Send Online Greeting Card dialog box.

3. Choose a theme from the Select a Theme from List. The *theme* is the overall design of the card.

4. Choose a title in the Select a Card Title list. The recipient's name will be placed after the words in the title you choose. Figure 3-8 shows where the title will go and the recipient's name — Dave — after the title. You can change the title later on.

5. Click the Next button. You see the second Greeting Card dialog box.

6. Enter a new title in the Title box if you don't like the title that ICQ supplied. Be careful, however, because ICQ places the recipient's name after the words you enter.

7. Enter a message in the Message box (refer to Figure 3-8).

8. Enter your name or nickname in the Sender box if you don't want your ICQ name to appear there (refer to Figure 3-8).

9. Click the Next button. A third dialog box appears.

10. Click the Preview the Card on Your Browser button. A browser window opens so that you can see what the card looks like.

11. Return to the Send Online Greeting Card dialog box and either click the Send button to send the card, or click the Back button to return to previous dialog boxes and make changes before sending the card.

Figure 3-8. Greeting cards like these are easy to send.

Sending and Receiving Files

You can send a file to or receive a file from someone else, but to make the transaction, both parties must be connected to ICQ. ICQ isn't like a conventional e-mail program in that the file goes directly from the sender's computer to the recipient's. ICQ can't store a file on its servers until the recipient comes online. You can give the order to send a file when the other party isn't connected to ICQ, but the file isn't delivered until both parties are connected.

A file is any file that is generated by a computer program — a Word file, spreadsheet, or .exe computer program. Read on to learn how to send and receive files in ICQ.

Sending a File

Follow these steps to send a file:

1. Click the name of the person on your Contact List to whom you will send the file.

2. Choose File on the pop-up menu. The Open dialog box appears.

3. Find and select the file or files that you want to send and then click the Open button. A Send Online File Request dialog box appears. The name of the file you selected is listed in the File Name(s) box. (If you selected more than one file, the number of files you selected is listed.)

4. Write a note to accompany your files in the Enter File(s) Description box. (You can click the Select File(s) button to add more files to the list.)

5. Click the Send button.

On the other end, the recipient either accepts or declines the file. If he or she declines it, you get a message saying as much or else nothing happens. But if the other party receives the file, the Sending Files To dialog box shown on the top of Figure 3-9 appears. The dialog box tells how many files are being sent, how long the transfer will take, and how fast the transfer occurs. When the file is delivered, you see the ICQ File Transfer Completed Successfully dialog box shown at the bottom of Figure 3-9.

Caution

Be careful about accepting files. Files can carry viruses.

Tip

To select more than one file in the Open dialog box, hold down the Ctrl key and click file names.

3

Communicating with
Others over ICQ

Tip

In the Sending File To dialog box, click the Skip File button if the transfer takes too long and you want to send the next file in the queue. Click the Abort button to stop the file transfer altogether.

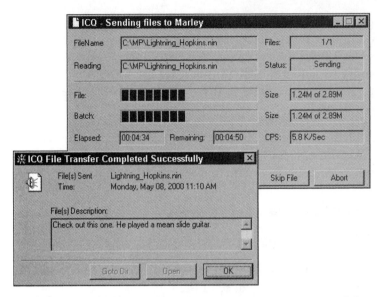

Figure 3-9. A file being sent (top) has been delivered successfully (bottom).

Two Fast Ways to Send Files

Here are a couple of fast ways to send files:

▼ In My Computer or Windows Explorer, find and select the file, and then drag and drop it over the name of the person on your Contact List that you want to send it to.

▼ Open My Computer or Windows Explorer, find the file you want to send, right-click it, and choose ICQ – Send to User on the shortcut menu. The names of people on your Contact List who are connected to ICQ appear on a submenu. Click the name of the person to whom you want to send the file to. Open the Send Online File Request dialog box and take it from there.

Receiving a File

When someone wants to send you a file, you see the file icon in the tray and/or beside a name on your Contact List. Double-click the icon and you see the Incoming File Request dialog box shown on the left side of Figure 3-10.

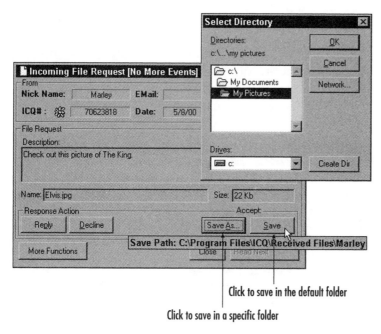

Click to save in the default folder

Click to save in a specific folder

Figure 3-10. Click the Save As or Save button to accept an incoming file.

In the dialog box, do one of the following to accept or decline the file:

▼ **Accept the file and store it in the default folder:** Click the Save button. As Figure 3-10 shows, you can move the pointer over the Save button to see where the file will be stored.

▼ **Accept the file and store it in a folder of your choice:** Click the Save As button, and, in the Select Directory dialog box shown in Figure 3-10, locate and select a folder. Then click OK.

Cross-Reference

Chapter 9 explains how incoming files are stored and how you can choose which folder on your computer they are stored in by default.

Tip

Click the Skip File button In the Receiving Files From dialog box if the transfer takes too long and you want to start receiving the next file in the queue. Click the Abort button to stop the file transfer altogether.

▼ **Decline the file:** Click the Decline button and choose a reason for declining from the pop-up menu. Or click the Reply button to send an instant message that explains why you can't accept the file.

Soon your computer and the sender's connect, and then you see the Receiving Files From dialog box. The dialog box tells you how many files are arriving, how much time remains in the transfer, and how fast the transfer occurs.

When the file transfer is complete, the ICQ File Transfer Completed Successfully dialog box appears. Click the Open button to open the file that was just sent to you, or click OK to close the dialog box.

Finding Out What Files Were Sent to You over ICQ

By default, files that were sent to you are kept in the `C:\Program Files\ICQ\Received Files\Sender's Name` folder. However, if you aren't sure where you stored a file, click the System Notice button and choose Incoming Files Folder on the pop-up menu. My Computer opens to the default folder where you keep incoming files. Double-click a folder named after someone who sent you files and you see all the files that the person sent you. (You'll see the files, provided you didn't save or move them elsewhere, of course.)

You can also follow these steps to open My Computer and find out which files someone sent you over ICQ:

1. Click the person's name on your Contact List.

2. Choose History on the pop-up menu.

3. Choose Incoming Files on the submenu.

The ICQ Phone Book: Fast Ways to Tell Others Where to Reach You

Of course, the fastest way to call another ICQ user is to move the pointer over his or her name on your Contact List, read the number, and start dialing. If the person you want to call lists phone numbers in the White Pages, the numbers appear above his or her name.

Most ICQ users, however, are more discreet — their phone numbers are not listed in the White Pages. To obtain someone's phone numbers, you could send an instant message asking as much, but a more efficient way is to take advantage of the Phone Book commands in ICQ.

As long as someone whose name is on your Contact List entered his or her phone numbers in the ICQ Phone Book, you can obtain the phone numbers and even dial one of them simply by clicking the name and choosing Phone Book⇨Find Phone# and Dial. ICQ dials phone numbers over your telephone handset by simulating the touch-tone frequencies over the computer's speakers.

The Phone Book feature also permits you to place an icon next to your name on others' Contact Lists to show whether you are available for telephone calls. The telephone icon lets others know when you can take phone calls. People who see the icon can click your name and choose Phone Book⇨Find Phone# and Dial to call you on the phone.

You can also send and receive phone call requests by choosing Phone Book⇨Send Phone Call Request. In the Phone Call Request dialog boxes that appear, you can tell others which telephone number to call and describe what you want to talk about.

Note

You must have a touch-tone phone, not a pulse phone, for ICQ to dial phone numbers for you.

Cross-Reference

Chapter 10 explains how to list your telephone numbers, and other information as well, in the ICQ White Pages.

Doing the Setup Work

The Phone Book is a very useful feature, but to take advantage of it, you have to do a bit of setup work:

▼ **Setup Step #1:** Enter telephone numbers in the Phone Book section of the View/Change My Details dialog box so that others whom you authorize know which numbers to call.

▼ **Setup Step #2:** Decide whether you want people who have put your name on their Contact Lists to obtain your phone numbers and configure your preferences accordingly.

▼ **Setup Step #3:** Enter your dialer settings so that ICQ knows how to make telephone calls for you. Believe it or not, ICQ can dial the telephone for you as long as your computer plays sound. To dial, you hold the telephone receiver to the computer speaker.

Read on to set up Phone Book phoning on your computer.

Setup Step #1: Entering Your Telephone Numbers

Follow these steps to enter your Phone Book phone numbers so that others can reach you quickly:

1. Click the ICQ button.

2. Choose View/Change My Details. The View/Change My Details dialog box opens.

3. Click the Phone Book section, as shown in Figure 3-11.

4. Click the Add button. You see the Add/Edit Phone and Fax dialog box.

5. Describe and enter the phone number. In the Type box, choose Home, Office, Cellular, Pager, or another name that clearly describes the telephone number from the pull-down menu. Notice the Extension box for entering extension numbers. Click OK to close the dialog box.

Note

The View/Change My Details dialog box offers another section for entering phone numbers — the Home section. However, phone numbers you enter there are entered in the White Pages for all to see. The phone numbers in the Phone Book section, on the other hand, are strictly for people who have put your name on their Contact Lists.

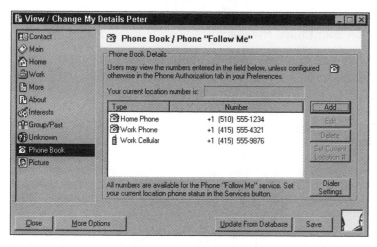

Figure 3-11. Adding phone numbers to the Phone Book section of the View/Change My Details dialog box.

6. Repeat Steps 4 and 5 to enter more telephone numbers, if necessary.

7. Select the telephone number where you can be reached right now and then click the Set Current Location # button. As you will discover shortly, you can notify others when you can be reached at a different phone number by selecting a number and clicking the Set Current Location # button.

8. Click the Save button.

9. Click the Close button to close the View/Change My Details dialog box.

The Edit and Delete buttons in the Phone Book section are for changing telephone numbers or removing them from the list.

Setup Step #2: Authorizing People to View Your Phone Numbers

After you enter telephone numbers, edit a telephone number, or choose a new current location telephone number in the Phone Book section of the View/Change My Details dialog box (refer to Figure 3-11), the next step is to decide who has authorization to obtain your phone numbers. Follow these steps:

1. Click the ICQ button.

2. Choose Preferences. You see the Owner Preferences For dialog box.

3. Click Phone Book to go to the Phone Book section.

4. Choose from the following options to determine who can obtain your phone numbers:

   ▲ **Set ICQ to Display a Response Dialog:** With this option, the Incoming Phone Authorization dialog box, as shown in Figure 3-12, appears whenever someone wants your phone numbers. In the dialog box, uncheck the boxes beside the phone numbers you *don't* want to offer and then click the Accept button. Or else click the Decline button to keep the person from obtaining your phone numbers.

   ▲ **Set ICQ to Automatically Accept:** Choose this option to let everyone obtain your phone numbers automatically.

   ▲ **Set ICQ to Automatically Decline:** Choose this option to prevent anyone from obtaining your phone numbers. Why choose this option? By choosing a Phone Book Alert/Accept mode, you can offer your phone numbers to people on your Contact List on a person-by-person basis. (I explain how shortly.)

▲ **Set ICQ to Automatically Decline from Users Who Are not on My Contact List:** When you select this check box, only people whose names are on your Contact List can obtain your phone numbers.

5. Click the Apply button.

Another strategy for handling phone numbers is to decide who gets your phone numbers on a person-by-person basis — and then you never have to make the decision again. With this technique, you click a name on your Contact List, choose Alert/Accept Modes on the pop-up menu, and click Phone Book to go to the Phone Book section of the User Preferences For dialog box. Next, check the Override General Prefs check box. Then, to give the individual permanent access to your phone numbers, click the Auto Accept option button; click the Auto Decline option button to permanently deny access to this individual. Now you can change your "Follow Me" Phone settings without having to authorize the person again.

Chapter 9 explains the Alert/Accept settings in the User Preferences For dialog box in detail.

Setup Step #3: Entering Your Dialer Settings

Dialer settings tell ICQ how to dial your telephone. As you will find out soon, ICQ can actually dial telephone numbers, but to do so it needs to know what your area code is, whether to dial a long-distance prefix, and what to dial for international numbers. Follow these steps to enter your dialer settings if you want ICQ to dial for you:

1. Click the ICQ button and choose View/Change My Details on the pop-up menu.

2. Click Phone Book to move to the Phone Book section of the View/Change my Details dialog box.

3. Click the Dialer Settings button to open the Dialer Settings dialog box.

4. Under I'm Dialing From, select the country in which you live and enter your area code.

A fast way to open the View/Change My Details dialog box is to click the View/ Change My Details button on the ICQuick shortcut bar.

3

Communicating with Others over ICQ

Choose which phone numbers to offer

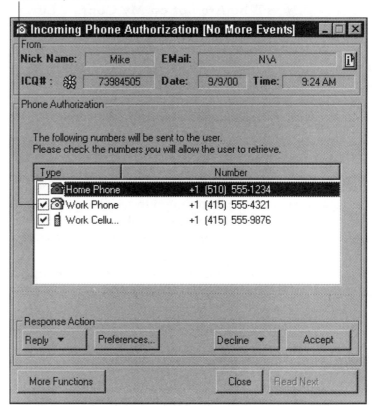

Figure 3-12. Choosing which phone numbers to volunteer and whether to volunteer them.

5. Under Dialing Prefix, enter the local, long–distance, or international prefixes you must enter to dial from your phone. In the United States, callers do not have to enter a local prefix. The long distance prefix in the United States is 1, the number you must dial to reach a number outside your area code. The international prefix in the United States is 011. That is the number you must enter to dial outside the country.

6. Click OK.

7. Click the Save button and then click the Close button.

For now, don't concern yourself with the Timing Prefix settings in the Dialer Settings dialog box. Probably the Medium settings will work. However, if you can't dial telephone numbers with the Medium settings, return to the Dialer Settings dialog box and try the Slow or Fast settings. If they don't work, follow these steps to experiment with the settings until you find the right ones:

1. In the Timing Prefix drop-down menu, choose Custom.

2. Click the Edit button. The Custom DTMF Settings dialog box appears. DTMF, which stands for Dual Tone Multiple Frequency, is the signaling system used in touch-tone telephone keypads. By experimenting with the Tone Time, Break Time, and Pause Time settings, you can help your telephone hear the frequency that ICQ generates.

3. Change the settings in the boxes. ICQ recommends these settings: Tone Time – 100, Break Time – 300, Pause Time – 3000.

4. Enter a bona fide telephone number in the Test Number box.

5. Hold your telephone's mouthpiece to the computer speaker and click the Play DTMF button.

6. If the call is completed successfully, click the OK button to close the Custom DTMF Settings dialog box.

7. Click the OK button in the Dialer Settings dialog box and then click the Save and Close buttons in the Phone Book section of the View/Change My Details dialog box.

Caution

As an anti-phreaking measure, newer electronic phones and office PBX systems no longer recognize DTMF tones played over the mouthpiece of telephones. If your telephone does not recognize DTMF tones, ICQ cannot dial numbers for you.

3

Communicating with
Others over ICQ

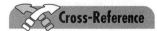

Earlier in this chapter, "Setup Step #1: Entering Your Telephone Numbers" explains how to enter phone numbers in the View/Change My Details dialog box.

Telling Others That You Want (Or Don't Want) to Take Phone Calls

After you enter your telephone numbers in the View/Change My Details dialog box, you can choose a simple command to tell everyone who put your name on their Contact List that you are available to take telephone calls. For that matter, you can also declare that you are too busy to take phone calls.

As shown in Figure 3-13, click the Services button, choose Phone "Follow Me"⇨Phone Status and then choose Available or Busy. A small telephone icon appears beside your name on others' Contact Lists:

▾ **Available:** A small yellow telephone icon appears beside your name so that others know you are taking phone calls.

▾ **Busy:** A red *X* is drawn across the yellow telephone icon so that others know not to bother you.

A small telephone icon appears as well on your System Notice button. It tells you that the telephone icon appears beside your name on others' Contact Lists. Choose the Don't Show command on the Phone Status submenu (see Figure 3-13) to make all the telephone icons disappear from others' Contact Lists.

Quickly Getting the Phone Number of Someone on Your Contact List

The next part of this chapter, "Sending Out a Phone Call Request," explains another way to get people on the phone — asking them to call you.

As long as a friend whose name is on your Contact List has made his or her "Follow Me" phone numbers available, you can quickly look up and even dial your friend's telephone number:

1. On your Contact List, click the name of the person you want to call.

2. Choose Phone Book on the pop-up menu.

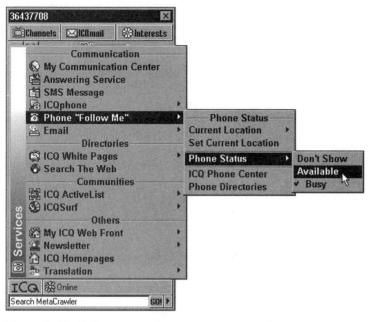

Figure 3-13. Telling others that you can receive phone calls.

3. Choose Find Phone# and Dial to open the Phone Book section of the User Details dialog box, as shown in Figure 3-14. The dialog box lists the telephone numbers where your friend can be reached. To find out where your friend can be reached at the present time, glance at the User Current Location Number box. (The number appears there, provided of course, that your friend has taken the time to update his or her phone number in the View/Change My Details dialog box.)

4. Either dial the telephone number yourself or select a number and then click the Dial button to tell ICQ to dial it. Be sure to hold the telephone mouthpiece beside the speaker on your computer if ICQ does the dialing.

5. Click the Close button.

A fast way to open the User Details dialog box is to move the pointer over a person's name on your Contact List and then click the Enter Phone # hyperlink in the box that appears.

See "Setup Step #3: Entering Your Dialer Settings" earlier in this chapter if ICQ can't successfully dial a telephone number for you.

Where the person can be reached

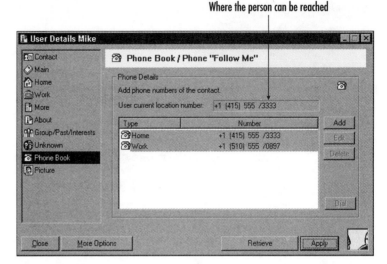

Figure 3-14. Looking up — and dialing — a friend's telephone number.

Sending Out a Phone Call Request

Note

To send a phone call request, both parties must be online and connected to ICQ.

A telephone call request is much like a message, except the telephone icon tells the person who receives your request that he or she is wanted on the telephone. What's more, you can include your telephone number in the request to make it easier for the other party to reach you. Follow these steps to send someone whose name is on your Contact List a telephone call request:

1. Click the person's name on your Contact List.

2. Choose Phone Book⇨Send Phone Call Request. You see the Send Online Phone Call Request dialog box, as shown in Figure 3-15.

3. Enter the subject of the telephone call in the text box.

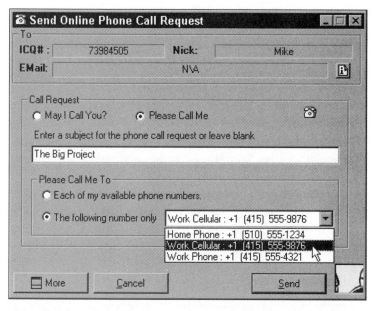

Figure 3-15. Asking someone to call you or accept a phone call.

4. To include the telephone number where you can currently be reached in the phone request message, do one of the following:

▲ Enter the phone number in the text box.

▲ Click the Please Call Me option button, click The Following Number Only option button, and choose a number from the drop-down list, as shown in Figure 3-15.

5. Click the Send button.

What happens next depends on how well your phone call request is received. The request might be ignored or denied. But if you get a response, it will appear in the form of a Send Online Phone Call Request dialog box. As the next part of this chapter explains, you can instruct someone when to call you in your reply to a phone call request. In the dialog box, look under User Response to find out when to call or expect a call.

Cross-Reference

In order to choose a telephone number from the Please Call Me drop-down list, you must have entered phone numbers in the Phone Book section of the View/Change My Details dialog box. See "Doing the Setup Work" earlier in this chapter.

3

Communicating with
Others over ICQ

Receiving a Telephone Call Request

You see the telephone icon on your Contact List and/or in the desktop tray when someone wants to speak to you on the telephone. Double-click the telephone icon, and you see the Incoming Phone Call Request dialog box, as shown in Figure 3-16.

The dialog box tells you what the subject of the proposed phone call will be. Sometimes a phone number appears as well. Click the Reply button to reply with an instant message or other communication, the Decline button to decline the request, or the Accept button to accept it. As shown in Figure 3-16, you can open the drop-down menu and tell the requester when to expect the call before clicking the Accept button.

Figure 3-16. Fielding a telephone call request.

Viewing Others' Photos (And Letting Them View Yours)

To see the face behind a name on your Contact List, you can obtain someone's photo. Likewise, you can make your photo available to people who have put your name on their Contact Lists. Before you can see someone else's photo, however, he or she must have given you permission to do so. And no one can see your photo unless they have permission first.

Read on to learn how to view someone else's photo, make your photo available to others, and grant permission to people to view your photo.

Viewing Someone Else's Photo

Follow these steps to see if you can view the photo of someone whose name is on your Contact List:

1. Click the name on your Contact List.

2. Choose User's Details/Address Book. You see the User Details dialog box.

3. Click Picture to go to the Picture section. If you have permission to view the photo, it appears in the Picture section, as shown in Figure 3-17.

4. Click the View Full Picture button to see a larger photo in a graphics program. (The picture appears in the default graphics program on your computer.)

Notice the Copy Thumbnail To File button. Click it to copy the file onto your computer so you can open the photo in a graphics program and perhaps edit it.

Making Your Photo Available to Others

Before anyone can see your photo, you have to make it available. After you have done that, you can decide who can view the photo (the subject of the next section in this chapter).

Tip

Click the Update from Database button in the User Details dialog box to get up-to-date information about the other person, including an up-to-date photo. The Picture section tells you when the photo was updated last.

Note

A photo also appears in the Contact section of the User Details dialog box.

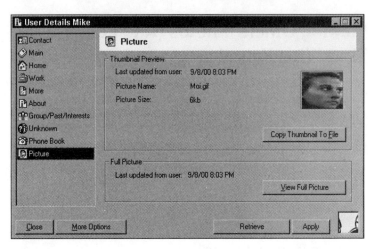

Figure 3-17. Others' photos appear in the Picture section of the User Details dialog box.

A photo you make available to other people over ICQ has to meet these standards:

Cross-Reference

Earlier in this chapter, "Sending and Receiving Files" explains how to send a file, including a graphics file, to someone else.

▼ It must be no larger than 7K in size. If your photo is larger than 7K, open it in a graphics program and crop it, turn it into a black-and-white image, or shrink it. If you can't make your photo smaller than 7K, send it to others in a file.

▼ It must be a GIF image, BMP or JPEG image file. Because GIF and BMP files are smaller than their JPEG counterparts, save your photo as a GIF or BMP file to keep it under the 7K size limitation.

Remember where the photo you want to make available to others is on your computer, and follow these steps to make the photo available:

1. Click the ICQ button.

2. Choose View/Change My Details. The View Change/My Details dialog box opens.

3. Click the Picture section. If you have already made a picture available but you are changing pictures, a picture already appears under "Thumbnail Preview."

4. Click the Browse button. You see the Open dialog box.

5. Find the photo, select it, and click the Open button. You return to the Picture tab, where the path to the photo appears.

6. Click the Save button.

7. Click the Close button.

Authorizing People on Your Contact List to View Your Photo

After you have pointed the way to your photo in the View/Change My Details dialog box (described in the previous setion of this chapter), the next step is to tell ICQ if you want to limit who can view your photo. (By default, anyone on whose Contact List you appear can see your picture.) Follow these steps to limit access to your photo:

1. Click the ICQ button.

2. Choose Preferences. You see the Owner Preferences For dialog box.

3. Click Picture to go to the Picture section.

4. Choose from the following options to determine who can view your photograph:

> ▲ **Set ICQ to Display a Response Dialog:** After selecting this option in your preferences, the Incoming Picture Authorization dialog box appears the next time the user on whose list you appear logs on to ICQ. In the dialog box, click the Accept or Decline button.

> ▲ **Set ICQ to Automatically Accept:** Choose this option to let everyone view your photo.

> ▲ **Sect ICQ to Automatically Decline:** Choose this option to prevent anyone from viewing your photo.

Tip

In the Open dialog box, click the Details button (the rightmost button) to see file types. In the Type column, look for GIF image and JPEG image — the file types you can use for ICQ photos.

3

Communicating with
Others over ICQ

▲ **Set ICQ to Automatically Decline from Users Who Are not on My Contact List:** When you select this check box, only people whose names are on your Contact List can obtain your photo.

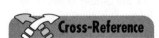
Cross-Reference

Chapter 9 explains the Alert/Accept settings in the User Preferences For dialog box in detail.

5. Click the Apply button

Another strategy for handling your photo is to decide on a person-by-person basis who gets to see it. Click a name on your Contact List, choose Alert/Accept Modes on the pop-up menu, and click Picture to go to the Picture section of the User Preferences For dialog box. Next, check the Override General Prefs check box. Then, to give the individual permanent access to your photo, click the Auto Accept option button; click the Auto Decline option button to permanently deny access to this individual.

Coming Up Next

Chapter 4 explains how to find old and new friends in ICQ. You discover how to add the names of friends and family to your Contact List, find out who in your address book is already a user, send out invitations to join ICQ, search for people on the Internet, and explore the PeopleSpace Directory.

Part

II

Reaching Out to Others in ICQ

Chapter

4

Finding and Adding Users

Quick Look

Searching for Friends and Family to Put Their Names on Your Contact List   page 78

ICQ offers a bunch of different ways to find the names of friends, family members, and associates so you can add their names to your Contact List. You can search with the Add/Invite Users command, scour the address books on your computer for ICQ users, and go on the Internet to search.

Keeping the Names of ICQ Friends on Your Contact List   page 85

When someone's name is on your Contact List, you know when he or she is online and connected to ICQ. All you have to do is click a name on the list and choose from many options for communicating with your friend. To put someone's name on your list, you may need his or her permission. As for others putting your name on their Contact Lists, you can decide whether or not they need your permission to do so.

Placing the Names of Non-ICQ Users on Your Contact List   page 95

Why put non-ICQ users on your Contact List? To make it easier to send them wireless pager messages or SMS (Short Messages Service) text messages. For that matter, you can talk to them by ICQphone.

Sending Out Invitations to Join ICQ   page 95

ICQ offers a command for sending e-mail invitations to join the club. Anyone who receives an invitation can click a hyperlink to join up. And when someone to whom you sent an invitation joins, ICQ alerts you.

Searching ICQ with the People Navigator   page 101

No matter what you want to search for in ICQ — user lists, chat rooms, interest groups, or ICQ Web Front pages — you can start in the People Navigator. Use the People Navigator to find new friends whose interests are the same as yours.

Chapter 4

Finding and Adding Users

This chapter describes how to search the ICQ databases, search the address books on your computer, and search the Internet for ICQ users so you can put their names on your Contact List and make your ICQ experience a better one. You are also introduced to the Contact List in this chapter. You find out how to add names to the list and get your name on others' lists. This chapter explains how to invite friends and family to join ICQ and send them your "four addresses" — all the different ways that you can be contacted in ICQ. Finally, you learn about the People Navigator, a way to find things quickly in ICQ.

Finding Friends and Family So You Can Put Them on Your Contact List

The more friends, family, and associates on your Contact List, the richer your ICQ experience will be. For that reason, ICQ offers many ways to find family and friends so you can invite them to join ICQ or put their names on your Contact List. Read on to discover how to find family and friends in the ICQ database with the Add/Invite Users command, how to look in the address books stored on your computer for ICQ users, and how to search the Internet.

After you find a family member or friend, you can invite him or her to join ICQ. If your friend or family member is already an ICQ user, you can place him or her on your Contact List.

Searching with the Add/Invite Users Command

The most straightforward way to search for friends and family members is to use the Add/Invite Users command. Go this route when you know an ICQ user's e-mail address, ICQ number, or name. Perhaps someone has given you a business card with an ICQ number on it and you want to enter your new associate's name on your Contact List. The Add/Invite Users command searches the ICQ user database. As Figure 4-1 shows, you can right-click a name in the Search results to add someone to your Contact List.

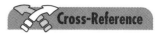

Cross-Reference

Later in this chapter, "Introducing the Contact List" explains how to add new names to your Contact List. "Sending Out Invitations to Join ICQ" explains how to invite somebody to be an ICQ user.

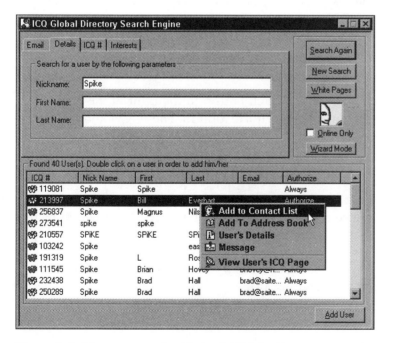

Figure 4-1. After you search with the Add/Invite Users command, you can enter a name you found on your Contact List.

The best way to search is by ICQ number because every user has a different number. Searching by e-mail address sometimes doesn't work, because not every user records his or her address with ICQ. Names can be problematic, since many of ICQ's millions of users share the same name.

Follow these steps to search the ICQ database for an ICQ user:

1. Click the Add/Invite Users button. You see the Find/Add Users to Your List dialog box, part of which is shown in Figure 4-2.

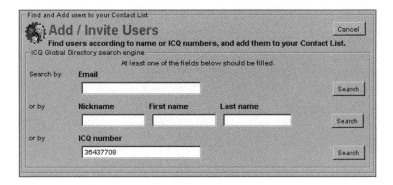

Figure 4-2. Searching for an ICQ user with the Add/Invite Users command.

2. Enter an e-mail address, first or last name, or an ICQ number.

3. Click the Search button to the right of the box you entered information in. The ICQ Global Directory Search Engine dialog box appears (refer to Figure 4-1). It lists ICQ users who were found in the search.

Later in this chapter, "Adding New Friends to Your Contact List" explains how to put a name on your Contact List after you've found it in the ICQ database.

What if your search came up empty? First, make sure you entered the e-mail address, name, or ICQ number correctly. If the entered information is in fact correct,, click the New Search button, select a different tab in the dialog box (Email, Details, or ICQ #), enter another search term, and try searching again.

Finding Out Whether Someone Whose Name Is in Your Address Book Is an ICQ Member

Maybe somebody you know is already registered with ICQ and you don't know it. One way to find out is to let ICQ search the e-mail address books on your computer. If ICQ finds an e-mail address that matches the e-mail address of an ICQ member, you are told as much. What's more, you can put the name of an ICQ member that ICQ found on your Contact List. And, if it turns out someone in your address book is not an ICQ user, you can send that person an invitation to join ICQ.

Follow these steps to search your e-mail address books for ICQ members:

1. Click the ICQ button.

2. Choose Add/Invite Users⇨Invitation to Join ICQ. You see the Invitation to Join ICQ dialog box.

3. Click the second button, ICQ Email Address Import. The ICQ Email Import dialog box appears. It lists the names of address books found on your computer.

4. Uncheck the boxes beside the names of address books you *don't* want to search.

5. Click the Start Address Book(s) Search button. ICQ conducts the search and you see the ICQ Email Import dialog box. The Searching notation tells you how many e-mail addresses in your address book have been compared to the e-mail addresses in ICQ's database. The top box shows the ICQ users the search found in your address books, whereas the bottom box shows non-ICQ users.

6. Click the double-arrows on the left side of the dialog box. The dialog box enlarges and looks like the one shown in Figure 4-3.

Tip

If you have already conducted a search, open the Type of Search drop-down menu and choose Search for New Contacts Added to My Address Books. This way, you don't have to wait while ICQ searches all your addresses. The Last Email Search Performed On dialog box tells you when you last conducted a search.

4

Finding and Adding Users

Check who you want to add to your contact list

Click to open full dialog box

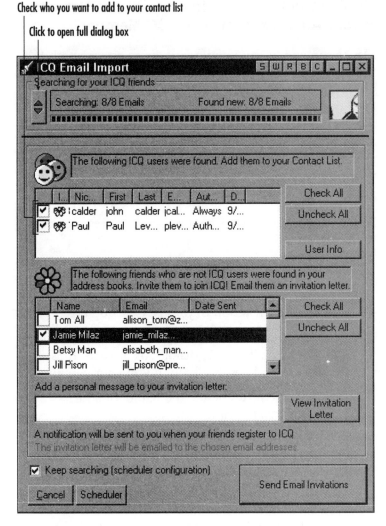

Figure 4-3. Finding out who in your address books is a member of ICQ and who you can invite to join ICQ.

7. Select the check boxes beside the names of the people you want to add to your Contact List.

8. Optionally, to invite people to join ICQ, check off names in the bottom half of the dialog box. ICQ will send e-mail invitations to the people whose names you check off. In the Add a Personal Message text box, you can enter a personal message to send along with the standard e-mail invitation.

9. Click the OK button (or the Send Email Invitations button if you are also sending invitations to join ICQ).

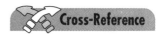 **Cross-Reference**

Later in this chapter, "Sending Out Invitations to Join ICQ" explains how invitations to join ICQ work.

ICQ gives you the opportunity to periodically check your address books for ICQ users. Click the ICQ button and choose Preferences. In the Owner Preferences For dialog box, click ICQ Email Import to go to the Email Import Scheduler tab. Then, in the Initiate Email Search Every X Day(s) text box, enter the frequency with which you want ICQ to search for users to add to your Contact List and click Apply.

Searching for People on the Internet to Put on Your Contact List

Another way to find friends and family who are not yet ICQ users and get the process rolling for putting their names on your Contact List is to search the Internet. After you find friends and family members, you can invite them to join ICQ. Follow these steps to search for a person on the Internet:

1. Click the ICQ button.

2. Choose Add/Invite Users⇨Invitation To Join ICQ on the pop-up menu. You see the Invitation to Join ICQ dialog box.

3. Click the Search in Other Email Directories button. You see the LDAP Search dialog box shown in Figure 4-4.

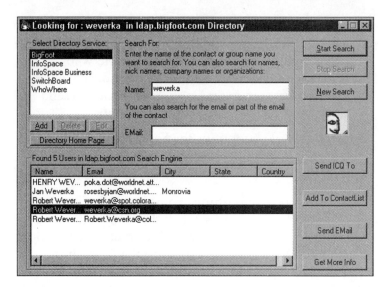

Figure 4-4. Searching for people so you can add their names to your Contact List.

4. Choose a directory in the Select Directory Service list.

5. Enter a name in the Name box.

6. If you know the e-mail address of the person you are looking for, enter it in the EMail text box.

7. Click the Start Search button. If the person can be found, his or her name and e-mail address, and perhaps other information as well, is listed at the bottom of the dialog box. (If the person can't be found, choose a different directory service and conduct the search again.)

8. Select the name of a person who you want to add to your Contact List and click the Add To Contact List button. You see the ICQ Global Directory Search Engine dialog box (refer to Figure 4-1)

If the person whose name you selected is a member of ICQ and his or her e-mail address has been recorded in the ICQ White Pages, the name appears on the bottom of the dialog box. Select the person's name and click the Add User button to add the person to your Contact List.

If the person isn't an ICQ user, you can invite him or her to join by clicking the Invite A Friend button. (See "Sending Out Invitations to Join ICQ" later in this chapter.)

Introducing the Contact List

The *Contact List* is a very important part of the ICQ window. The Contact List is where the names of your ICQ friends and family are kept. After you learn your way around the Contact List, you will know when your friends are connected to ICQ and be able to get in touch with them quickly.

ICQ offers different ways of displaying names on the Contact List. You can display only the names of people who are online and connected to ICQ, or you can display all the names, as shown on the left side of Figure 4-5. When you display all the names, the names of the people who are connected to ICQ are blue and are listed under the Online heading; the names of people who are not connected are red and appear under the Offline heading.

As shown on the right side of Figure 4-5, you can also organize names into groups such as Family or Friends. Organizing names into groups is the way to go if many names are on your Contact List.

By glancing at the online status icon next to someone's name on the Contact List, you can tell whether he or she is online, away, or occupied. Move the pointer over someone's name and you can read the person's address and phone numbers (if that person chose to display them), availability status, ICQphone status, and phone status.

Cross-Reference

Chapter 2 describes the online status icons.

4

Finding and Adding Users

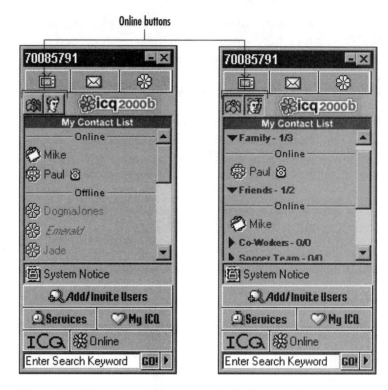

Figure 4-5. Click the tab buttons to display Contact List names in different ways.

Clicking a name brings up a pop-up menu. From the menu, you can send someone a message, invite someone for a chat, or do any number of things — and do them quickly.

How does someone's name get on your Contact List? You put it there. And that is the subject of the following pages.

Adding New Friends to Your Contact List

Throughout ICQ, you have many opportunities to put other peoples' names on your Contact List. For example, the ICQ Global Directory Search Engine dialog box (refer to Figure 4-1) has an Add User button that you can click to put someone on your list. The method you use to add a name to your Contact List depends on whether you need authorization to put it there:

▼ If you need authorization to put someone's name on your Contact List, you have to get permission from the person first.

▼ If you don't need authorization, the name is entered on your Contact List as soon as you give the command for putting it there.

If you need authorization, you see the Privacy – User's Authorization Is Required dialog box, shown at the top of Figure 4-6, when you try to put someone's name on your Contact List. But if you don't need authorization, you see the User Has Been Added dialog box shown at the bottom of Figure 4-6. Read on to learn the details of putting someone's name on your Contact List

Cross-Reference

The start of Chapter 10 explains how to tell ICQ whether others need permission to put *your* name on *their* Contact Lists.

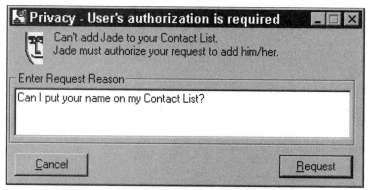

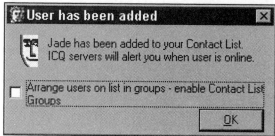

Figure 4-6. These dialog boxes tell you when you need permission to place a name on the Contact List (top) and when you don't need permission (bottom).

Putting a Name on Your Contact List
When You Need Permission

When you try to put someone's name on your Contact List but you need authorization to do it, you see the Privacy - User's Authorization Is Required dialog box (refer to Figure 4-6). Introduce yourself in the Enter Request Reason box, click the Request button, and click OK in the confirmation box. Your authorization request is sent to the person you want to add to your Contact List.

On your Contact List, the name of the person whose permission you are seeking appears under the heading "Awaiting Authorization." The name stays there until your request has been accepted or denied:

> ▼ **Accepted:** A System Message icon appears beside the person's name. Double-click the icon and you see the Incoming "Authorization" Request Accepted dialog box shown on the top of Figure 4-7. Click Close and then click OK in the User Has Been Added message box.

> ▼ **Denied:** Either you see the Incoming "Authorization" Request Denied dialog box, as shown on the bottom of Figure 4-7, or nothing happens because the other party doesn't respond to your request.

Putting a Name on Your Contact List
When You *Don't* Need Permission

When you don't need permission to put someone's name on your Contact List, the User Has Been Added dialog box (refer to Figure 4-6) appears right away and the name is entered on your list. Meanwhile, the person whose name was added to your list is notified that his or her name is on your Contact List.

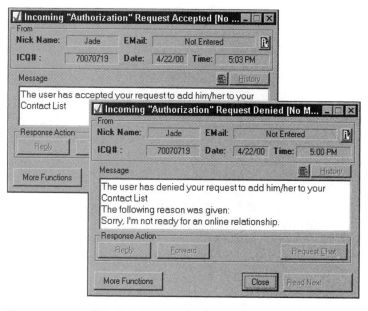

Figure 4-7. A request to put a name on a Contact List has been accepted (top) and denied (bottom).

Following Up a Request for Authorization

Sometimes the other party simply doesn't respond to your request, and the name sits on your Contact List under "Awaiting Authorization." When that happens, either try again or give up:

▼ **Send out another request:** Click the name and choose Re-Request Authorization on the pop-up menu. Then enter a word or two in the Resend Request dialog box and click the Request button.

Continued

Following Up a Request for Authorization
(continued)

▼ **Tell ICQ to send out more requests:** Click the person's name under "Awaiting Authorization" and choose Authorization Status on the pop-up menu. You see the Request for Authorization Follow Up Service dialog box. To have ICQ resend the request every three days for the next nine days, select a name and click the OK button. While you're at it, you can check the Send Email check box (if it's not grayed out) to send the request by e-mail. Click the Stop Service check box if you want ICQ to stop sending authorization requests after nine days.

▼ **Give up:** Click the name and choose Delete on the pop-up menu. Then click Yes in the confirmation box.

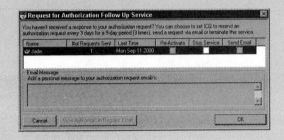

Fielding Requests from Others to Put Your Name on Their Contact Lists

Cross-Reference

The start of Chapter 10 explains how to require others to get permission to put your name on their Contact Lists.

When you registered with ICQ, you made an important decision about allowing others to put your name on their Contact Lists. How others place your name on their lists depends on whether they need permission first.

If others *don't* need permission, you get a System Notice message when someone puts your name on a Contact List. When you open the message, the Incoming "You Were

Added" dialog box tells you the person's name, ICQ number, and perhaps their e-mail address, as shown in Figure 4-8. While the dialog box is open, you can click buttons to perform these useful tasks:

▼ **Get information about the person from the White Pages:** Click the Get User Info button to open the User Details dialog box and learn more about the person.

Chapter 5 explains how to send names on your Contact List to other people.

▼ **Send names from your Contact List to the person:** Click the Send Contacts button.

▼ **Add the person's name to your Contact List:** Click the Add to Contact List button.

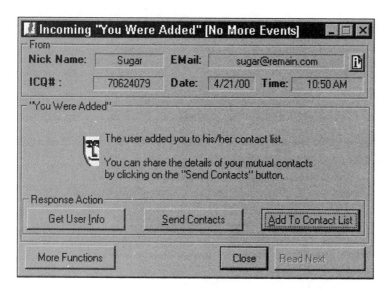

Figure 4-8. You see the Incoming "You Were Added" dialog box if others don't need permission to put your name on their Contact Lists.

When people want to put your name on their Contact List and they need permission to do so, you get a System Notice message. Open the message and you see the Incoming

Request for Authorization dialog box shown in Figure 4-9. Follow these instructions to grant or deny the other person permission to put your name on his or her list:

User Details button

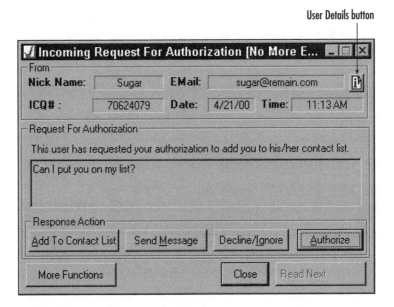

Figure 4-9. You see the Incoming Request for Authorization dialog box if others need permission.

Click the User Details button (the *i*) in the Incoming Request for Authorization dialog box to open the User Details dialog box and get more information about the person who wants to put your name on his or her list. You'll find the button in the upper-right corner of the dialog box.

▼ **Give permission:** Click the Authorize button.

▼ **Deny permission:** Click the Decline/Ignore button and then choose one of these options from the drop-down menu:

  ▲ **Decline — Without a reason:** A notice is sent to the person: "The user has denied your request to add him/her to your Contact List."

  ▲ **Decline — Enter a reason:** A dialog box opens so you can explain why you have chosen not to allow your name to be put on the list. When you click OK, the explanation is sent along with the standard message: "The user has denied your request to add him/her to your Contact List."

▲ **Add To Ignore List:** The person's name is placed on the Ignore List so that you don't receive communications from him or her anymore.

▲ **Close (Ignore):** Nothing happens. The other person doesn't hear from you. However, your name remains on the other person's Contact List under the Awaiting Authorization heading. The other person can click your name and ask again that you give permission to be put on his or her Contact List.

Chapter 10 explains the Ignore List.

The Incoming Request for Authorization dialog box (refer to Figure 4-9) offers two more helpful buttons for fielding Contact List requests:

▼ **Add to Contact List:** Places the person's name on your Contact List (although you may need to get permission first).

▼ **Send Message:** Opens the Send Message dialog box so you can send a message and learn more about the person.

For Microsoft Outlook Users: Adding Contact Names to Your ICQ Contact List

If you who have installed Microsoft Outlook 2000 on your computer, you can search the Contacts folder in Outlook for people who are ICQ users. And if you happen to know that someone on your Outlook Contacts folder is an ICQ user, you can assign that person a name from your ICQ Contact List. By doing so, you can send ICQ events — instant messages, chat requests, URLs, and files — to the person from inside Outlook.

Chapter 8 explains how you can send ICQ events from inside Outlook.

Open Outlook 2000 and follow these steps to search for ICQ users or tell ICQ which of your Outlook contacts are users of ICQ:

1. Click the Contacts icon from the Outlook icon list to go to the Contacts folder, as shown in Figure 4-10.

If you select an e-mail message in your Inbox, the ICQ bar immediately lets you know if the sender is a recognized ICQ user. A white flower icon means that the sender is not recognized; a red flower means that the sender is an ICQ user but is presently offline, and a green flower means that the sender is both an ICQ user and online. ICQ recognizes an e-mail address for a user only if the user has listed this particular address in the View/Change My Details dialog box. If the sender is using a different e-mail address than the one listed in ICQ, you need to assign the correct ICQ name to that address.

Click the Flower button

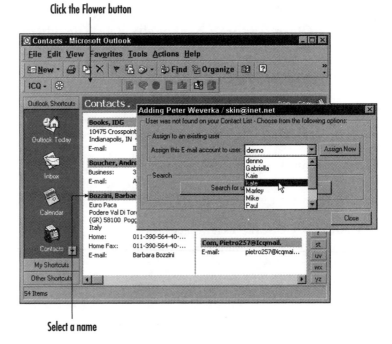

Select a name

Figure 4-10. Searching for people so you can add their names to your Contact List.

2. Select a name on the Contacts list.

3. Click the Flower button on the ICQ bar to find out if the person whose name you clicked is an ICQ user. As shown in Figure 4-10, the Adding dialog box appears.

4. Do either or both of the following:

▲ **Search the ICQ database:** Click the Search for User on ICQ Database button. The ICQ Global Directory Search Engine dialog box appears. If the e-mail address in Outlook matches an e-mail address in the ICQ database, the person's name appears in the search results. You can click the Add User button to place the person's name on your ICQ Contact List.

If you don't see the ICQ bar, choose View➪Toolbars➪ ICQ bar.

▲ **Assign the person to a name on your Contact List:** If you know that the person in question is on your Contact List, open the Assign this E-Mail Account to User drop-down menu and choose a name from your Contact list. Then click the Assign Now button and click OK in the confirmation box.

Adding a Non-ICQ User to Your Contact List

A person doesn't have to be an ICQ user to be on your Contact List. If you intend to send wireless pager messages or SMS (Short Messages Service) text messages to someone, you can put his or her name on your Contact List and send the messages by way of ICQ. You can also communicate by ICQphone to people on your Contact List who are not ICQ users.

The names of non-ICQ users can be found on the Contact List under "Non ICQ Contacts." Follow these steps to put a non-ICQ user on your Contact List:

1. Click the ICQ button.

2. Choose Add/Invite Users⇨Add Non ICQ Contact. The Add Non ICQ Contact dialog box appears.

3. Enter a name, e-mail addresses, and phone numbers in the Main and Phone Book areas.

4. Click the Save button and the Close button.

Tip

Non-ICQ users who are on your Contact List cannot take advantage of all the features that ICQ offers. Only put a non-ICQ user on your list if you can't place him or her there as a regular ICQ user. For that matter, encourage non-ICQ users to become users of ICQ.

4

Finding and Adding Users

Sending Out Invitations to Join ICQ

ICQ is a very exciting and useful way to communicate with other people over the Internet. And the more people that join ICQ, the better ICQ becomes. In that spirit,

ICQ offers a special command for sending e-mail invitations to join the network. The invitation reads as follows (italics show where your name and ICQ number appear):

Hello!

I have tried to contact you through ICQ but couldn't find you in the ICQ Community! If you are using ICQ, please send me your ICQ number by ICQ EmailExpress to
YourICQNumber@pager.mirabilis.com.

If you are not using ICQ, I would like to invite you to join the ICQ Community so we can send messages, chat, and find more friends to join us.

Download ICQ by going to:
http://www.icq.com/download

Once you do so, we can communicate online.

Seek you @ ICQ

Your name

Your ICQ number

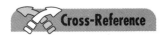

Cross-Reference

Later in this chapter, "Telling Others about Your Four Addresses" describes the four ways that people can reach you in ICQ.

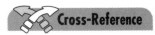

Cross-Reference

The next section in this chapter explains how to send several invitations at once to join ICQ.

The bottom of the message also describes the four ways that your friend can contact you by way of ICQ. The rest of this section tells you how to send the invitation and what happens if the invitation is accepted.

Sending an Invitation to Join

Follow these steps to invite someone to join ICQ:

1. Click the ICQ button in the ICQ window.

2. Choose Add/Invite Users⇨Inviation To Join ICQ on the pop-up menu. The Invitation to Join ICQ dialog box appears.

3. Click the Invite a Friend button. The Invitation to Join ICQ dialog box shown in Figure 4-11 appears.

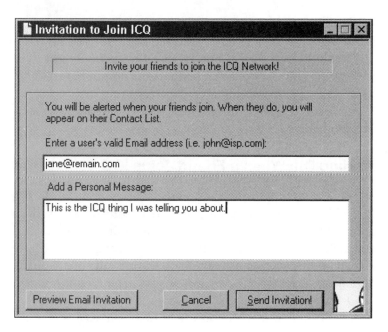

Figure 4-11. Inviting someone to join ICQ.

4. Enter your friend's e-mail address in the text box.

5. In the Add a Personal Message text box, enter a sentence or two explaining why you like ICQ. The words you enter will appear at the top of the message.

6. Click the Send Invitation button. The Preview dialog box appears so you can read the message before you send it. (Click No if you want to return to the Invitation to Join ICQ dialog box and rewrite your message.)

7. Click the Send Invitation button on the Preview dialog box.

If the person to whom you sent the invitation is not an ICQ user, a Future Users Watch area appears on the bottom of your Contact List. Under the new heading, you will find the e-mail address of the person to whom you sent the invitation. The name will stay there until you

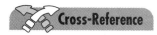

Cross-Reference

Chapter 8 explains how to configure ICQ to send e-mail and tell ICQ what your SMTP address is.

4

Finding and Adding Users

delete it or the name is entered on your Contact List. But if the person is an ICQ user, you see the User Was Found! dialog box. Click the Yes button to send the invitation anyway, or else use the Add/Invite users command to enter the person's name on your Contact List. (See "Searching with the Add/Invite Users Command" earlier in this chapter.)

Finding Out When a Friend Joins ICQ

Suppose the friend to whom you sent an invitation joins ICQ. How do you find out about it? If your friend, in the course of registering, enters the e-mail address to which you sent the invitation, the ICQ system recognizes the e-mail address as the same one you entered in the original invitation to join ICQ. As soon as your friend connects to ICQ for the first time, ICQ sends your friend a message about putting your name on his or her Contact List.

Cross-Reference

Earlier in this chapter, "Adding New Friends to Your Contact List" explains the ins and outs of putting names on the Contact List.

If your friend agrees to put your name on his or her list, the System Message icon appears beside your friend's e-mail address under the Future Users Watch area on your Contact List. Double-click the icon and the Incoming:You Were Added dialog box tells you that your name was added to your friend's Contact List.

If your friend doesn't, however, enter his or her e-mail address when registering with ICQ, you may never know if your friend registers with the network, unless, of course, you ask. You can, of course, search for your friend using the Add/Invite User command and other means of searching.

Telling Others About Your Four Addresses

When you become an ICQ user, you get four "addresses." Other ICQ users can reach you at all four addresses, but non-ICQ users can reach you only at three of the four. Here are the four addresses:

- ▼ **Your ICQ number:** The number by which other ICQ users know you.

- ▼ **Your WorldWide Pager address:** Anyone can go on the Internet to your Personal Communication Center at `wwp.mirabilis.com/`*`your ICQ number`* and write a note to you in the WorldWide Pager, a form that you can find on your Personal Communication Center Web page. Try visiting your Personal Communication Center on the Web by clicking the Services button and choosing My Communication Center.

- ▼ **Your Email Express address:** Anyone can write an e-mail message to you at this e-mail address: *`Your ICQ number@pager.icq.com`*. The message arrives as soon as you log on to ICQ.

- ▼ **Your Web Front:** As long as you have created it, anyone can visit your ICQ homepage, known as the Web Front, on the Internet by going to this address: `members.icq.com/`*`your ICQ number`*.

Here is the message your friends will receive (italics show where your name and ICQ number appear):

> Greetings,
>
> As I am a member of the ICQ Network I would like to provide you with my four ICQ addresses which will enable you to contact me.
>
> 1) My ICQ Number is *Your ICQ number*. If you are a member of the ICQ Network you will be able to contact me through this number. If you would like to join, you can download the program from `http://www.icq.com`.

Chapter 8 describes receiving e-mail messages from sources outside of ICQ.

Chapter 14 explains how to create a personal ICQ homepage.

2) My Personal Worldwide Pager address: You can find my Worldwide Pager on the Web in my ICQ Personal Communication Center page at `http://wwp.mirabilis.com/`*your ICQ number*. From this page on the Web you can send me a real time message. This message will reach me and pop up on my screen. If I'm online — immediately, if I am offline — as soon as I log on to the Internet wherever I may be.

3) My EmailExpress Address is *your ICQ number*@pager.mirabilis.com. You can send me an Email Express. This Email will be delivered directly to my screentop wherever I may be.

4) My Personal ICQ homepage is members.icq.com/*your ICQ number*. Through this page you will be able to communicate with me two ways even if you don't have the ICQ program.

Seek you @ ICQ

Your name

Your ICQ number

To tell your friends who aren't members of ICQ how to reach you at the four addresses, you can send a message that describes the addresses. Here's how:

1. Click the My ICQ button.

2. Choose Send My Four ICQ Addresses on the pop-up menu. You see the Send My Four ICQ Addresses dialog box shown in Figure 4-12.

3. Enter your friend's e-mail address in the text box.

4. If you want to, enter a word or two in the Add a Personal Message text box. The words you write will appear at the top of the message.

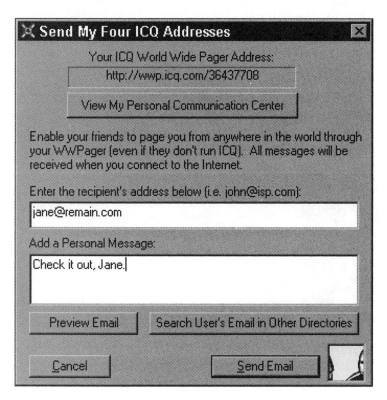

Figure 4-12. Telling others the four ways to reach you in ICQ.

5. Click the Send Email button. The Preview dialog box appears in case you want to read the message before you send it. (Click No if you want to return to the Send My Four ICQ Addresses dialog box and rewrite part of the message.)

6. Click the Send Address button.

People Navigator: Searching for Items in ICQ

No matter what you want to search for in ICQ, you can start in the People Navigator. Its opening page is shown in Figure 4-13. Starting from the People Navigator, you can

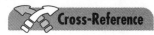

Appendix B describes the general areas and subcategories in the People Navigator.

search for several different items at once — user lists, chat rooms, interest groups, and ICQ Web Front pages — and in so doing find people who share your interests.

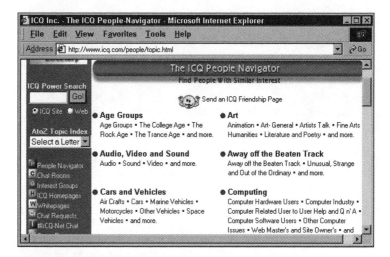

Figure 4-13. You can search for items starting in the People Navigator.

Follow either of these instructions to open the People Navigator in your browser:

▼ Go to this address in your browser: `www.icq.com/people/topic.html`.

▼ Click the Add/Invite Users button, click the Topic Directories tab in the Find/Add Users to Your List dialog box, and click the People Navigator hyperlink.

After you arrive at the People Navigator, follow these instructions to conduct the search:

▼ **Drill down into the topics:** Click the name of a general area, click a subcategory name, and click a topic name. Each time you click, you see a new Web page with subcategories or topics. Eventually, you arrive at what you are looking for. Click the Back button in your browser if you need to back up and start your search in a different direction.

▼ **Search by letter:** Choose a letter from the A to Z Topic Index (the index doesn't appear on some Web pages). You see a list of items whose names begin with the letter you chose.

After you select a general area and subcategory in the People Navigator, you see several letters that tell you whether user lists, chat requests, chat rooms, and so on are available for the topic, as shown in Figure 4-14. By clicking a letter, you can go to a Web page in ICQ. By clicking the letter C, for example, you can go to chat rooms where the topic is discussed. Click the letter M to go to a message board where the topic is being debated.

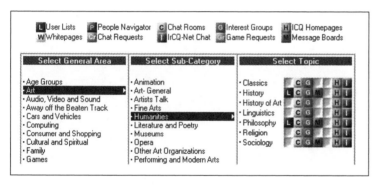

Figure 4-14. Items are organized by general area, subcategory, and topic in the Navigator Directory.

Coming Up Next

Throughout this chapter, you learned how to find and add friends and family to your Contact List. In the next chapter, you find out how to manage all those names you just added. You discover how to organize long lists, put names in groups, and view the list in different ways. You also find out how to send names on your Contact List to others.

Chapter

5

Managing Your Contact List

Chapter 5

Managing Your Contact List

IN THIS CHAPTER

▼ Changing views to work more comfortably in the Contact List

▼ Keeping Contact List names in groups

▼ Renaming and removing Contact List names

▼ Exchanging Contact List names with other ICQ members

The names of ICQ friends, family, and associates appear on your Contact List. This chapter looks into what you need to know to manage a Contact List. You find out how to view the list in different ways. You also find out how to organize Contact List names into groups, remove names, rename people on the list, and change the appearance of the Contact List. Finally, this chapter describes how to trade Contact List names with others.

Different Ways of Viewing Contact List Names

If you forget who someone on your Contact List is, click his or her name and choose User Details/Address Book on the pop-up menu. You can read about the person in the User Details dialog box.

As the Contact List gets longer (and it tends to do that), finding a name gets harder. To remedy the situation, ICQ offers different ways of viewing the Contact List. Instead of viewing everyone's name on the list (and having to scroll the list to read the names), you can see only the names of people who are online and connected to ICQ. And, instead of arranging names on the list in alphabetical order, you can arrange them by group.

In Advanced mode, click these buttons at the top of the Contact List to change views:

▼ **Online Mode button:** When you click this button and you see the green flower, only the names of people who are connected to ICQ are shown, as you can see on the left side of Figure 5-1. Clicking the Online Mode button is a great way to find someone to chat or exchange messages with.

When the Online Mode button is not selected and you see the green-and-red flower, all the names appear — first the names of people who are online and then the rest of the names. As shown on the right side of Figure 5-1, you have to scroll to see all the names on your Contact List.

Tip

Here's a fast way to find a name on a large Contact List: Click the words "My Contact List" in the ICQ window and then, on your keyboard, press the first letter of the name you are looking for. The name is highlighted.

Online mode button

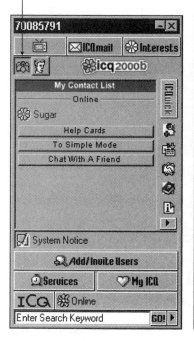
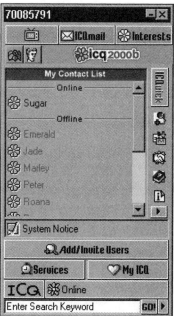

Figure 5-1. Click the Online Mode button to see either only people connected to ICQ (left) or all names on the Contact List (right).

Cross-Reference

Later in this chapter, "Groups for Managing Really Large Lists" explains how to open and close groups, create a new group, and move names from group to group.

Floating Names on the Contact List

Most people multi-task when they use ICQ — they do one or two other things while ICQ is running. That's great, or course, but sometimes the ICQ window gets in the way when you are trying to do other tasks. You can handle that dilemma, however, by floating a name on your Contact List. This way, you can minimize your Contact List and still exchange events with a user or users.

Floating a name means to drag it from the Contact List to a corner or side of the computer screen. When you click a floating name, you see the same pop-up menu that you get when you click a name on the Contact List. Incoming event icons appear next to the name so you know when someone wants your attention. The floating name acts as a mini-ICQ window — one that sits conveniently on the side of the window.

Follow either of these instructions to make a name on the Contact List float:

▼ Click the name and drag it out of the ICQ window.

▼ Click the name and choose "Floating" On from the pop-up menu.

> Follow either of these instructions to move a name back onto the Contact List:
>
> ▼ Drag the name back onto the Contact List.
>
> ▼ Click the name and choose "Floating" Off from the pop-up menu.
>
> If more than one name is floating and you want to move all floating names back to the Contact List, click a floating name and choose All Floating Off.

▼ **Contact List Groups button:** When this button is pressed down and two faces appear on it, names are sorted by group. You can file names under the General, Family, Friends, or Co-Workers group, as well as groups you create yourself. Non-ICQ Contacts constitute their own group.

When the Online Mode button and the Contact List Groups button are pressed down, only the names of people in each group who are connected to ICQ appear.

Names are listed in alphabetical order, but you can move a name up or down the Contact List by clicking and dragging it upward or downward. To alphabetize the list, right-click the Online Mode button, choose Sort, and then choose By Name.

Groups for Managing Really Large Lists

As the left side of Figure 5-2 shows, clicking the Contact List Groups button in Advanced mode arranges the names on the Contact List into groups. ICQ gives you four groups to start with: General, Family, Friends, and Co-Workers. But you can create groups of your own as well.

Contact List Groups button

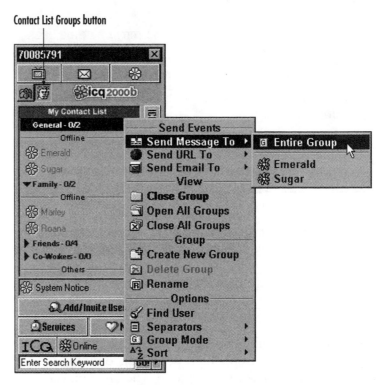

Figure 5-2. Click the Contact List Groups button to arrange names by group on the Contact List.

Obviously, keeping names in groups makes finding names easier. Instead of scrolling through a long list, you can look in a group. And groups offer another advantage: You can send the same message, URL, or e-mail message to all the people in a group and save yourself the trouble of sending the same event several different times (refer to the right side of Figure 5-2). The captain of a softball team, for example, can put the names of all the players in the same group and send the team schedule to everyone at once.

Cross-Reference

Chapter 4 explains how to put the non-ICQ users on your Contact List.

With the exception of external contacts, names you put on your Contact List are put in the General group by default, but moving a name from one group to another is easy. As the following sections explain, you can change the way groups are displayed, view the names in some groups but not in others, change the names of groups, and delete groups.

Displaying and Reading Group Names

Within each group, the names of people who are connected to ICQ appear first under the Online heading. Other names appear under the Offline heading. The following list shows you how to open or close groups on your Contact List:

Tip

Click the Online Status Mode button to see, within each group, only the names of people who are currently connected to ICQ.

- ▼ **Open a group so you can read its names:** Either double-click the group's name or click the name and choose Open Group from the pop-up menu. The triangle beside the group name points down when a group is open.

- ▼ **Close a group to make more room on the Contact List:** Either double-click the group's name or click the name and choose Close Group from the pop-up menu. The triangle points to the right when a group is closed.

Note

You can't move the name of a non-ICQ contact into a group.

- ▼ **Open or close all groups:** Click any group name and choose Open All Groups or Close All Groups from the pop-up menu.

Next to each group name are two numbers separated by a slash. The first number tells you how many people from the group are online; the second number tells you the total number of people in the group. For example, "General - 2/8" tells you that, of the eight people in the General group, two are connected to ICQ.

Moving Names from Group to Group

Names you add to your Contact List are placed in the General group by default. However, moving a name to a different group is easy enough. ICQ offers two ways to move a name on the Contact List from one group to another:

- ▼ **Drag the name to a new group:** Click the name you want to move, hold down the mouse button, drag the name over the name of a group, and release the mouse button.

Changing the Order of Group Names

You can decide for yourself in which order group names appear on the Contact List. To change the order of group names, follow these steps:

1. Click any name and choose Close All Groups on the pop-up menu. Now you can see all the groups and decide what order to put them in.

2. Drag the names up or down the list until they are in the proper order.

▼ **Choose the Move To Group command:** Click the name you want to move, choose Move To Group on the pop-up menu, and click the name of a group on the submenu.

Creating a New Group

Create a new group when you want to categorize the names on your Contact List in a different way. For example, people working on a project with you can be in one group, and the members of your soccer team (if you are on a soccer team) can be in another group. Follow these steps to create a new group for the Contact List:

1. Click the name of any group on the Contact List.

2. Choose Create New Group on the pop-up menu. You see the Create New Group dialog box shown in Figure 5-3.

You can also create a new group by right-clicking the Contact List Groups button and choosing Create New Group.

Figure 5-3. Creating a new group for the Contact List.

3. Enter a descriptive name for the group.

4. Click the Create button.

The new group is placed on the bottom of the Contact List. However, you can drag its name to move it higher on the list.

Renaming a Group

The name of a group isn't descriptive enough? Follow these steps to change its name:

1. On the Contact List, click the name of the group that you want to change.

2. Choose Rename on the pop-up menu. The group name is highlighted.

3. Type a new name and press the Enter key.

Deleting a Group

When you delete a group, you also get the opportunity to either delete the names in the group or move them to another group. You cannot delete the General group. Follow these steps to delete a group on the Contact List:

1. Click the name of the group you want to delete.

2. Choose Delete Group on the pop-up menu. The Confirm Delete Group dialog box appears, as shown in Figure 5-4.

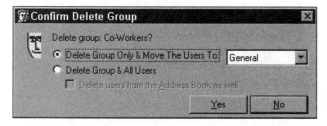

Figure 5-4. Deleting a group on the Contact List.

Sending Messages or URLs to All or Most of the People in a Group

One of the advantages of categorizing names in groups on the Contact List is being able to send messages or URLs to all or most of the people in the group. Instead of laboriously writing messages to six different people, for example, you can write one message and send it to six people at once.

You can send ICQ messages, URLs, or e-mail messages to the people in a group. Follow these steps to do so:

1. With groups displayed on the Contacts List, click the name of the group to whom you want to send messages or URLs.

2. Choose one of the Send Events option at the top of the pop-up menu and then choose Entire Group (the option at the top of the submenu).

3. In the Send Multiple Recipients dialog box, type your message or URL.

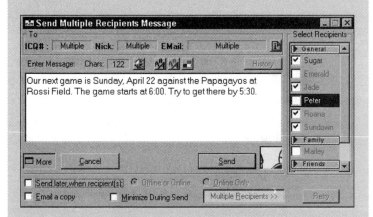

4. Under Select Recipients on the right side of the dialog box, select the names of the people to whom you want to send a message or URL.

5. Click the Send button.

3. Choose one of the following options to either move the names to another group or to delete the names as well as the group:

> ▲ **Delete Group Only and Move the Users To:** Open the drop-down menu and choose where to move the names.

> ▲ **Delete the names as well as the group:** Click the Delete Group & All Users option button. To delete all records of the people whose names you are deleting from the Message Archive, check the Delete Users from the Address Book As Well check box.

4. Click the Yes button.

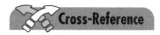

Chapter 12 describes the Address Book.

Chapter 12 explains the Address Book and the Message Archive.

Removing Names from the Contact List

When the Contact List gets too long, prune the list. Review the list and remove the names of the people with whom you no longer correspond. As part of removing a name, ICQ asks if you want to delete the name from the Address Book as well as the Contact List. Keep the name in the Address Book if you want to get in touch with the person later on. Names and ICQ numbers are kept on file in the Address Book.

Follow these steps to remove a name from the Contact List:

1. Click the name you want to remove.

2. Choose Delete on the pop-up menu. The Confirm Delete User dialog box appears.

3. Check the Delete User from the Address Book As Well check box if you anticipate never wanting this person's name on your Contact List again or you don't care to review your correspondence with this person in the Message Archive.

4. Click the Yes button.

Finding Someone on Your Contact List

Suppose you try to find someone on your Contact List, but try as you might, you can't find the name you are looking for. For such occasions, ICQ offers the Find User command. Follow these steps to find a lost name on the Contact List:

1. Right-click the Online Mode button or Contact List Groups button.

2. Choose Find User on the pop-up menu. The Find User dialog box appears.

3. Enter a nickname, name, e-mail address, or ICQ number. After you enter the first few letters or numbers, the bottom of the dialog box opens and you see the name of the person you are looking for — if ICQ can find the person.

4. Right-click the person's name and choose an option from the menu to get in touch with him or her.

Changing a Name on the Contact List

Change a name on the Contact List so that you can easily identify someone. Sometimes two people on the list have the same name. Sometimes remembering a person's name is difficult. Sometimes the nicknames people give themselves in ICQ are not the names you know them by. For times like those, give someone on your Contact List a new name.

People whose names have been changed never know it — they never know it as long as you don't call them the wrong name. And when you want to know the name under which someone has registered in ICQ, all you have to do is move the pointer over the name on the Contact List. As shown in Figure 5-5, the name under which the person is registered appears.

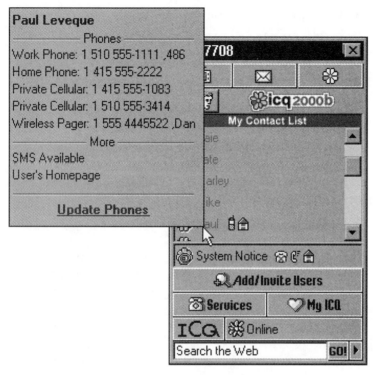

Figure 5-5. Finding someone's official name.

To change a name on the Contact List, click the name and choose Rename on the pop-up menu. The name is high-lighted on the Contact List. Type a new name and press the Enter key.

Redesigning the Contact List

Some people find the Contact List a little dull. The gray background bores them. They want the names of people who are connected to ICQ to be any color but blue. If you are one of these people, ICQ gives you the opportu-nity to change the color scheme of the Contact List by following these steps:

1. Click the ICQ button.

2. Choose Preferences. You see the Owner Preferences For dialog box.

3. Click Contact List on the left side of the dialog box.

4. Click the Colors tab, as shown in Figure 5-6.

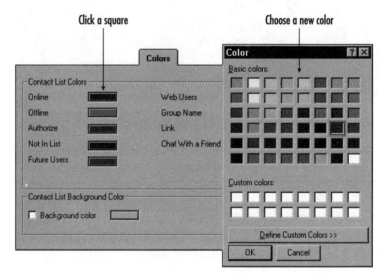

Figure 5-6. Fashioning a color scheme for the Contact List.

5. Click the square beside the Contact List element whose color you want to change. As shown in Figure 5-6, the Color dialog box appears. Table 5-1 describes the Contact List elements whose colors you can change.

6. Click to choose a new color and then click OK.

7. Repeat Steps 5 and 6 to redesign different parts of the Contact List.

8. Click the Apply button in the Owner Preferences For dialog box.

Table 5-1. Contact List Elements

Element	Description
Online	Names of people on your Contact List who are connected to ICQ
Offline	Names of people on your Contact List who aren't connected to ICQ
Authorize	Names of people waiting to be authorized for the Contact List
Not in List	Names of people who sent you items but are not/haven't been added to your Contact List
Future Users	Names of people whom you invited to join ICQ
Web Users	Names of people who sent you items from the Web
Group Name	Group names
Link	URL links in messages
Chat with a Friend Users	Names of people who found you with the Chat with a Friend command
Background Color	Background color of the ICQ window

Suppose you alter the color scheme of the Contact List but regret doing so? To return to the original color scheme, open the Owner Preferences For dialog box (click the ICQ button and choose Preferences) and click the Restore ICQ Defaults button.

Chapter 4 explains how
Contact List authorization
works.

To select all the names in the
Export Users dialog box,
click the first name and then
Shift+click the last one before
clicking the Select button.

Trading Contact List Names with Others

You can send others the names on your Contact List. And
others can send their Contact List names to you. However,
passing around Contact List names doesn't excuse you
from getting permission to put names on your list. If authorization is what the person wants, you still have to get
permission to add a name to your Contact List, even
though someone else sent the name to you.

To send Contact List names to someone else, he or she
must be on your Contact List. You can't send Contact List
names to strangers. Read on to learn how to send Contact
List names to others and what to do when Contact List
names are sent to you.

Sending Out Names on Your Contact List

Follow these steps to send names on your Contact List to
someone else:

1. On your Contact List, click the name of the person
   to whom you want to send the names.

2. Choose Contacts on the pop-up menu. The Export
   Users on Your Contact List to a Member dialog box
   appears, as shown in Figure 5-7. The names of people on your Contact List are on the left side of the
   dialog box.

3. Ctrl+click each name that you want to send.
   Ctrl+click means to hold down the Ctrl key while
   clicking the mouse.

4. Click the Select button. The names you selected are
   moved to the right side of the dialog box. If you selected a name accidentally, click it in the right side
   of the dialog box and then click the Remove button.

5. Click the Send button.

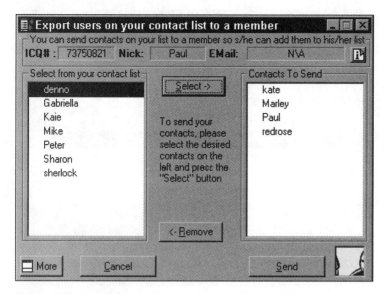

Figure 5-7. Sending names on your Contact List to someone else.

Getting Contact List Names from Somebody Else

The Contacts icon appears beside a name on your Contact List when someone sends you Contact List names. After the names arrive, you can review them one at a time to see if you want to put them on your Contact List.

Double-click the Contacts icon to open the Incoming Contacts List dialog box shown in Figure 5-8. Then follow these steps to investigate each name in the dialog box and perhaps add it to your list:

1. Click a name.

2. Click the Get User Info button. The User Details dialog box appears.

3. Click areas in the dialog box to read about the person. Then click the Close button.

4. Click Add to Contact List to put the person on your list.

Cross-Reference

Chapter 4 explains the ins and outs of putting a new name on the Contact List.

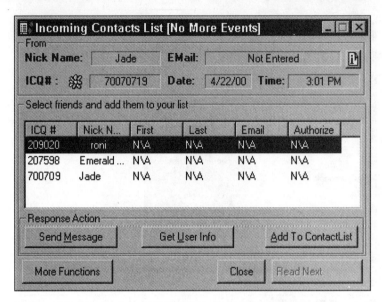

Figure 5-8. You see this dialog box when someone sends you names to add to your Contact List.

What happens next depends on whether you need permission to put the name on your Contact List. Either you see the Privacy - User's Authorization Is Required dialog box or the User Has Been Added dialog box.

Coming Up Next

The next chapter looks at chatting on ICQ. You find out how to invite someone to chat and make the best use of the Chat window. And you learn how to include more than one person in a chat and chat with IrCQ-Net.

Chapter

6

Chatting on ICQ

Chapter 6

Chatting on ICQ

ICQ is famous for chatting. People from all over the world chat on ICQ. ICQ has made it easy to find others to chat with and to engage others in a chat. This chapter explores the chief means of chatting in ICQ. You learn how to engage someone in a chat. You also discover the myriad ways that the Chat window can make chatting more fun. This chapter also explains how to gracefully quit a chat and chat with more than one person. Finally, you discover how to navigate the vast IrCQ-Net and find a chat room there.

Inviting Someone Else to Chat

Cross-Reference

Chapter 5 explains the Contact List and how to put someone's name on it.

To invite a friend to chat, his or her name must be on your Contact List. Not only that, but your friend must be online and connected to ICQ (if you want to start chatting right away, that is). You can tell who on your Contact List is connected to ICQ by glancing at the list and looking at the Online area.

Follow these steps to invite someone for a chat:

1. In Advanced mode, click the person's name.

2. Choose ICQ Chat on the pop-up menu. You see
the Send Online Chat Request dialog box shown in
Figure 6-1.

Figure 6-1. Inviting someone to chat.

3. Write an invitation to chat in the Enter Chat
Subject text box.

4. Click the Chat button.

If your invitation is accepted, you see the Chat window
and you can start chatting. If your invitation is declined,
you see a message box telling you as much. Click OK in
the message box.

What happens on the other end when someone receives
your invitation to chat? Keep reading.

Cross-Reference

Later in this chapter, "Making
Good Use of the Chat
Window" explains how the
Chat window works.

Fielding a Request for a Chat

Anyone who has put your name on his or her Contact List can invite you for a chat. You can tell when you have been invited for a Chat because the Chat icon (a speech bubble with a few lines of indecipherable text) appears in the tray and/or on your Contact List, if the person who invited you for a chat is listed there, as shown in Figure 6-2.

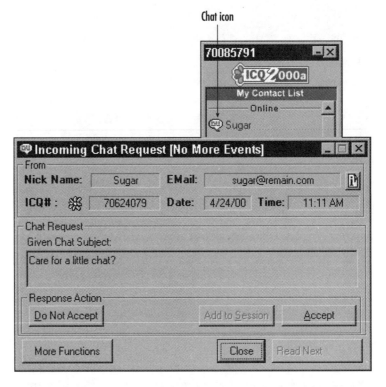

Figure 6-2. Double-click the Chat icon to see the Incoming Chat Request dialog box.

Follow these steps to field a chat request and accept or decline it:

1. Double-click the Chat icon on the Contact List or in the tray to open the Incoming Chat Request dialog box (refer to Figure 6-2).

2. Accept or decline the invitation:

   ▲ **Accept the Invitation:** Click the Accept button. The Chat window appears so you can start chatting. The next section in this chapter describes how to handle the Chat window.

   ▲ **Decline the Invitation:** Click the Do Not Accept button and choose a Decline option from the drop-down list.

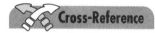

Chapter 9 explains how you can automatically accept or decline all chat requests, both from an individual on your Contact List or from everyone who wants to chat with you.

Making Good Use of the Chat Window

The Chat window appears in all its glory after a chat request invitation has been accepted. Notice that both chatters' names are listed at the top of the Chat window and that your partner's name appears as well above his or her half of the Chat window, as shown in Figure 6-3. When you enter text, your words appear in your half of the window. Your partner's words, meanwhile, appear on his or her half. You don't have to press the Enter key to send your message to your partner, because he or she sees the words as you type them. Only press the Enter key when you want to skip down a line.

The Chat window is designed to make chatting comfortable and easy. You can do much to change the look of the Chat window. By clicking toolbar buttons and choosing options from the menu, you can make the Chat window work the way you want.

Move the pointer over a toolbar button in the Chat window to read the button's name.

Your contributions to the chat

Names of chatters

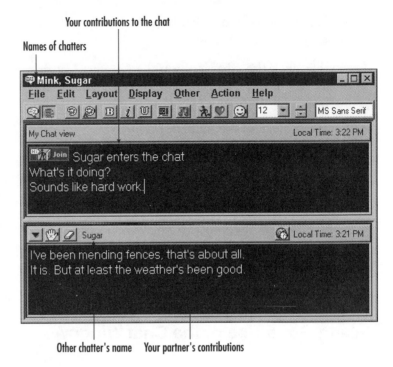

Other chatter's name   Your partner's contributions

Figure 6-3. The Chat window offers many ways to make chats livelier, speedier, and more fun.

These pages explain the many different ways to make the Chat window a livelier and more comfortable place to chat with friends. You will find advice on these pages for the following:

▼ Changing fonts, font sizes, and text color to make chats easier to read.

▼ Choosing a new background color for the window.

▼ Imposing your screen appearance choices on your partner's side of the Chat window. No matter what you do to your side of the window, the other side exhibits your partner's choices, not your own, but you can make the other side of the window look like your side if that makes the chat easier to read.

▼ Changing the layout of the Chat window. Besides a split screen, you can opt for an IRC-style screen so that chatters' names appear next to their comments.

▼ Including emotes, actions, and smileys to make on-line chats more closely resemble real-life chats.

▼ Handling long chats that occur while you are doing several things at once on our computer. You can put the Chat window to sleep, beep your partner to awaken him or her, and freeze the tasks, among other things.

Making the Text Easier to Read

By default, text in the Chat window is white on a black background; the font is MS Sans Serif; and the font size is 12 points. What's your favorite way to display text? You can change the font, font size, and color of text in the Chat window by following these instructions:

▼ **Font:** Open the Font drop-down list on the right side of the toolbar and choose a new font, as shown in Figure 6-4. You might have to enlarge the window to see the down-arrow that you click to open the list.

▼ **Font Size:** Open the Font Size drop-down list and choose a point-size option (refer to Figure 6-4).

▼ **Text Color:** Click the Color button and choose a color on the drop-down list (refer to Figure 6-4). You can also choose Display⇨Color, and select a color in the Color dialog box. Be careful which color you choose. If you choose black text on a black background, for example, you can't read the text.

Tip

To change the font, font size, and text color all at once, choose Display⇨Font. Then choose Font, Size, and Color options in the Font dialog box.

Color button   Font Size menu   Font menu

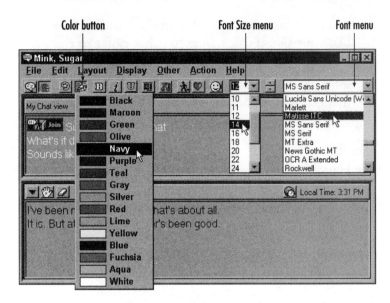

Figure 6-4. Change the look of text by opening a drop-down list or going to the Font dialog box.

Changes you make to the font, font size, and color of text take effect when you start typing. Text that is already in the Chat window stays the same.

Changing the Background Color of the Chat Window

The background color is black by default, but perhaps you prefer another color. Follow either of these instructions to change the background color of the Chat window:

▼ Click the Background Color button and choose a color from the drop-down list.

▼ Open the Display menu and choose Back Color. Then select a color in the Color dialog box and click OK.

Be careful which color you choose, because you can't read the text if it is the same color as the background.

Imposing Your Screen Choices on Your Partner

No matter how strenuously you redecorate your side of
the Chat window, your partner's side exhibits his or her
choices, as shown in Figure 6-5. What if you find your
partner's side of the window hard to read? You can follow
one of these instructions to impose your screen choices on
your partner's side and thereby make reading chats easier:

▼ Click the Override Font & Color button.

▼ Open the Display menu and choose Override
Format.

Note

When you change the
appearance of your partner's
side of the Chat window, he
or she doesn't notice the difference. The changes don't
appear in your partner's
window.

6

Chatting on ICQ

Override Font & Color button

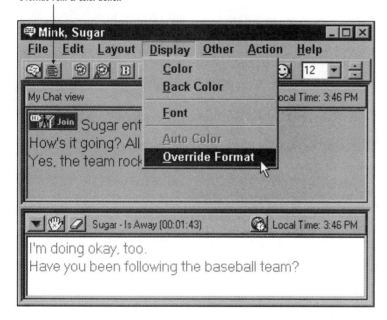

Figure 6-5. Making your partner's side of the window look like your
side.

Changing the Layout of the Chat Window

The Chat window is like any other program window. You
can click its title bar and drag it from place to place. Move
the pointer over the perimeter of the window and start

dragging to make the window larger or smaller. To give more room to one side the window, move the pointer over the division between the sides, click when you see the double arrow, and start dragging.

So much for the standard techniques for rearranging the Chat window. As shown in Figure 6-6, you can also split the window vertically or choose an IRC (*Internet Relay Chat*)-style window instead of a split window.

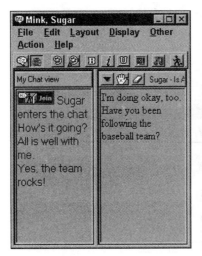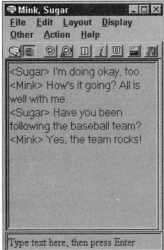

Figure 6-6. A screen split vertically (left) and an IRC-style screen (right).

Note

ICQ switches to an IRC-style window automatically when more than five people are chatting at once.

Here are the three ways to lay out the Chat window:

▼ **IRC-style:** Text appears in the order in which it was entered and chatters' names appear beside their comments. To enter a comment, type it in the space along the bottom of the window and press the Enter key.

▼ **Split screen horizontal:** Your comments appear on the top half of the window; your partner's appear on the bottom half.

▼ **Split screen vertical:** Your comments appear on the left side of the window; your partner's appear on the right side.

Follow these instructions to change the layout of the Chat window:

1. Open the Layout menu.

2. Choose Vertical, Horizontal, or IRC-style.

Emotes, Actions, and Smileys for Making Chats More Lively

One of the drawbacks of chatting on ICQ, of course, is not being able to accompany your remarks with facial expressions, hand gestures, voice inflections, and other things that make real-life conversations roll along.

To help remedy that problem, you can include *actions, emotes,* and *smileys* in your chats. The following list gives you the lowdown on these features:

▼ **Action:** The word *Action* followed by a dramatic description of you performing an action of some kind appears in the Chat window, as shown in Figure 6-7.

Tip

The fastest way to switch between a split and an IRC-style window is to click the Style button on the toolbar.

Tip

Here's a neat way to convey your feelings in a chat: Open the Other menu and choose LOL (or press Ctrl+L). You hear a laughing voice and the letters *LOL* (for laugh out loud) as well as a smiley face, :-), appear in the Chat window.

6

Chatting on ICQ

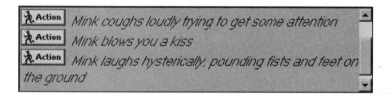
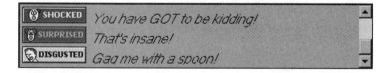
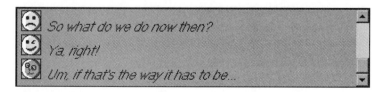

Figure 6-7. Examples of actions (top), emotes (middle), and smileys (bottom).

▼ **Emote:** A picture of a face, a word describing a facial expression, and a bit of text you enter yourself appears in the Chat window, as shown in Figure 6-7.

▼ **Smiley:** A picture of a smiley face appears in the Chat window, as shown in Figure 6-7. You can choose from different smiley faces, each with a different facial expression.

Including an Action in a Conversation

Click the Send Action button on the toolbar and you will see a list of words. Click one of those words and enter the word *Action* and one of the sentences in Table 6-1 (refer to the top of Figure 6-7). Each sentence starts with your name. In the table, the name *Peter* is used as the sample name and the action word, if it appears in the sentence, is italicized.

Table 6-1. Actions for the Chat Window

Action	Sentence That Is Entered
grin	Peter *grins* mischievously.
drool	Peter *drools* with desire.
scream	Peter opens wide eyes and *screams* excitedly.
yawn	Peter *yawns* showing deep boredom.
cough	Peter *coughs* loudly to get some attention.
kicks	Peter *kicks* and screams.
hug	Peter gives you a big warm *hug.*
laugh	Peter *laughs* hysterically, pounding fists and feet on the ground.
kiss	Peter blows you a *kiss.*
ignore	Peter puts his nose in the air making a hmmpf sound, *ignoring* that remark.

Action	Sentence That Is Entered
amazed	Peter opens eyes wide with *amaze*ment.
think	Peter scratches his head, deep in *thought*.
flower	Peter picks a *flower* and hands it to you.
confused	Peter moves eyebrows inward in puzzlement.
jump	Peter *jumps* up and down ecstatically.
scold	Peter points a finger at you, *scold*ing you for your actions.
apology	Peter begs for your forgiveness.
brb	Peter will *be right back*.
excuse	Peter asks to be *excused* and heads for the toilet.
listen	Peter gives you complete attention.

Besides entering one of the sentences in Table 6–1, you can enter an Action sentence of your own by following these steps:

1. Click the Action menu on the menu bar.

2. Choose Send Action. The Action Event dialog box appears.

3. Describe the action but *omit your name*. ICQ will enter your name at the start of the sentence. For example, if you enter **scares the horses with his antics** and your name is Joe, ICQ will enter this action: "Joe scares the horses with his antics."

4. Click the Send button.

Tip

Pressing Ctrl+A is the fastest way to bring up the Action Event dialog box.

6

Chatting on ICQ

Putting an Emote in a Chat

You can convey your emotional state to your chat partner very quickly by entering an emote. Follow these steps to do so:

1. Either click the Send Emote button or open the Action menu and choose Send Emote. The Gesture Event dialog box appears, as shown in Figure 6-8.

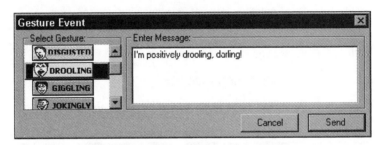

Figure 6-8. Spicing up a conversation with an emote.

2. In the Select Gesture list, choose the option that best describes the way you feel.

3. In the Enter Message text box, enter a comment to accompany the emote.

4. Click the Send button.

Putting a Smiley in the Chat Window

Most people would tell you that a smiley is a bundle of punctuation marks that you type to form a little picture. Popular smileys include the happy face, :-), the devlish wink, ;->, and the frown, :-(. Typically, people type smileys in chats and instant messages to describe how they feel, but you don't have to type them yourself in ICQ because you can choose them from the Send Smiley drop-down list, as shown in Figure 6-9.

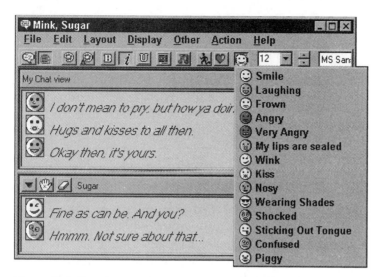

Figure 6-9. Entering a smiley in the Chat window.

Follow these steps to enter a smiley in the Chat window:

1. Click the Send Smiley button on the toolbar.

2. Choose a Smiley from the drop-down list that appears (refer to Figure 6-9).

A Few Tricks for Handling Chats

Here are a few tricks for handling chats and making them even more fun:

▼ **Making your chat partner snap to attention:** Open the Other menu and choose Beep Users (or press Ctrl+G) to get your partner's attention. Your partner will hear two car-horn beeps, and the words *Beep! Beep!* will appear on his or her screen. That ought to get your partner's attention!

▼ **Minimizing the Chat window until your partner comes alive**: No point in leaving the Chat window on-screen if your chat partner appears to have fallen asleep on you. Instead, open the Other menu and choose Sleep (or press Ctrl+S). The Chat window is minimized until your partner starts typing again. As soon as he or she starts typing, the Chat window leaps on-screen and you can continue the conversation.

▼ **Letting your partner know when you are focused elsewhere:** Choose File⇨Send Focus to tell your chat partner you have minimized the Chat window. When the option is selected and you minimize the window, the words *Is Away* appear after your name in your partner's Chat window. A timer even shows how long you are away.

▼ **Keeping the Chat window on top of other windows:** If the Chat window is where you want it to be, you can choose Layout⇨Always on Top. Now the Chat window will stay in the forefront when you switch to another window or computer program.

▼ **Freezing your partner's words:** In a small Chat window that you have tucked in a corner of your computer screen, text can fly by before you get a chance to read it. To make your partner's words stand still, click the Freeze button, one of three buttons on the small toolbar on your partner's side. (The hand graphic of the Freeze button is animated in frozen mode.) Click the Freeze button again to let the text scroll.

▼ **Wiping the text from the Chat window:** Choose File⇨Clear Buffer to erase all the text from the Chat window. To erase only the text on your partner's side of the window, click the Clear button (the one that looks like an eraser on your partner's side of the window).

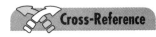
Cross-Reference

Chapter 12 explains the Message Archive, including how to replay or print a chat that you have saved.

Quitting a Chat

All good things, including chats, must come to an end. When you quit chatting, ICQ gives you the opportunity to save the chat in the Message Archive. A chat that you save in the Message Archive can be replayed or printed later on.

How a chat is closed down depends on whether you close it yourself or your chat partner closes it first. If you want to quit a chat without saving it in the Message Archive and you quit it before your partner does, all you have to do is choose a few simple commands. Follow either of these instructions to quit a chat without saving it in the Message Archive:

▼ Click the Close button (the X) and choose Quit⇨ Don't Save Chat Session, as shown in Figure 6-10.

▼ Choose File⇨Quit⇨Don't Save Chat, as shown in Figure 6-10.

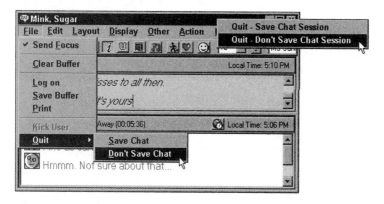

Figure 6-10. The two ways to quit a chat without saving it in the Message Archive.

But if your partner closes the chat before you do, or if you quit the chat and decide to save it in the Message Archive, you see the Chat Session Ended dialog box shown in Figure 6-11. The dialog box offers options for printing the chat, saving it as a text file, or replaying it before you save it in the Message Archive.

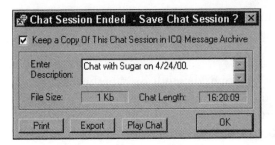

Figure 6-11. Saving a chat so you can review it later.

Uncheck the Keep a Copy of This Chat Session in the ICQ Message Archive check box and click OK if you decide *not* to save a chat. But if you want to quit a chat and save it in the Message Archive, follow these steps:

1. Either click the Close button and choose Quit⇨ Save Chat Session or choose File⇨Quit⇨Save Chat. The Chat Session Ended dialog box appears (refer to Figure 6-11).

2. Check the Keep a Copy of This Chat Session in the ICQ Message Archive check box.

3. Enter a descriptive name for the chat in the Enter Description text box.

4. Click OK to store a transcript of your chat session in the Message Archive.

Besides storing a transcript of your chat session in the Message Archive, the Chat Session Ended dialog box provides you with a number of other ways to keep track of a chat session. Before you save a chat, you can do the following:

Cross-Reference

Chapter 12 explains the ICQ Chat File Player.

▼ **Print the text of the chat:** Click the Print button and then click OK in the Print dialog box. To be able to read the chat, however, reset the text of the chat to a dark color. Unless you do so, the text will print in white, and you won't be able to read it!

▼ **Save the chat as a text (.txt) file:** Click the Export button and choose To Text File. Then save the file in the Save As dialog box. When you print the file, it will appear in IRC mode, where chatters' names appear next to their comments.

▼ **Replay the chat:** Click the Play Chat button and replay the chat in the ICQ Chat File Player dialog box.

Engaging in a Chat-with-a-Friend Chat

One of the fastest ways to make new friends in ICQ is to engage in a Chat-with-a-Friend chat. For that matter, making yourself available to strangers who are looking for a Chat-with-a-Friend chat is also a fast way to make friends. ICQ members' Contact Lists are filled with the names of people whom they met during Chat-with-a-Friend chats.

At any given time, thousands upon thousands of ICQ members volunteer for Chat-with-a-Friend chats. ICQ offers a special button called Chat With a Friend to help you get in touch with them. Read on to learn how to engage in and volunteer for Chat-with-a-Friend chats.

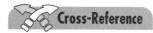 **Cross-Reference**

Chapter 5 explains what a Contact List is and how to enter the names of friends on your Contact List.

Finding a New Friend to Chat With

To start off, make sure you are connected to ICQ and you have chosen Available/Connect on the Status menu. Then follow these steps to find a new friend to chat with:

1. Click the Chat With a Friend button in the center of the ICQ window. The Chat with a Friend dialog box appears.

2. Click the Finding tab.

3. Open the Group drop-down list and choose an option to tell ICQ with whom you want to chat — Romance, Games, or one of the other eight groups.

Cross-Reference

Chapter 2 explains the Status menu and how to change your status.

4. Click the Find an Online Chat Friend button. What
   happens next depends on whether ICQ can find
   someone else who wants to chat. If the search goes
   on too long and nothing happens, click the Stop
   Search button, select a new option from the Group
   drop-down list, and try again. If a volunteer is
   found, the Finding tab lists information like that
   shown in Figure 6-12.

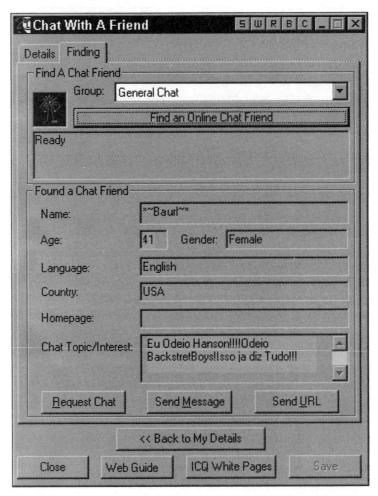

Figure 6-12. Read the Finding tab, and click Request Chat if the
person seems worth chatting with.

5. Read the volunteer's self-description on the Finding tab. Does the volunteer seem worth chatting with?

6. Click the Request Chat button. The Send Online Chat Request dialog box appears.

7. Enter an opening remark in the Enter Chat Subject box and click the Chat button.

And if the other person doesn't seem worth chatting with? Click the Find an Online Chat Friend button to start searching anew. You might try choosing a new group from the Group drop-down list as well.

Volunteering for Chat-with-a-Friend Chats

You meet the nicest people in Chat-with-a-Friend chats. Follow these steps to volunteer yourself for a chat with a stranger:

1. Click the Chat with a Friend button.

2. Select the I Want to Be Available to Chat with a Friend check box.

3. Describe yourself on the text boxes and drop-down list boxes. Others will see the information you enter if your name comes up in a Chat-with-a-Friend chat (refer to Figure 6-12).

4. Enter an enticing reason why you want to chat in the Enter Your Chat/Topic Interest text box. What you enter there will encourage or discourage others from engaging you in a chat.

5. Click the Save button and then the Done button.

Make sure you are connected to ICQ. Unless you click the Status button and choose Available/Connect, no one can engage you in a chat.

If someone wants to chat with you, a new name appears on your Contact List under the Random heading and the Chat Request icon appears beside the name as well as in the tray. Double-click the Chat Request icon and the Incoming Chat Request dialog box appears.

Tip

The personal details on the Details tab come from the White Pages. You can change your self-description, however, without regard to your description in the White Pages. Chapter 11 explains how to describe yourself in the White Pages.

Cross-Reference

Chapter 2 explains how to change your online status.

Chatting with More Than One Person

When more than two people are chatting, choose Display⇨Auto Color to assign a different color to each chatter's contributions.

More than two people can engage in a chat. In fact, that Chat window can accommodate an unlimited number of people. When a new chatter arrives, a new area is added to the Chat window. Instead of being divided into two parts, it is divided into three or four or five. However, if more than five people participate in a chat, the Chat window switches automatically to IRC mode, and chatters' names appear next to their comments.

Read on to learn how to invite someone to participate in a chat that you are in the midst of. You will also find instructions for inviting someone who invited you to chat to a chat you're already having.

Inviting Someone from Your Contact List to Participate in an Ongoing Chat

Suppose you are chatting with someone and you notice on your Contact List that a friend has connected to ICQ. You say to yourself, "Why not invite her to chat, too?" Follow these steps to include a person whose name is on your Contact List in a chat that you're having already:

1. In Advanced mode, click the person's name on the Contact List and choose ICQ Chat. You see the familiar Send Online Chat Request dialog box.

2. Enter a chat invitation in the Enter Chat Subject text box.

3. Click the Join Session button at the bottom of the dialog box and, from the drop-down list that appears, choose the chat to which you want to invite the person.

4. Click the Chat button.

Bringing Someone Who Sent You an Invitation into a Chat

You're chatting along when suddenly you get an invitation to chat with someone else. Rather than engage in two chats at once, you can invite the person who sent you the invitation to participate in the chat you are already having. Follow these steps:

1. In the Incoming Chat Request dialog box you receive from the other user, click the Add to Session button, as shown in Figure 6-13.

2. From the drop-down list, click the chat in which you want to include the other person.

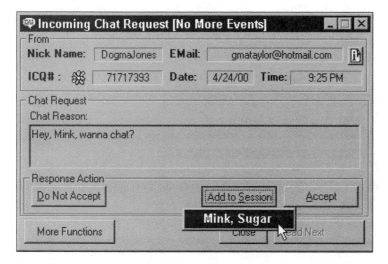

Figure 6-13. When an invitation to chat comes, you can invite the person into an ongoing chat.

Booting a Third (Or Fourth or Fifth) Person Out of a Chat

Majority rules in ICQ. As long as the majority of chatters support it, you can boot someone out of a chat. That's right — you can kick out someone who is using profanity or is otherwise being a boor. After one chatter proposes kicking someone out, all the chatters vote, and if the majority favors giving one party the boot, he or she is booted.

When someone is nominated for ousting, you see the Remove User? dialog box. It lists the name of the person who has been nominated. Click OK to remove the user named in the dialog box or click Cancel to vote against removing him or her. If the majority favors kicking out the chatter, the User Kicked (or the You Were Kicked) dialog box appears.

Follow these steps to attempt to kick someone out of a chat:

1. In the Chat window, open the File menu.

2. Choose Kick User. The ChatDirect Session - Kick User dialog box appears, as shown in Figure 6-14.

Figure 6-14. Nominating someone to be kicked out of a chat.

3. Double-click the name of the person you want to kick out or click the name and then click the Kick User button.

4. Click OK in the Confirmation box.

Other chatters vote whether to kick the chatter out. Look at the bottom of the ChatDirect Session - Kick User dialog box for the results of the vote (refer to Figure 6-14).

Chatting on the IrCQ-Net

The IrCQ-Net is a giant online social club with many different chat rooms. At any given time, thousands upon thousands of people are chatting on IrCQ-Net. The network offers 40 chat rooms as well as the numerous chat rooms that visitors create. Chats take place in a special window, not in ICQ dialog boxes. In fact, you don't have to be connected to ICQ to visit an IrCQ-Net chat room.

Instead, you go to the Web site of IrCQ-Net, where you give yourself a nickname and decide which chat room to enter. Then the IrCQ-Net window opens, you enter the chat room, and you start chatting away. Each room is devoted to a particular subject, although chatting being what it is, the subject tends to change frequently.

Participating in different chat rooms is easy — so is going from chat room to chat room. The makers of IrCQ-Net have made entering emotions (also known as emotes) and changing the color of text simple. If you want to chat directly with someone whose name you see in a Chat window, that is easy, too. Keep reading.

Entering a Chat Room at IrCQ-Net

Follow these steps to go to IrCQ-Net and enter a chat room so you can chat with others:

1. In your Web browser, go to the following address: `www.icq.com/ircqnet`. You arrive at the Web page shown in Figure 6-15.

6

Chatting on ICQ

Figure 6-15. This page is the starting point for engaging in IrCQ-Net chats.

After you enter the IrCQ-Net window and start chatting, you can change your nickname. To do so, click the Nick button, and in the Change Nickname dialog box, enter a new name and click OK.

2. Enter a nickname in the Your Nickname text box. Other chatters will know you by the name you enter. You don't have to use your ICQ nickname. Names cannot include blank spaces.

3. Optionally, enter your ICQ number and e-mail address as well. If you enter your ICQ number, it will appear after your nickname in Chat windows so others know how to contact you in ICQ.

4. Scroll down the page and click a room you would like to enter. Don't worry about choosing precisely the right room. As the following pages explain, you can enter another room easily enough.

The IrCQ-Net window appears, as shown in Figure 6-16. Notice the Status tab and the tab named after the room you chose near the top of the screen. If you enter other rooms, their tabs will appear as well.

Choose another room   Chatters

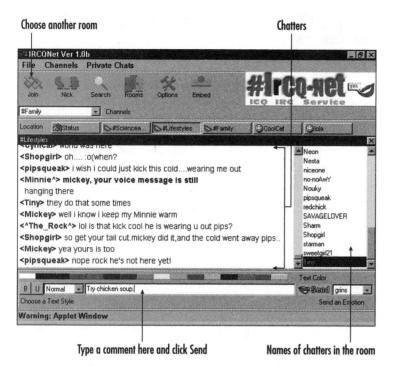

Figure 6-16. Chats take place in the IrCQ-Net window.

Type a comment here and click Send   Names of chatters in the room

To contribute to a chat, type your comment in the text
box near the bottom of the window and click the Send
button or press the Enter key. Chat contributions appear in
the window. The names of chatters in the room appear on
the right side of the window.

Besides the chat rooms that you can enter from the IrCQ-
Net Web page, IrCQ-Net offers many more chat rooms
that were created by visitors to the network. To get to
them, however, you have to be inside the IrCQ-Net window. Read on.

Entering Other Rooms and Chatting Directly with Others

Most people open two or three chat rooms at the same time and flutter from room to room as their interests take them elsewhere. If someone in a chat room seems worth talking to in private, you can double-click his or her name on the right side of the IrCQ-Net window for a private chat.

A tab appears in the IrCQ-Net window for each chat you are engaged in. To go from chat to chat, click a tab. On the tabs, the names of chat rooms you have entered are preceded by a number sign (#) and are marked by red lips; chats you have in private are marked with a smiley face.

IrCQ-Net offers no less than three different ways to enter another chat room. The Channels drop-down menu and the Join button offer 25 chat rooms, but you can access all the rooms, including those created by visitors to IrCQ-Net, by clicking the Rooms button:

▼ **Open the Channels drop-down list:** From the Channels drop-down list, choose another chat room. You will find the list above the room tabs.

▼ **Click the Join button:** Click the Join button, choose a new chat room in the IRCQNet Join Room dialog box and click OK.

▼ **Click the Rooms button to open the Rooms list:** Click the Rooms button to open the Rooms list of all the chat rooms, as shown in Figure 6-17. Then scroll down the list, find a room that looks promising, and double-click its name to enter it. IrCQ-Net puts a new tab in the window — the Rooms tab — so you can return to the Rooms list and perhaps enter another room.

After you have opened the Rooms list, you can click the Rooms button again to get an up-to-date list of rooms and the number of chatters in each room.

Double-click a chat room to enter it

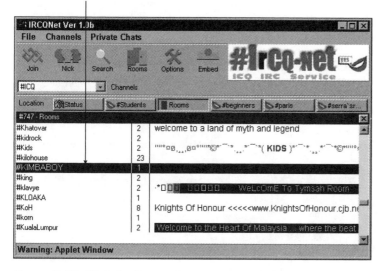

Figure 6-17. Click the Rooms button to visit chat rooms that visitors to IrCQ-Net created.

To chat privately with someone whom you met in a chat room, double-click his or her name on the right side of the IrCQ-Net window. A new tab opens in the IrCQ-Net window so you can start chatting.

Sending an Invitation to Chat on IrCQ-Net

If you are chatting away in an IrCQ-Net and you realize all of the sudden that someone on your Contact List belongs in the chat, you can invite him or her to come to the chat room. To do so, click the person's name on your Contact List and choose IrCQ-Net Invitation. The Send Online IrCQ-Net Invitaiton dialog box appears.

From the Categories drop-down menu, choose where the channel you want your friend to visit is found. Then click the name of a chat room on the Chat Rooms drop-down menu and click the Send button to send the invitation.

6

Chatting on ICQ

Making a Chat Room Livelier

Here are a few techniques for making chats a little livelier in the IRCQ-Net window:

> ▼ **Change the color of text:** Click one of the Text Color buttons at the bottom of the IRCQ-Net window, as shown in Figure 6-18, and start typing.

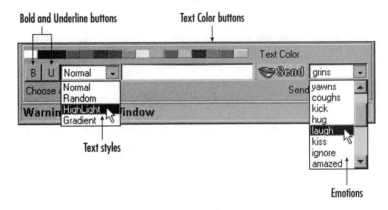

Figure 6-18. Techniques for making a chat livelier.

> ▼ **Boldface or underline text:** Click the Bold (B) or Underline (U) button and start typing (refer to Figure 6-18).

> ▼ **Send an emotion:** Choose an option from the Send an Emotion drop-down list (refer to Figure 6-18).

> ▼ **Choose a text style:** Open the Choose a Text Style drop-down list and choose Random, Highlight, or Gradient, and start typing (refer to Figure 6-18). Experiment with these options to find out what they are. If you want to change a style, click the Options button, and in the IRCQNet Options dialog box, click the SpecialFX button. Then choose an Effect from the menu and change the settings.

Cross-Reference

Earlier in this chapter, "Emotes, Actions, and Smileys for Making Chats More Lively" explains what an emotion is.

Coming Up Next

The next chapter explores how to make new friends in
ICQ. You discover ActiveLists and the various places in
ICQ where you can go to meet new and exciting people.
You also explore the ins and outs of posting messages and
chat requests so you can find friends.

Chapter

7

Making New Friends in ICQ

Quick Look

Chapter 7

Making New Friends in ICQ

This chapter explores the numerous ways that you can find new friends in ICQ. It explains searching the White Pages, ActiveLists, user lists, interest groups, the message boards, the Chat Request page, and public chat rooms. What are all those things? Keep reading. The first section in this chapter explains them.

A Look at the Ways to Find Friends

ICQ offers more than a few ways to make new friends:

▼ **White Pages:** Search the ICQ White Pages for people whose interests are the same as yours, who live in your town, or who share a common past, among other things. See "Searching the White Pages for New Friends."

▼ **ActiveLists:** Being a member of an ActiveList puts you in touch with people who share your interests whenever you connect to ICQ. After you join an ActiveList, you can see its members' names on your Contact List. You can tell who is online and get in touch with them quickly. See "Exploring ActiveLists."

▼ **User lists:** A user list is a list of people who are devoted to the same hobby or pursuit. ICQ users maintain user lists on their Web sites. Go to a user list and you can find the names — and contact information — of people who share your interests. See "Looking for Friends on User Lists."

▼ **Interest groups:** ICQ maintains interest groups at its Web site so that like-minded people can stay in touch with one another. From an interest group page, contacting a group member is easy. After you join an interest group, others can find you quickly as well. See "All about Interest Groups."

▼ **Message boards:** Post or reply to a message on the message boards. Topics are organized into categories and folders to make it easy to find the subject you want to discuss. See "Paying a Visit to the Message Boards."

▼ **Chat requests:** ICQ users can post invitations to chat on the Chat Request Page. Go to the page to find someone to chat with or invite others to chat. See "Visiting the Chat Request Page."

▼ **Chat rooms:** Any ICQ user can create a public chat room. The names of rooms appear on the Contact List. When a room is up and running, you can click its name and choose ICQ Chat to join the conversation. See "Locating and Joining a Public Chat Room."

Cross-Reference

Chapter 11 explains in detail how to describe yourself in the ICQ White Pages. The techniques for entering information about yourself are the same as the techniques for describing who you want to find in the White Pages Search Engine.

Searching the White Pages for New Friends

Everyone who registers with ICQ is encouraged to describe themselves in the ICQ White Pages. Besides the basics, such as your nickname, age, and the place where you live, you can describe your occupation, interests, and affiliations. You can list the schools you attended and the clubs and organizations you belong to.

Information about all ICQ users is kept in the White Pages. By searching the White Pages, you can find people who share your interests, grew up in the same place as you, have the same occupation as you, or went to the schools you went to. You can find ICQ users who are or who have done any number of things.

Figure 7-1, for example, shows a search for people who live in San Francisco and attended the University of California at Santa Barbara. With the names gathered from this search, you could arrange a little college reunion. As the figure shows, you can right-click a name in the search results area at the bottom to send an instant message to someone whose name is on the list.

Follow these steps to conduct a search of the White Pages:

1. Click the Services button.

2. Choose ICQ White Pages⇨Search ICQ White Pages. The ICQ White Pages Search Engine dialog box appears (see Figure 7-1).

3. Check or uncheck the Show Only Online Users check box. When the box is checked, only people who are currently connected to ICQ are uncovered in the search. Check the box if you intend to contact the people whom you find immediately or you want the search to go faster. The search goes faster, because ICQ searches only for people who are connected to ICQ.

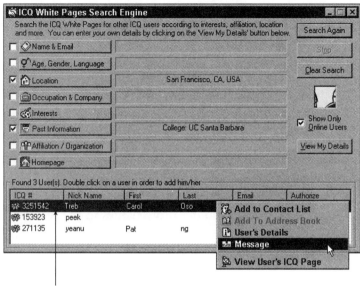

Right-click a name to contact a person

Figure 7-1. Searching the White Pages.

4. Click buttons and fill in dialog boxes to describe
who you want to search for. You don't have to click
all the buttons and fill in all the dialog boxes. Only
enter information that you want to find in the
White Pages.

5. Click the Search button.

Eventually, the names of people who match the search
conditions you entered appear in the search results area.
Right-click a name to contact someone on the list or add
him or her to your Contact List.

In some cases, your search doesn't work out. If no match is
found, you see the No User(s) Were Found message box.
Or if too many matches are found, the Too Many Results
message box appears. In any event, try these techniques to
undertake a more productive search:

▼ **Wrong results:** Change the search conditions. Or
uncheck the check box next to a button to tem-
porarily remove a search condition from the search.

7

Making New Friends in ICQ

By unchecking, you can check the box later on and use the search condition without having to re-enter it into a dialog box.

▼ **Too many names:** Change the search conditions to make them narrower. You can also check the Show Only Online Users check box (if you unchecked it before) to get only the names of people who are connected to ICQ.

▼ **Too few names:** Change the search conditions to make them broader. And try unchecking the Show Only Online Users check box (if you checked it before). This way, you get more names in the search results.

Exploring ActiveLists

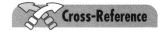

Cross-Reference

Chapter 11 explains how to own and administer an ActiveList.

An *ActiveList* is like an online social club. Each ActiveList is devoted to a particular interest or theme. ICQ users create and maintain ActiveLists. Being the member of an ActiveList puts you in touch with people who share your interests whenever the list is online — that is, whenever the owner or administrator is connected to ICQ.

After you join an ActiveList, the names of all the members become accessible to you. As shown in Figure 7-2, you can make the name of an ActiveList to which you belong appear where the Contact List normally appears. The names of members who are online are shown at the top of the list. By clicking a name, you can contact a member in the normal way — by sending an instant message or a chat request, for example. By clicking the name of the ActiveList, you can see a menu for sending all members an instant message, chatting with several members at once, reading the club news, and doing any number of other things, as Figure 7-2 demonstrates.

Click the Active List to see the pop-up menu

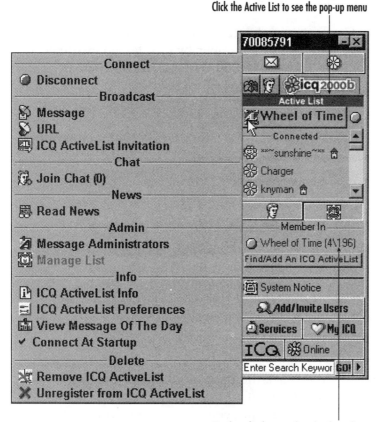

Number of online members/total members

Figure 7-2. Click the Services button and choose ICQ ActiveList⇨ Show ICQ ActiveLists to see the ActiveLists to which you belong.

Read on to learn how to join an ActiveList, handle list names and member names in the ICQ window, get information and messages from the owner of the list, send events to members, engage members in a chat, and unregister from an ActiveList.

Later in this chapter,
"Sending and Receiving an
Invitation to Join an
ActiveList" explains another
way to join an ActiveList —
by invitation.

Joining an ActiveList

ICQ offers these different ways to search for and join an
ActiveList: by its ID number, by its title, and by category.
Follow these steps to find an ActiveList and perhaps join it:

1. Click the Services button and choose ICQ
ActiveList⇨Find/Add an ICQ Active List.

2. Click an option button to search by ID number,
name, or category:

▲ **Search by List ID:** Enter the number of the
Active List if you happen to know it.

▲ **Search by List Title:** Enter the name of the
ActiveList if you know it.

▲ **Search by Category:** If you choose this option
and click the Next button, the dialog box asks
you to select a category and a language. Select
the Language check box and choose a language
from the drop-down list.

To choose a category, click the check box and
then click the Press to Edit Topic/Keywords button. In the ICQ Interests Selection dialog box,
choose a topic, choose a category, and choose a
subcategory, as shown in Figure 7-3. Then click
the Add button. You can enter more than one
subcategory. Click OK to return to the
ActiveList Search Wizard dialog box.

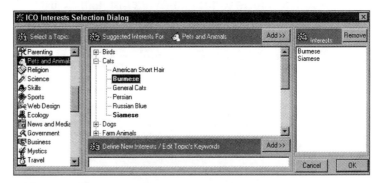

Figure 7-3. Searching by topic/keyword for an ActiveList.

3. Select or deselect the Show Only Online ActiveLists box. Deselect the box if you want to search only for ActiveLists whose owners are online. As I point out shortly, owners have to be online for you to obtain the names of people on an ActiveList. By checking Show Only Online ActiveLists box, you can obtain names faster.

4. Click the Next button. If ICQ can find ActiveLists, the ICQ ActiveList Search Wizard dialog box appears. (If ICQ can't find lists, ICQ tells you as much. Click the Back button and try again.) Besides the ID number of the ActiveList, its title, its subject, and a description, the dialog box offers this important information:

   ▲ **The number of administrators/members:** The # of Users column tells you, first, how many list owners or administrators are currently online and, second, how many people have joined the list altogether. The larger the list, the more you will get out of it.

   ▲ **Authorization:** Whether you need authorization from the owner of the list or its administrators to join.

5. Select a list that you are interested in and click the More List's Info button. You see the ICQ ActiveList Info dialog box, as shown in Figure 7-4.

6. Read the Main, More, and Owner tab of the dialog box to learn more about the ActiveList, and then click the Cancel button to return to the ICQ ActiveList Search Wizard dialog box.

7. Click the Add List button in the ICQ ActiveList Search Wizard dialog box if you decide to join the ActiveList.

7

Making New Friends in ICQ

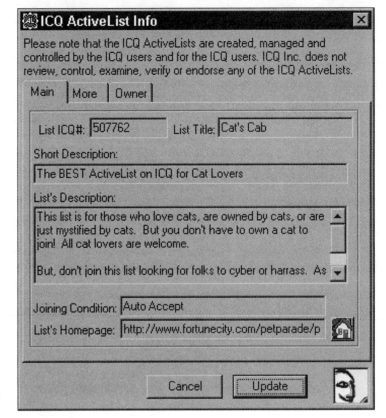

Figure 7-4. The ICQ ActiveList Info dialog box tells you much about an ActiveList.

You can tell by glancing in the ICQ ActiveList Search Wizard dialog box whether any ActiveList owners are on-line. When owners are on-line, the green online status indicator appears in the ICQ# column.

Later in this chapter, "Unregistering from an ActiveList" explains how to remove yourself from an ActiveList.

What happens next depends on whether you need authorization to join the list, whether the list owner or any list administrators are online, and whether any members of the list are online. When you join an ActiveList, the names of its members are sent to your computer.

In the case of an ActiveList that you need authorization to join, only the list owner or an administrator can authorize your membership. Here are the different scenarios for what happens after you click the Add List button in the ICQ ActiveList Search Wizard dialog box:

▼ **You don't need authorization to join and an ActiveList member is online:** You see the Join ICQ ActiveList dialog box shown on the left side of Figure 7-5. Click the Next button to download the list of members to your computer. In a moment, the dialog tells you that the names have been downloaded. Click the Done button.

Figure 7-5. Joining an ActiveList when you don't need (left) and do need (right) authorization.

▼ **You don't need authorization to join and no members are online:** A message box tells you that the ActiveList has been added to your Contact List. You will find the name of the ActiveList under the Guest In heading. Later, when a owner of the list comes online, the circle beside the list's name will turn green (like a traffic light). At that point, you can click the name of the list and choose Join List on the pop-up menu. You will see the Join ICQ ActiveList dialog box shown on the left side of Figure 7-5. Click the Next button to download the members' names to your computer.

▼ **You need authorization to join:** You see the Join ICQ ActiveList dialog box shown on the left side of Figure 7-5. Click the Next button and the dialog box shown on the right side of Figure 7-5 appears. Enter the reason you want to join and click the Next button.

7

Making New Friends in ICQ

Tip

If the owner or the administrators of the ActiveList are slow in approving your membership, click the name of the list, choose Ask Authorization on the pop-up menu, and try again.

**Sending and Receiving an Invitation
to Join an ActiveList**

One way to join an ActiveList is to do so by invitation. If
someone sends you an invitation to join an ActiveList,
you can be pretty sure that the list is worth joining.
Follow these steps to send someone an invitation:

1. Click the person's name on your Contact List.

2. Choose ICQ ActiveList Invitation. You see the Send
   Online ICQ Active List Invitation dialog box. It lists
   each ActiveList you belong to.

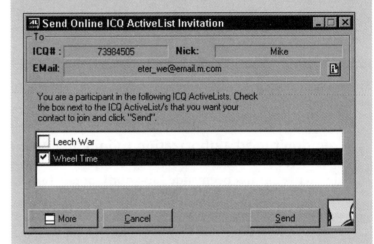

3. Check the names of the ActiveLists for which you
   want to send invitations.

4. Click the Send button.

To send an invitation to several people at once, click the
name of an ActiveList in the ICQ window and choose
ICQ ActiveList Invitation. Then in the Send Multiple
Recipients dialog box, check the names of lists for
which you want to send invitations, check the names of
people to whom you want to send invitations, and click
the Send button.

When you receive an invitation to join an ActiveList, the ActiveList Invitation icon appears beside a name on your Contact List. Double-click the icon and you see the Incoming ICQ ActiveList Invitation dialog box. Follow these steps to see if the ActiveList is worth joining and perhaps join it:

1. Click the Add an ICQ ActiveList button. Soon you see the ICQ ActiveList Search Wizard dialog box.

2. Click the More List's Info button. The ICQ ActiveList Info dialog box opens. It describes the ActiveList, tells you who its owner is, and shows the acceptance requirements.

3. Click Cancel to close the ICQ ActiveList Info dialog box.

4. Click the Add List button if you decide to join the ActiveList and take it from there. (See the previous section of this chapter for details.)

The ActiveList appears in the ICQ window under the Guest In heading if members were online when you attempted to join, or the ActiveList appears under the Awaiting Authorization heading if no members were online. Later, if the owner or an administrator of the list authorizes you to join, you receive a System message telling you so. After that, you can click the name of the list when one of its members is online, choose Join List on the pop-up menu, and click the Next button in the Join ICQ ActiveList dialog box to download the members' names to your computer.

Once you become a member of an ActiveList, all the other members know when you are online. They can click your name to contact you or click the name of the ActiveList to send events to everyone on the list.

Click the Show/Hide ICQ ActiveLists button on the ICQuick shortcut bar to hide or display ActiveLists in the window.

Click the Online Mode button (the Flower button directly beneath the Channels button on your Contact List) to view only ActiveList members who are connected to ICQ. Click the button a second time to view all members.

Handling ActiveLists in the ICQ window

Click the Services button, choose ICQ ActiveList on the pop-up menu, and check the Show ICQ ActiveLists command to view lists you have joined in the ICQ window. ActiveLists appear in the bottom half of the window, as shown in Figure 7-6.

A green circle beside an ActiveList name means that the owner of the list is connected to ICQ. The numbers that come after list names mean, first, how many members are online and, second, how many members are in the ActiveList altogether. After you select a list, the names of its members appear at the top of the ICQ window.

Follow these instructions to handle ActiveLists in the ICQ window:

▼ **View a different ActiveList:** Scroll to and click the name of the list. You can also right-click the ActiveList button, choose Show ICQ ActiveList, and select a list (refer to Figure 7-6).

▼ **Switch between ActiveLists and your Contact List:** Click the ICQ List or ActiveList button. You can also right-click the ActiveList button and choose Show Contact List or choose Show ICQ ActiveList and select the list you want to view (refer to Figure 7-6).

▼ **View only your Contact List:** Click the Show/Hide ICQ ActiveLists button on the ICQuick shortcut bar, or click the Services button, choose ICQ ActiveList on the pop-up menu, and uncheck the Show ICQ ActiveLists command.

Communicating with the other Other Members

Besides posting and reading news items (the subject of the next section in this chapter), you can communicate with the other members of an ActiveList in the following ways:

Switch between Contact List ActiveLists

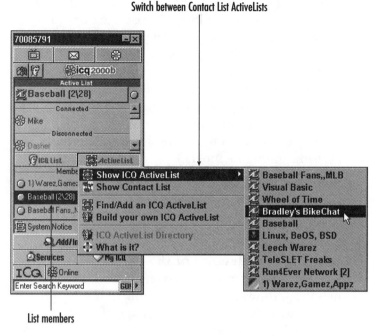

List members

Figure 7-6. The names of ActiveLists appear in the bottom half of the ICQ window.

▼ **Broadcasting and receiving a message or URL:** To send a message or URL (Web page address) to ActiveList members who are online, click the name of the ActiveList and choose Message or URL on the pop-up menu. Then in the Broadcast dialog box, enter the message or a note to accompany the URL, and click the Broadcast button. You can click the Specify Recipients button to send the message or URL to some, not all, of the ActiveList members who are online.

When you receive a message or URL, the ActiveList message or ActiveList URL icon appears in the tray and beside the name of the ActiveList. Double-click the icon to read the message or URL.

Note

You can always communicate with an ActiveList member in the usual way — by clicking his or her name and choosing a command on the pop-up menu. Instant messages and other events you send this way are not shared with all the members of the ActiveList who are online.

▼ **Starting or joining a chat:** Click the name of an ActiveList and choose Join Chat on the pop-up menu to start a chat among the members. If members are already chatting, you see a number in parentheses after the Join Chat command. The number tells you how many people are chatting at present. Click the Join Chat command and the Chat window appears on-screen so you can chat with other members. (Some ActiveLists do not permit chatting among members.)

▼ **Sending a message to the owner administrators:** Click the name of the ActiveList and choose Message Administrators to send a message to the owner and administrators of the ActiveList.

▼ **Reading the Message of the Day:** The owner of an ActiveList can post a Message of the Day for members. To read it, click the name of the ActiveList and choose View Message of the Day from the pop-up menu.

To find out who the owner of an ActiveList is, click the list's name and choose ICQ ActiveList Info. Then click the Owner tab in the ICQ ActiveList Info dialog box.

Reading and Spreading the News

ActiveList members can post messages for others to read, as well as respond to messages that others have posted. To read news from other members, click the name of the ActiveList and choose Read News on the pop-up menu. (Some ActiveLists do not permit members to post messages.) You see the News Board dialog box, as shown in Figure 7-7. Click the Download Next 50 button to find out if anyone has posted messages.

The titles of messages (and their replies) appear in the top of the dialog box. Click the plus sign (+) next to a message title to see its replies. To read a message, select it in the top of the dialog box and read it in the bottom. Follow these instructions to post and reply to messages:

Select a message . . .

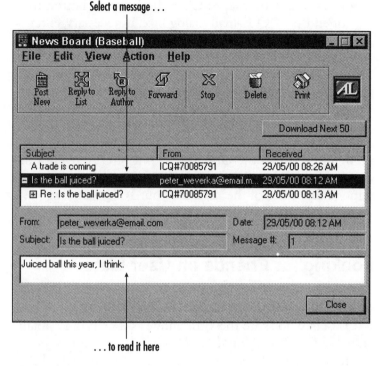

. . . to read it here

Figure 7-7. Getting the news from other members of an ActiveList.

▼ **Post a new message for all to read:** Click the Post New button. In the Message dialog box, enter a title for your message and the message itself.

▼ **Reply to a message:** Select the message that needs a reply and click the Reply to List button. Then enter a title and write your reply in the Re: Message dialog box. The message you enter will appear below the message to which you are responding. To read your message, others will click the plus sign (+) beside the message you are replying to (refer to Figure 7-7).

▼ **Reply to the author privately:** Click the Reply to Author button. The ICQ E-mail dialog box appears. Enter an e-mail address in the To box, if necessary. Then write your reply and click the Send button.

Cross-Reference

Chapter 8 explains how to send messages by ICQ E-mail.

▼ **Forward a message:** Click the Forward button to open the ICQ E-mail dialog box. If necessary, enter an e-mail address in the To box and click the Send button.

Unregistering from an ActiveList

To unregister from an ActiveList, click the name of the list and choose Unregister from ICQ ActiveList on the pop-up menu. Then, in the Unregister from ICQ ActiveList dialog box, click the Next button. Click Next again to remove the name of the list from your ICQ window.

Looking for Friends on User Lists

A *user list,* also known as a *User Created List,* is a list of ICQ users who share the same interests. The lists are maintained by ICQ users on their Web sites. When someone creates a user list, he or she submits its name to ICQ. ICQ enters the name of the user list in the PeopleSpace Directory so that ICQ users can find, visit, and perhaps join it.

Usually, the Web page where the user list is found offers a form that you can fill out if you want to join. Also on the Web page are members' names and ICQ numbers. A user list is like an address book for people who share the same passion or hobby. After your name is entered on a list, others can find you easily.

Anyone can visit a user list with or without joining. Follow these steps to find and visit a list that interests you:

1. Go to the User Created Lists page at ICQ by doing one of the following:

   ▲ Click the ICQ button and choose Add/Invite Users⇨Users' List.

   ▲ Go to this address in your browser: `www.icq.com/icqlist`.

2. Click general areas and subcategories until you find a topic that intrigues you.

3. Click the name of the topic. As shown in Figure 7-8, names and descriptions of user lists appear.

Click to visit a user list

Figure 7-8. Look for user lists in the PeopleSpace Directory.

4. Click a View List button or logo to visit the user list on the Internet.

All about Interest Groups

An *interest group* is a collection of people who are interested in the same topic. Unlike user lists, interest groups are maintained on computers at ICQ. Getting in touch with a member of a group is simply a matter of clicking the Message Me or Page Me button. To examine groups and perhaps join one, you search the ICQ Interests Groups page. After you join an interest group, returning to it is easy, because ICQ maintains a special page for you on the Internet where it keeps the names of interest groups to which you belong.

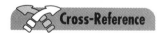

Cross-Reference

Chapter 11 shows how to create your own interest group.

Read on to discover how to find an interest group, join one, and visit a group that you belong to.

Looking for and Joining an Interest Group

Here are instructions for searching for interest groups and joining them. Not every interest group you find is worth joining, but you are sure to find one you like if you look long enough.

Note

If you have already joined an interest group, clicking the Interest Groups hyperlink in the Topic Directories tab of the Find/Add Users to Your List dialog box takes you to the Service Area page, which lists groups that you have joined. To look for a new group to join from there, click the Join a Group hyperlink.

Follow these steps to search for an interest group:

1. Do one of the following to go to the Welcome to the ICQ Interest Groups page at ICQ.

   ▲ Click the Add/Invite Users button, click the Topic Directories tab in the Find/Add Users to Your List dialog box, and click the Interest Groups hyperlink.

   ▲ Open your browser and go to this address: `groups.icq.com/main.asp`

2. Search the ICQ Interests Groups page until you come to a list of interest groups like the one in Figure 7-9. Groups are ranked in order by number of members (but you can click the Name or Date option button to put groups in alphabetical order or date-of-creation order).

3. Click the View button beside the name of an interest group that looks intriguing.

You come to a Web page where members' names and ICQ numbers are listed. At the top of the page is the name of the *interest group master,* the person who created the group. To learn more about the group, click the Message Me button and query the interest group master. While you're at it, click members' names or the Zoom Me button to read members' profiles in the White Pages and see if the people in the interest group are your kind of people.

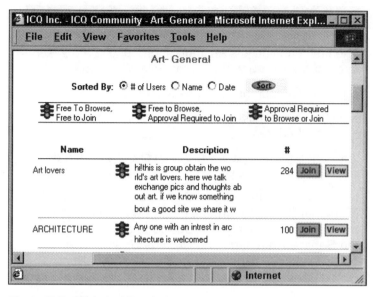

Figure 7-9. Click the View button to visit an interest group.

If you find an interest group you like, follow these steps to join it:

1. Either click the Join This Group link (you will find it under Activities) on an interest group page, or if you are looking at a list of interest groups (refer to Figure 7-11), click the Join button. You come to the Your Details page.

2. In the Group Specific Details box, describe what you hope to get out of the group. The words you enter will appear in the Details for Group column on the interest group page.

3. Click the Save button.

4. Click Continue to go to your Service Area page, or View This Group to return to the interest group you just joined. Your Service Area page lists interest groups that you have joined (see "Visiting an Interest Group to which You Belong").

Note

If this is the first time you have joined an interest group, you have to enter some information about yourself. See "Joining Your First Interest Group."

7

Making New Friends in ICQ

Joining Your First Interest Group

The first time you join an interest group, you are asked to enter the following "Personal Details" information:

▼ Your ICQ number and password.

▼ Personal details such as your name, age, and e-mail address.

▼ An image of a face, which you choose from a dozen or so faces on a list.

No matter how many interest groups you join, your "Personal Details" information stays with you. You only have to enter it once. If you decide to change it, go to the Service Area page and click the Update More Details link (see "Changing Your Details or Quitting a Group" later in this chapter).

Incidentally, when someone clicks the Zoom Me button on an interest group page, he or she sees your profile in the White Pages, not the personal information you enter when you join an interest group for the first time. But when someone clicks your name in an interest group, he or she sees your "Personal Details" information.

Visiting an Interest Group to which You Belong

Do either of the following to go to your Service Area page and visit an interest group that you belong to:

▼ Click the Add/Invite Users button, click the Topic Directories tab in the Find/Add Users to Your List dialog box, and click the Interest Groups hyperlink.

▼ Open your browser and go to this address:
`groups.icq.com/service-area.asp`

The Service Area page lists the interest groups that you belong to. Click a View button to go to an interest group. Click the Update More Details link to change the "personal details" you entered the first time you joined an interest group.

Changing Your Details or Quitting a Group

To change your self-description or quit an interest group to which you belong, start by going to your Service Area page (see the previous section in this chapter). Then click the Edit button beside the name of the interest group that you want to quit or change your self-description in. You come to the Edit Info For page, where you can do the following:

- ▼ **Change your personal details:** Click the Personal Details hyperlink to change the "personal details" you entered when you joined your first interest group.

- ▼ **Change your group-specific details:** Click the Group Specific Details hyperlink to change the words you wrote for the Details for Group column of the interest group page.

- ▼ **Quit the group:** Click the Remove Yourself from This Group hyperlink. Then click Yes when ICQ asks you if you really want to quit the group.

Paying a Visit to the Message Boards

The message boards are places to debate topics, trade stories, exchange information, and meet new people. The ICQ message boards work very much like other message boards. You can post messages and reply to messages that others posted. Others can do the same to you.

Read on to learn how to search the message boards, find discussions that interest you, register and log in, post or reply to a message, and bookmark discussions so you can return to them later.

7

Making New Friends in ICQ

Reading Messages on the Message Boards

To visit the message boards and read messages, click the Add/Invite Users button, click the Topic Directories tab in the Find/Add Users to Your List dialog box, and click the message boards link. You go to the Message Boards page of the PeopleSpace Directory (`www.icq.com/boards`).

From there, you can either navigate the Message Boards section of the PeopleSpace Directory until you find a topic you are interested in or you can search by keyword for messages. Messages on the message boards are stored in folders (and sometimes subfolders as well) and *discussions*. A *discussion* is a collection of messages that pertain to the same topic. Keep burrowing deeper until you come to a message that interests you. As Figure 7-10 demonstrates, ICQ shows the trail you took in the form of hyperlinks and pointing hands. To retrace your steps, click a hyperlink to return to a topic, folder, or discussion.

Figure 7-10. To backtrack through the message boards, click a hyperlink.

Often the best way to find messages that interest you is to search for them. To do that, click the Search button. (You can usually find it, along with other buttons, at the bottom of pages.) On the search form that appears, enter a keyword for the search, and click an option button to search all the message boards or merely the folder you are in. (The top of the search form tells you which folder that is.) Then click the Search button.

Registering (and Choosing Your Preferences) so You Can Post Messages

Before you can post or reply to a message on the message boards, you have to register and obtain a password. Click the Register button to register. (You'll find the button near the bottom of most message boards.) You see the New User Registration form. Fill it out and click the Register button. And while you're at it, either write down your password or commit it to memory.

You need the password to enter messages on the message board. The password ensures that no one enters messages under your name.

When you see the Registration Complete page, click the Preference button. You see a form for entering the preferences. How you fill out the form determines what others can learn about you when you post a message. Your name and the second line of information (if you enter a second line) will appear prominently at the top of messages. As for these parts of the form, people who read your messages will be able to click your name, go to a second Web page, and learn the following:

Note

After you choose your preferences, the Preference button appears at the bottom of pages on the message board. You can always click the Preference button to change your preferences.

▼ **Your homepage:** Others can click a link on the second page to go to the Web page you enter.

▼ **Personal information:** Others can read the description you enter here after clicking your name.

▼ **Your favorite URLs:** Others can click the descriptions of your favorite URLs to go to those Web page addresses. As the form indicates, enter the Web page address, then a blank space, and then the description.

Click the Set Preference button at the bottom of the page when you are finished choosing what others can learn about you on the message boards.

The first time you post a message after arriving at the message boards, you will be asked to log in. On the Login page, enter the name and password you gave ICQ when you registered on the message boards.

Tip

Instead of waiting for ICQ to ask you to log in, you can simply click the Login button to get to the Log In page and enter your log-in information. You will find the button at the bottom of most message board pages.

7

Making New Friends in ICQ

Posting a Message on the Message Boards

Here are instructions for posting and replying to messages on the message boards:

To delete a message you wrote, find the message and click the Delete button. You will find this button beside your message.

▼ **Starting a new discussion:** A discussion is a collection of messages about the same topic. Start a discussion when you want to gather opinions about a matter. As shown in Figure 7-11, discussions on the message boards are marked with the lips icon.

To start a discussion, click the Add Discussion button. Then enter a title and description on the Web page that appears. Click the Add Discussion button at the bottom of the page when you are finished.

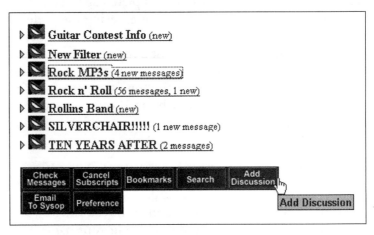

Figure 7-11. Click the Add Discussion button to start a discussion like the ones shown here.

▼ **Replying to a message:** At the bottom of every message is a form for entering a reply. Enter a title, enter your reply, and click the Post My Message button. On the message boards, your reply appears below the original message.

▼ **Replying directly to someone who posted a message:** Click the person's name (if the poster entered his or her name). You come to a new Web page with links that you can click to send e-mail to the poster or visit the poster's Personal Communication Center (and write the person a message from there).

Bookmarking Discussions so You Can Revisit Them

Suppose you want to keep track of a discussion on the message boards. Or maybe you want to return to a message you posted to see if anyone has replied. To be able to return to a discussion quickly, click the Bookmark button. You will find this purple button at the bottom of the first message in a discussion. (Don't click the blue Bookmarks button, which takes you to a Web page that lists discussions you have bookmarked.)

After you click the Bookmark button, you go to the Bookmarks page. If you want, enter a comment about the discussion and click the Set button. To visit the Bookmarks page, click the blue Bookmarks button that is found at the bottom of most pages on the message boards. From the Bookmarks page, click a discussion name to return to it. Click the Delete button to delete a bookmark.

Another way to find messages you posted is to search for them. Click the Search button and enter your name as the keyword for the search.

You must log in before you can bookmark a discussion.

Be sure to click the Refresh button in your browser from time to time to update the list on the Chat Request page.

Visiting the Chat Request Page

Besides chat-with-a-friend chatting, which is explained in Chapter 6, you can find a stranger to chat with by going to the Chat Request page, a Web page where ICQ members can offer themselves for chats or engage someone else in a chat.

Figure 7-12 shows the Chat Request page. To get to this Web page, do one of the following:

▼ Click the Add/Invite Users button. In the Find/Add Users to Your List dialog box, click the Chat tab, and then click Chat Request, the fourth hyperlink in the first group of hyperlinks.

View chat requests

Invite others to chat

Figure 7-12. Read the list of topics and click View to see who's chatting.

▼ Go to this address in your browser: www.icq.com/chatrequest

Chatters submit their invitations in topics. You can tell how many chatters have submitted invitations in each topic by glancing at the numbers.

You can you tell if someone you want to chat with is on-line by glancing at the status indicator, the Flower icon beside his or her name. Chapter 2 explains the status indicator and how you can use it to reveal or hide your online status.

To find someone to chat with on the Chat Request page, scroll down the page, read the list of topics, and find a topic that interests you. Then click the View button beside the topic's name. You see a Current Chat Requests page similar to the one in Figure 7-13. Read the chat invitations, and when you find one that seems promising, click the Chat with Me button.

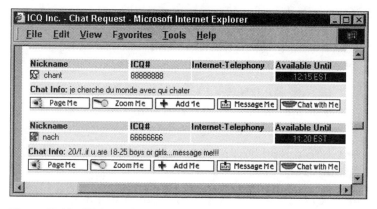

Figure 7-13. Click the Chat with Me button to engage someone in a chat.

To put out your own request to chat on the Chat Request page (refer to Figure 7-12), find the category where you want to leave your invitation and click the Request button in the category. You see the Post a Chat Request page. Fill in the form. Under Time, state how long you will be online. Be sure to enter an enticing invitation to chat in the Description box.

Tip

Leave invitations to chat in more than one category. Doing so increases your chances of finding someone to chat with.

Cross-Reference

Chapter 6 explains how to create your own public chat room.

Locating and Joining a Public Chat Room

A *public chat room* is one that is maintained by an ICQ user. Any ICQ member can create one. After you join a public chat room, its name appears on your Contact List. You know when the room is open and receiving chatters, because its name appears under the Contact List's Online heading. To enter the chat room, you click its name and choose ICQ Chat on the pop-up menu. Then the Chat window opens so you can start chatting away.

7

Making New Friends in ICQ

ICQ keeps a list of public chat rooms that are currently online in the ICQ Chat Rooms Directory. Do either of the following to go to the there and start searching for a public chat room:

▼ Click the Add/Invite Users button, click the Chat tab in the Find/Add Users to Your List dialog box, and then click the Chat Rooms Directory link.

▼ Go to this address in your browser:
   `www.icq.com/icqchat`

The ICQ Chat Rooms Directory only lists public chat rooms that are currently open. When you find a chat room you want to join, click the Add Room to Contact List button, as shown in Figure 7-14. Whether you can join right away depends on whether you need authorization from the chat master, the person who maintains the public chat room. On the Contact List, the names of public chat rooms are preceded by an ampersand (&).

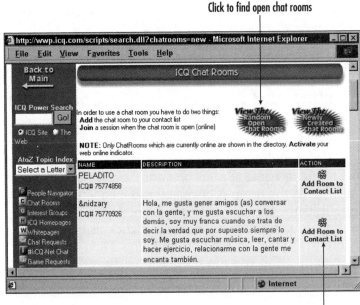

Figure 7-14. Go to the PeopleSpace Directory to search for and join a public chat room.

Because a chat room must be online for you to join it, finding a chat room to join can be problematic. However, you can always click the Random Open Chat Rooms link to examine chat rooms that are open. You will find this link on many pages in the ICQ Chat Rooms Directory. You can also find open chat rooms by clicking the Add/Invite Users button, clicking the Chat tab in the Find/Add Users to Your List dialog box, and then clicking the Find a Random Chat Room link.

Coming Up Next

The next chapter describes the e-mail services that ICQ offers. You learn how to subscribe to and use ICQmail, the free service that is available to all ICQ users. You also find out how to send e-mail to sources outside the ICQ network and how to receive e-mail from outside sources. The chapter even explains how you can be alerted in ICQ when e-mail has arrived in your private e-mail accounts.

Trading E-Mail
Messages over ICQ

Quick Look

ICQmail and ICQ E-mail — What's the Difference?　　　page 189

ICQ offers two ways to send and receive e-mail: by ICQmail and ICQ E-mail. For people to send and receive ICQmail, they must first subscribe to the ICQmail service. All ICQ users can send and receive ICQ E-mail without having first to subscribe; moreover, any ICQ user can receive ICQ E-mail from non-ICQ users as well.

Take Advantage of Free ICQmail Service　　　page 190

ICQmail is free to all ICQ users. After you register, you get an e-mail account from which you can send e-mail and files to others. You can also receive e-mail, keep an address book, and store messages in your ICQmail account. You don't have to be connected to ICQ to send and receive ICQmail.

Send ICQ Events While You Are
Working in Microsoft Outlook　　　page 209

You can send ICQ events — instant-messages, chat requests, URLs, and files — while you are inside the Microsoft Outlook 2000 program. All you have to do is select the name of an ICQ user on your Outlook Contacts list and click a button on the ICQ Integration for Outlook toolbar.

Chapter 8

Trading E-Mail
Messages over ICQ

This chapter explains the various and sundry e-mail features of ICQ. ICQ offers a special e-mail service called ICQmail. After you subscribe and get your ICQmail account, you can send and receive ICQmail e-mail. Whether you subscribe to ICQmail or not, people can send e-mail to you in ICQ — the messages arrive the same way that instant messages arrive, for example. What's more, you can send e-mail to addresses outside the ICQ network. This chapter explains how you can be alerted in ICQ when e-mail has arrived at the mailbox you keep with your Internet Service Provider. Finally, for users of Microsoft Outlook, this chapter describes how to send ICQ events from Outlook.

The Difference between ICQmail and ICQ E-Mail

ICQ offers two e-mail services, ICQmail and ICQ e-mail:

- ▼ **ICQmail:** A free e-mail service that all ICQ users can subscribe to and use. The service works like MSN hotmail, Yahoo mail, and other free e-mail services. First, you register. Then you get an e-mail address to which others — ICQ users or not — can send you e-mail. You can send e-mail from your account to others as well. ICQmail is a Web-based e-mail service: All the sending and receiving of messages is done inside your Web browser on a Web page, not in the ICQ window. You don't have to be connected to ICQ to send or read ICQmail, although you can quickly access your ICQmail from the ICQ window.

- ▼ **ICQ E-mail:** A feature whereby you can send e-mail to or receive e-mail from others in the ICQ window. You don't have to subscribe to ICQ E-mail to send and receive messages — the service is available to all ICQ users by way of their normal e-mail accounts. Sending and receiving ICQ E-mail is much like sending and receiving instant messages: You have to be connected to ICQ to send and receive. When e-mail arrives in ICQ, you see the EmailExpress icon in the desktop tray. When you double-click the EmailExpress icon, you can see and read the e-mail message.

Figure 8-1 shows an EmailExpress and ICQmail icon in the ICQ window. When you receive a message by ICQ E-mail, the EmailExpress icon appears. The ICQmail icon appears on the System Notice button when you get a message by ICQmail.

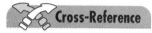

Cross-Reference

The next section in this chapter, "Subscribing to and Using the ICQmail Service," explains ICQmail. See "Receiving ICQ E-Mail from Sources Outside the ICQ Network" and "Sending ICQ E-Mail Messages to Mail Boxes Outside ICQ" later in this chapter to learn about ICQ E-mail.

Definition

EmailExpress: The ICQ term for an e-mail message that an ICQ user sends to a mailbox outside ICQ, or an e-mail message sent from outside ICQ to an ICQ user.

EmailExpress message from outside ICQ

Message to your ICQmail account

Figure 8-1. ICQ offers two kinds of e-mail: ICQ E-mail and ICQmail.

Subscribing to and Using the ICQmail Service

ICQmail is free to all ICQ users. Not only that, ICQmail makes sending and receiving e-mail easy. After you open an ICQmail account, you get a free e-mail account at this address: *a name@icqmail.com*. Anyone can send e-mail, and files as well, to your ICQmail address. When items arrive, you are notified in ICQ, but you can collect and send ICQmail messages without running ICQ as well. If you're on the road, for example, you can collect and send ICQmail from an Internet café by logging into the ICQmail Web site. You can also keep an address book, and you can even store e-mail correspondence in different folders in the ICQmail Web site to stay organized.

Subscribing and using ICQmail doesn't require you to load special software on your computer. Everything is done inside your browser window. Messages are placed on a Web page after they arrive so you can read them. To obtain a file that was sent to you, you click a hyperlink on a Web page. Your addresses are kept on a Web page as well.

This section discusses how to do the following in ICQmail:

▼ Receive and read ICQmail messages

▼ Receive and read ICQmail messages, when you are on the road, without connecting to ICQ

▼ Write and send a message to someone else

▼ Send and receive files

▼ Delete messages

▼ Store messages in folders (also known as pages)

▼ Keep an address book

However, before you do anything, you have to register. Read on.

Registering for ICQmail

Follow these steps to register for ICQmail:

1. Click the ICQmail button at the top of the ICQ window.

2. Choose Register New Account on the pop-up menu. Your browser window opens to the Register for ICQmail page (`www.icq.com/icqmail/client.html`).

3. Enter your ICQ number, enter an ICQ password, and click the Continue button. You come to a Terms of Use page.

4. Read the terms of use and click the I Accept button. You see the Request an Email Address page.

Caution

ICQmail allows each subscriber to store up to 5 megabytes of data in his or her account. If you often receive large files, be sure to collect your ICQmail regularly. Files cannot be delivered if you exceed the 5-megabyte limit.

Note

You can register more than once and maintain several different ICQmail accounts.

8

Trading E-Mail
Messages over ICQ

Tip

Very likely, your name or nickname have already been taken. To get an e-mail address that is easy to remember, try entering a number after your name or nickname.

Note

Your ICQmail e-mail address is entered automatically in the Main section of the View/Change My Details dialog box after you register for ICQmail. Click the ICQ button, choose View/Change My Details, and click Main to read your address.

Cross-Reference

Later in this chapter, "Handling your ICQmail on the Road" explains how you can retrieve and read ICQmail messages without connecting to ICQ first.

5. In the first text box, enter what you would like the *your name* side of your ICQmail address to be, and, in the second and third text boxes, enter other words that ICQ can use to generate an e-mail address. Then click the Continue button.

If one of the names you want has not been taken, a Web page tells you what your ICQmail address is. Very shortly, an ICQmail message is sent to your newly opened ICQ mail account and the ICQmail icon appears on your System button. Shortly thereafter, your browser opens automatically so you can read the message. It welcomes you to ICQ and briefly describes the many things you can do with ICQmail.

If the name you entered isn't available, however, either click the option button next to one of ICQ's suggestions for a name and click the Register button, or click the Back button and start all over.

Retrieving and Reading ICQmail Messages

When new ICQmail messages arrive, the ICQmail icon appears on the System Notice button (refer to Figure 8-1) or beside the sender's name on the Contact List. Double-click the icon (or click it and choose Receive) to open the Incoming ICQmail Message dialog box. As soon as the dialog box opens, so does a new page in your browser window. As shown in Figure 8-2, the new page shows the message so you can read it.

Notice the buttons on the top of the message for replying, replying to all who received the message if more than one person received it, and forwarding the message. When you click the Reply, Reply All, or Forward button, the Write Mail page appears so you can write your reply or forward the message. On the page, an address has already been entered if you are replying. To forward a message, enter an address.

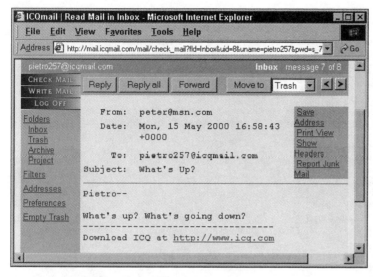

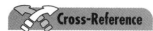

Later in this chapter, "Writing and Sending a Message" explains the Write Mail page.

Figure 8-2. Reading an ICQmail message.

To read e-mail messages that have already arrived in your account, click the ICQ button, choose the name of your account on the pop-up menu, and choose Read Mail (Inbox) on the submenu. Doing so takes you to a Web page where new messages appear, as shown in Figure 8-3. From there, click the Check Mail button to collect your ICQmail messages.

Messages that you have not read yet are shown in boldface type. Click a message subject in the Inbox to open it in your browser and read it (refer to Figure 8-2).

Writing and Sending a Message

To send an ICQmail message, click the ICQmail button, choose the name of your account on the pop-up menu, and choose Read Mail (Inbox). You can also click the Write Mail button if you are looking at the Inbox in your browser window. Either way, you see the Write Mail page shown in Figure 8-4. Fill out these text boxes and click the Send button:

8

Trading E-Mail
Messages over ICQ

Click a message to read it

Click to collect your mail   Unread message

Messages from ICQmail subscribers

Click to go to other folders

Figure 8-3. The Inbox, where messages arrive.

Handling Your ICQmail on the Road

Good news: You don't have to run ICQ or be connected to the ICQ network to collect your ICQmail, send ICQmail messages, or organize messages in folders. As long as you can access the Internet, you can collect your ICQmail and write messages to others, no matter where you are.

To collect your ICQmail without running ICQ, go to this address in your Web browser: `www.icq.com/icqmail`. You land in the Log In to ICQmail page. Enter your e-mail address, enter your ICQ password, and click the Login button. You see the Inbox (refer to Figure 8-3).

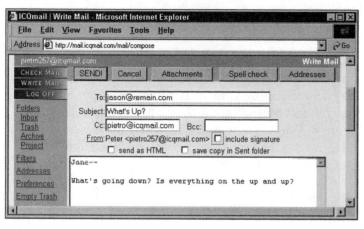

Figure 8-4. Writing and sending an ICQmail message.

▼ **To:** Enter the recipient's e-mail address. To send the same message to more than one person, enter a semicolon (;) and a second e-mail address.

▼ **Subject:** Briefly describe your message. The recipient will see what you type here first.

▼ **Cc:** If you want to, enter an e-mail address here to send a copy of the message to a third party.

▼ **Bcc:** Enter an e-mail address here to send a blind copy. When you send a blind copy, the primary recipient of the message isn't told that a copy was sent to a third party.

▼ **Include Signature:** Select this box if you want to include a signature at the bottom of your message. A signature is a snippet of text that appears at the bottom of an e-mail message. By default, the signature reads, "Download ICQ at `http://www.icq.com/icqmail/signup.html`."

▼ **Send as HTML:** Select this box if you intend to include HTML code in your e-mail message.

▼ **Save Copy in Sent Folder:** Select this box to save a copy of the message in the Send folder so you can review it after you send it. (ICQmail creates the Send folder when you place your first copy there.)

Tip

To quickly enter an address that is filed in your Address Book, click the Addresses button. On the Address Book page, select the To, Cc, or Bcc check box next to a name, and then click the Address Message button to return to the Write Mail page. Later in this chapter, "Keeping an Address Book in ICQmail" explains how to maintain an address book.

8

Trading E-Mail
Messages over ICQ

Don't forget to click the Spell Check button to correct misspellings in your message before you send it.

Sending a File Along with a Message

To send a file along with an ICQmail message, click the Attachments button on the Write Mail page (refer to Figure 8-4). You arrive in the Attachments window shown in Figure 8-5. For each file you want to send along with your message, follow these steps:

1. Click the Browse button. The Choose File dialog box appears.

2. Locate the file, select it, and click the Open button. The path to and the name of the file you chose appear in the Locate File to Attach box.

3. Click the Attach button. The name of the file is listed at the bottom of the Attachments page.

If you change your mind about sending a file, go to the bottom of the Attachments page, select the check box next to the name of each file you *don't* want to send, and click the Remove Selected button.

After you have attached the file, click the Return to Message button to return to the Write Mail page. Click the Send button to send the file and the message.

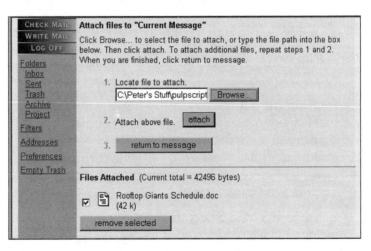

Figure 8-5. Sending a file with an ICQmail message.

Receiving a File over ICQmail

You know when you have received a file along with an
e-mail message because, under Attachments at the bottom
of the message, the file or files are listed, as shown in
Figure 8-6. If you want to open the file immediately, simply click the name of the file to view it. If you want to
download the file to a folder before you open it, right-
click the name of the file and choose Save Target As (or
Save Link As) from the menu that appears. Then, in the
Save As dialog box, locate and select the folder where you
want to save the file and click the Save button.

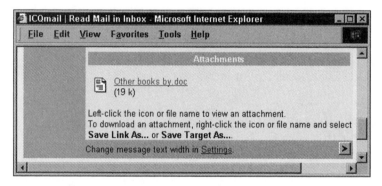

Figure 8-6. Look at the bottom of a message for file attachments.

Storing and Managing Messages

The Inbox is the starting point for storing and managing
messages. Click the Inbox link under Folders on the left
side of a page to see the Inbox page (refer to Figure 8-3).
Besides opening messages there, you can delete them or
move them to different folders (also known as pages).
What's more, you can create folders of your own and in so
doing organize messages to make retrieving them easier.

Read on to learn how to delete messages, create new folders, move a message to a different folder, and display messages in folders.

Choosing How to Display Messages in Folders

Unless you change the settings, each folder (or page) lists ten messages. To see the rest of the messages, if there are more than ten, open the Go To drop-down list in the lower-right corner of the Inbox Web page and choose another set to view. You can also click the Forward or Previous button.

However, you can display more than ten messages at a time by following these steps:

1. Either click Preferences on the left side of the ICQmail Web page, or click the ICQmail button on the ICQ window, choose the name of your account, and choose ICQmail Preferences on the submenu.

2. On the Preferences page, click the Settings link.

3. On the Preferences | Settings page, enter the number of messages to display on each page in the text box.

4. Click the OK button.

Deleting Messages

To delete a message, select the check box to the left of its name, open the Move To drop-down menu, choose Trash, and then click the Move To button. Messages you delete are moved to the Trash page. Click the Trash link on the left side of a page to view messages on the Trash page.

When you log off ICQmail, all messages on the Trash page are deleted permanently. However, you can delete them whenever you want by clicking the Empty Trash link, the bottommost link on the left side of pages.

Creating Folders for Storing Messages

To keep better track of messages, store them in different folders (or pages), one for each project you are working on or sender (a friend or family member) you are working with. Follow these steps to create a new folder:

Tip

To delete several messages at once, select the check boxes next to the ones you want to delete or click the Select All button.

1. Click the Folders link. You will find it on the left side of the page above the Inbox link. The Folders page appears.

2. Scroll to the bottom of the page, where you will find text boxes and menus for creating, renaming, and deleting folders, as shown in Figure 8-7.

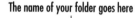

The name of your folder goes here

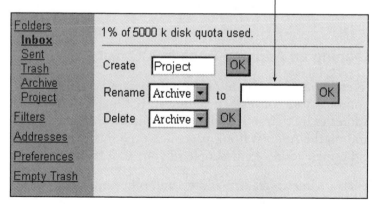

Figure 8-7. Creating a new folder (also known as a page).

3. Enter a name in the Create text box and click OK. The name of your new folder appears in the Folders list on the left side of any ICQmail page.

To rename a folder, select it in the Rename drop-down list, enter a new name, and click OK. Do the same to delete a folder, but choose it instead in the Delete drop-down list. Messages in a folder you delete are deleted as well.

Moving Messages to Different Folders

To move messages to a different folder (also known as a page), start by selecting the messages. To do so, select the check boxes to the left of their names. Then open the Move To drop-down list, as shown in Figure 8-8, choose a folder name, and click the Move To button.

The fastest way to address an ICQmail message is to click an e-mail address on the Address Book page. The Write Mail page appears with the address already entered. All you have to do is write the message. It's already addressed for you.

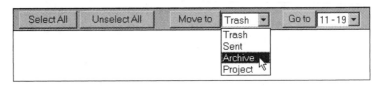

Figure 8-8. Moving messages to another folder.

Others can also send you EmailExpress messages from your Personal Communication Center. See Chapter 14.

The next section in this chapter describes the ICQ Email dialog box and how to configure ICQ so you can send e-mail messages.

Keeping an Address Book in ICQmail

To enter an address (and phone number and other information as well) or read an address in ICQmail, click the Addresses link. (You'll find it below the list of folders.) You land on the Address Book page. The page lists the names and e-mail addresses of people in your address book.

Click a name to read an address and other information that you entered about a person.

To enter information, click the New Person button, enter information or choose options on the New Person page, and click OK. Or else click the Add More Detail button before clicking OK to enter detailed information about the person.

Receiving ICQ E-Mail from Sources Outside the ICQ Network

Every ICQ user gets an e-mail address in ICQ: *Your ICQ number*@pager.icq.com. For example, if your ICQ number is 987654, anyone — from inside or outside ICQ — can address an e-mail message to you at 987654@pager.icq.com.

You know when a message arrives because the Email Express icon appears on your Contact List in the Web Message area, as shown in Figure 8-9. After you open the message, you see the Incoming EmailExpress Message dialog box, also shown in Figure 8-9.

As long as an e-mail address is on file for you in the White Pages, you can click the Reply By Email button to reply to the sender. After the ICQ Email dialog box opens, enter your reply and click the Send button. Your message will be sent outside the ICQ network to the original sender.

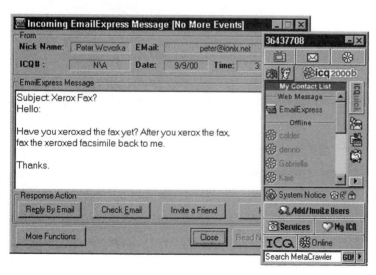

Figure 8-9. EmailExpress messages are sent from outside ICQ.

Chapter 11 explains how to file an e-mail address in the White Pages — and do it in such a way that others can't see it.

In the case of people whose names are on your Contact List, you can send a copy of an EmailExpress message to the person by ICQ E-mail as well as in the form of an instant-message. To do so, choose the Send Email & Notify command.

Sending ICQ E-Mail Messages to Mail Boxes Outside ICQ

An advantage of using the Contact List is that, if an individual is on your Contact List, you don't have to remember that person's e-mail address in order to send him or her an e-mail; ICQ remembers the address for you. If someone you want to reach is not on your Contact List, however, or has not filed his or her e-mail address in the White Pages, don't despair, because you can send an e-mail address from ICQ to anyone if you know their e-mail address. People's names don't have to be on your Contact List for you to send them e-mail. Follow these steps to send ICQ e-mail to addresses outside of the ICQ network:

1. Either start from the Contact List or the Services button:

   ▲ **Sending to someone on your Contact List:** Click the person's name, choose Email on the pop-up menu, and choose Send Email. If the Send Email command is grayed out, the person's e-mail address is not on file in the White Pages. Try clicking the Services button to send your e-mail message.

   ▲ **Sending to someone whose name isn't on your Contact List:** Click the Services button, choose Email on the pop-up menu, and choose Send Email on the submenu.

   You see the ICQ Email dialog box shown in Figure 8-10. If you started out by clicking a name on your Contact List, an address is already entered in the To box. If you started out by clicking the Services button, you still need to enter the recipient's e-mail address manually.

2. If necessary, enter an address in the To box.

3. Enter an e-mail address in the CC box if you want a copy to go to a third party.

4. Enter the message in the message box.

5. Click the Send button.

Notice the Voice Message and File Attachment buttons in the ICQ Email dialog box (refer to Figure 8-10). Click the down arrow on either of those buttons to record a voice file or send a file along with your message.

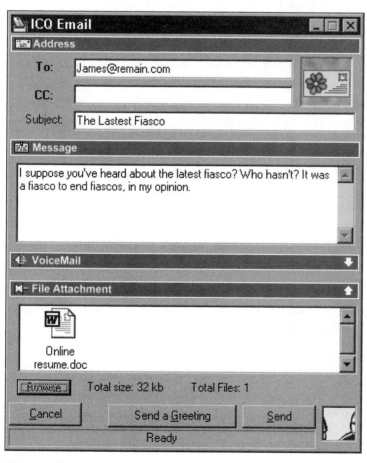

Caution

For security reasons and to prevent bulk-mailing by advertisers, not all ISPs permit you to be alerted when incoming mail has arrived. Many ISPs prevent outside accounts (not from their domain) from retrieving e-mail. If that is the case with your ISP, ICQ cannot alert you when incoming mail has arrived.

Figure 8-10. Sending an e-mail message to an address outside of ICQ.

Being Alerted in ICQ When Your E-Mail Accounts Receive Mail

ICQ can alert you when mail arrives in other e-mail accounts that you maintain. Suppose you keep an e-mail account with an Internet Service Provider (ISP) called `Remain.com`. Instead of having to start your e-mail program and connect to `Remain.com` to see if e-mail has arrived, ICQ can inform you when it arrives. This way, you spare yourself the trouble of connecting to your ISP.

ICQ checks every ten minutes to find out if new e-mail has arrived in one of your other accounts. When it has arrived, the E-Mail Message icon appears in the desktop tray so you can open the ICQ Email Check dialog box and see what the messages are. The subjects of the messages and the names of the senders appear in a dialog box. At that point, you can double-click a message to read its first twenty lines. Read on to learn how to configure ICQ so you can be alerted to incoming mail and check for incoming mail in your private e-mail accounts without leaving ICQ.

Configuring ICQ So You Can Be Alerted

To be alerted when mail arrives at a private account, you have to configure ICQ so it can obtain information from your Internet Service Provider about incoming mail. And to do that, you have to know the following information about the account:

- ▼ The address of the mail server where the account is kept.

- ▼ Your user name. The user name is the part of the e-mail address that appears before the at sign (@). In the address `jane@remain.com`, for example, *jane* is the user name.

▼ Your password. You chose a password when you established the e-mail account.

How do you obtain the address of the mail server where the account is kept? The easiest way is to call your Internet Service Provider and ask. Tell your provider that you need the POP3 (Post Office Protocol) address of the server where incoming mail is kept. However, you can also obtain the mail server address by opening the software program you use for e-mailing and clicking a few commands. Here are instructions for finding the mail server address in popular software programs:

▼ **Microsoft Outlook Express and Microsoft Outlook:** Open the Tools menu and choose Accounts. Then click the Mail tab in the Internet Accounts dialog box, select the account, and click the Properties button. In the Properties dialog box, click the Servers tab and look in the Incoming Mail (POP3) box.

▼ **Navigator Mail:** Open the Edit menu and choose Preferences. Then double-click Mail & Groups in the Category box and choose Mail Server. Look in the Incoming Mail Server box for the address.

▼ **Eudora:** Open the Tools menu, choose Options, and click Checking Mail in the Category box. Look under POP account for the address.

With the information you need on hand, follow these steps to configure ICQ so it can alert you when e-mail arrives at your private e-mail account:

1. Click the Services button.

2. Choose Email on the pop-up menu.

3. Choose Preferences on the on the submenu. As shown in Figure 8-11, you see the Email Alerts tab of the Owner Preferences For dialog box.

Tip

As e-mail programs are upgraded, the procedures for obtaining mail server addresses change. Go to this Help page in ICQ to get up-to-date instructions for obtaining mail server addresses in popular programs: www.icq.com/email/pop3.html.

8

Trading E-Mail
Messages over ICQ

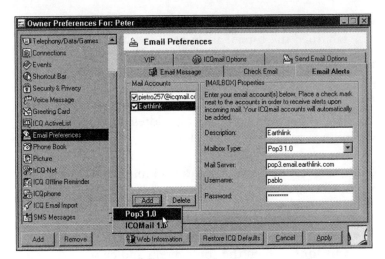

Figure 8-11. Telling ICQ how to alert you to incoming mail at your ISP.

4. Click the Add button (the one on the Email Alerts tab) and choose Pop3 1.0 from the pop-up menu. (The other option, ICQMail 1.0, pertains to people who subscribe to ICQmail.)

5. In the Description text box, enter a name for your ISP. The name is used for identification purposes only. You can enter any name you wish.

6. In the Mail Server text box, enter the incoming mail (POP3) address.

7. In the Username text box, enter your username.

8. In the Password text box, enter the password for the account (not your ICQ password).

9. Click the Apply button.

Checking for the Arrival of New E-Mail Messages

After you complete the setup work, you can find out whether you have any new messages. ICQ offers two ways to find out whether new messages have arrived. Choose the method that suits you best:

- ▼ Click the Services button, choose Email, and choose Check Incoming Email.

- ▼ Wait until you see the E-Mail Message icon in the desktop tray and then double-click it. By default, ICQ checks for new messages every ten minutes. The E-Mail Message icon appears in the desktop tray when new messages have arrived.

Whether you choose the Check Incoming Email command or double-click the E-Mail Message icon, you see the ICQ Email Check dialog box shown in Figure 8-12. It lists new messages, their subjects, when they were sent, and their sizes. When applicable, ICQ numbers and ICQ user's online status are also displayed.

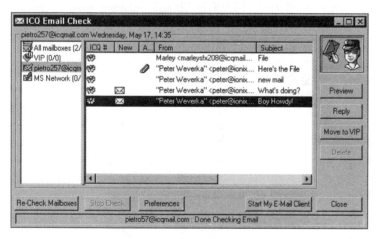

Figure 8-12. The ICQ Email Check dialog box tells which new messages have arrived.

The ICQ Email Check dialog box offers several buttons for handling e-mail messages. Select a message and then click one of these buttons:

- ▼ **Preview:** Opens the E-Mail Preview dialog box so you can read the first twenty lines of the message.

- ▼ **Reply:** Opens the ICQ Email dialog box (refer to Figure 8-10) so you can reply by ICQ E-mail. You can also open the dialog box by double-clicking a message.

Cross-Reference

The next section in this chapter, "Choosing How You Want to Be Alerted to New E-Mail," explains the VIP list.

▼ **Move to VIP:** Places the sender's e-mail address on your VIP list. You can play special sounds when mail arrives from people whose addresses are on the list.

▼ **Delete:** Removes the e-mail message from your account.

▼ **Re-Check Mailboxes:** Runs another check for arriving e-mail.

▼ **Stop Check:** Stops a check.

▼ **Preferences:** Opens the Owner Preferences For dialog box (refer to Figure 8-11) so you can choose settings for receiving e-mail.

▼ **Start My E-Mail Client:** Opens the software program that you use for sending and receiving e-mail so you can open the e-mail messages in their entirety.

Choosing How You Want to Be Alerted to New E-Mail

The Email Preferences section of the Owner Preferences For dialog box has six tabs for telling ICQ how you want to be alerted to incoming e-mail messages. Follow either of these instructions to open the Email section of the Owner Preferences For dialog box:

▼ Click the Services button, choose Email, and choose Preferences.

▼ Click the ICQ button, choose Preferences, and select Email Preferences on the left side of the Owner Preferences For dialog box.

Starting with the Check Email tab, check or uncheck boxes to do the following under these headings:

▼ **Check Email:** First choose whether to see e-mail messages you haven't opened yet or only newly arrived messages in the ICQ Email Check dialog box (refer to Figure 8-12). Then enter a number to tell ICQ how often to check for new e-mail.

▼ **Launch:** Choose whether to check for new e-mail each time you start ICQ, and whether to open your e-mail software whenever ICQ detects a newly arrived message.

▼ **Display Options:** Choose whether to make the e-mail message icon appear in the desktop tray, whether to display headers in the ICQ Email Check dialog box (refer to Figure 8-12), and how many lines to display when you click the Preview button in the ICQ Email Check dialog box.

The VIP tab is for entering the e-mail addresses of people you are anxious to hear from on your VIP List. After you put names on the list, check the Play WAV box and choose a WAV sound file in the Open dialog box. When mail arrives from someone on your VIP list, the sound is played. To enter a name on the VIP list, either choose a Contact List name from the ICQ Users drop-down menu and click the Add button, or click the Other Users option button, enter an e-mail address, and click Add.

Definition

Header: In e-mail terminology, the subject of an e-mail message, the sender's name, the recipient's name, and the date.

Tip

You can start the ICQ program from inside Outlook 2000. To do so, click the ICQ button on the ICQ Integration for Outlook toolbar and choose Launch ICQ on the pop-up menu. If you don't see the ICQ Integration for Outlook toolbar, choose View➪Toolbars➪ICQ Integration for Outlook.

For Outlook Users: Sending ICQ Events from Inside Outlook

Users of Microsoft Outlook 2000 can send ICQ events from inside the Outlook program. That's right — as long as ICQ is running while Outlook is open, you can send instant-messages, chat requests, URLs, or files to any ICQ user on your Outlook Contacts list. You can also reply to an e-mail that was sent to you in Outlook from an ICQ user with an ICQ message. You can even use ICQ to forward e-mail you received in Outlook to other ICQ users.

Sending an ICQ Event to an Outlook Contact

Follow these steps to send an ICQ event to someone whose name is on your Outlook Contacts list:

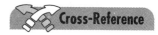

Cross-Reference

Chapter 4 explains how to tell Outlook which people on your Outlook Contacts list are ICQ users.

8

Trading E-Mail
Messages over ICQ

1. In Outlook, click the Contacts icon to display the Contacts list, as shown in Figure 8-13.

2. Select the name of the person to whom you will send the event. To send an event, the recipient must be an ICQ user. When you select the name of an ICQ user, the words "Message To" appear beside his or her name on the ICQ Integration for Outlook toolbar. A status icon also appears to tell you the person's online status (refer to Figure 8-13).

3. Click a button on the ICQ Integration for Outlook toolbar to send an event. (Click the Message To button to send an instant message.) A Send dialog box appears.

4. Fill in the Send dialog box and click the Send button.

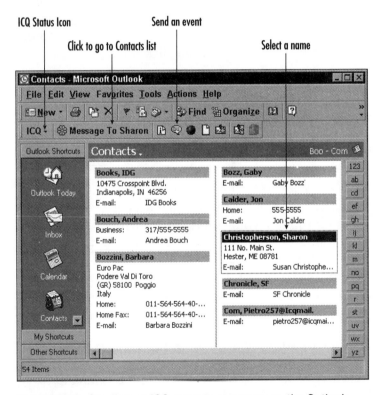

Figure 8-13. Sending an ICQ event to someone on the Outlook Contacts list.

Forwarding an Outlook E-Mail with ICQ

Suppose an e-mail message lands in your Outlook Inbox folder and you want to forward it in ICQ to one or more ICQ users. Yes, it can be done. In the Inbox folder, select the message and then follow these instructions:

▼ **Forwarding a message:** Click the Forward with ICQ Message button on the ICQ Integration for Outlook toolbar .You see the Send Multiple Recipients Message dialog box, where you can add a word or two of your own to the message and select names from your ICQ Contact List.

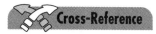
Cross-Reference

Chapter 3 explains the Send Multiple Recipients Message dialog box and how to send a message to more than one person.

▼ **Forwarding a file that was sent to you:** Click the Forward Attachments button on the ICQ Integration for Outlook toolbar. The names of ICQ users on your Contact List who are currently online appear on a drop-down menu. Choose a name on the menu.

Coming Up Next

Chapter 9 explains how to customize ICQ so you can get more out of the program. You find out how to be alerted when certain people come online or certain types of messages arrive. You discover how to write customized status messages and accept or reject messages, chat requests, files, and URLs automatically. The chapter also explains how to customize the ICQuick shortcut bar, assign your own sounds to events, and tell ICQ where to store incoming files.

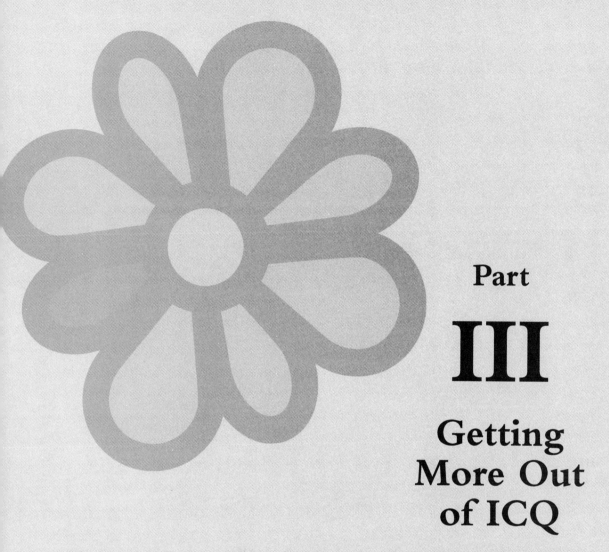

Part

III

Getting More Out of ICQ

Chapter

9

Customizing ICQ

Quick Look

Decide How You Want to Be Notified of Incoming Events   page 216
When someone sends you an event — a message or chat request, for example — an icon starts blinking. Sometimes you hear a sound as well. You can, however, make all kinds of bells and whistles go off when a new event arrives.

Make Special Considerations for Someone on Your Contact List   page 219
Do you want to hide from someone when you are online? You can make the Away, N/A, Occupied, or DND status icon appear next to your name on Contact Lists when you are on-line. You can accept chat requests and files from someone automatically, write a personalized status message for someone, and make a special sound play when someone comes online, among other things.

Write Your Own Tailor-Made Status Messages   page 231
When you are in Away, N/A, Occupied, DND, or Free for Chat mode, others can click your name, choose Read Message, and read a status message. Instead of the standard status messages that ICQ supplies, you can write exciting messages of your own.

Customize the ICQuick Shortcut Bar   page 234
Put your own favorite buttons on the shortcut bar. While you're at it, you can rearrange the buttons or auto-hide the shortcut bar so it appears only when you need it.

Choose Where to Keep Incoming Files   page 236
When someone sends you a file, it lands by default in the `C:\Program Files\ICQ\ Received Files` folder, but you can decide for yourself where to put incoming files.

Choose the Sounds that ICQ Plays   page 238
ICQ squeaks, squawks, and talks. A sound plays whenever someone sends you an event and under other circumstances as well. You can decide which sounds are played and disable sounds as well.

Chapter 9

Customizing ICQ

This chapter describes how to make ICQ work your way. The program gives you many opportunities for choosing how you want to receive events — messages, chat requests, files, and more. In this chapter, you find out how to automatically receive events without having to negotiate dialog boxes, and how to automatically decline events as well. You discover how to treat individuals on your Contact List in different ways, how to write your own status messages, and how to customize the ICQuick shortcut bar. Finally, this chapter shows how to choose a default folder for incoming files and assign sounds to different ICQ events.

Cross-Reference

The next part of this chapter, "Making Special Allowances for People on Your Contact List," explains how to tell ICQ to alert you when certain people on your Contact List send you events or connect to ICQ.

Choosing How You Want to Be Alerted to Incoming Events

When an event arrives over ICQ, an icon starts blinking in the system tray. You hear a sound or phrase, too. However, you can decide for yourself exactly how you want to be alerted to incoming events by going to the Events and Contact List sections of the Owner Preferences For dialog box. Figure 9-1 shows the Events section.

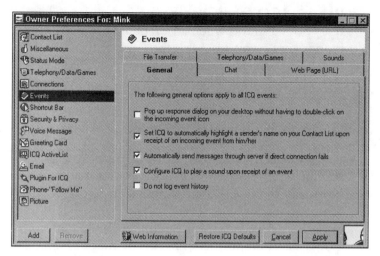

Figure 9-1. Choosing how you want to be alerted to incoming events.

To open the Owner Preferences For dialog box, click the ICQ button and choose Preferences on the pop-up menu.

Click Events on the left side of the Owner Preferences For dialog box and then click the General tab to choose among these settings:

▼ **Make dialog boxes appear when someone sends you an event:** Normally, you have to double-click an icon to open a dialog box when someone sends you an event. However, you can make the dialog box appear right away by selecting the first check box, Pop Up Response Dialog on Your Desktop Without Having to Double-Click on the Incoming Event Icon.

▼ **Keep ICQ from selecting senders' names on the Contact List:** When someone on your Contact List sends you an event, the name is highlighted, but you can prevent that by deselecting the Set ICQ to Automatically Highlight a Sender's Name on Your Contact List Upon Receipt of an Incoming Event from Him/Her.

Cross-Reference

Later in this chapter, "Assigning Your Own Sounds to Events" explains how to choose the sound you hear when an event arrives over ICQ.

▼ **Prevent ICQ from Playing Sounds:** Normally, ICQ plays a sound when an event arrives, but if the sounds annoy you, uncheck the Configure ICQ to Play a Sound Upon Receipt of an Event check box.

Click Contact List on the left side of the Owner Preferences For dialog box to choose among these settings on the Options tab, shown in Figure 9-2:

▼ **Keep the ICQ window from appearing on-screen when someone sends you an event:** Normally, the ICQ window jumps on-screen when someone sends you an event so you know that an event has arrived, but you can uncheck the Popup Contact List Upon Incoming Event check box if you prefer that the window stay minimized.

▼ **Keep the names of people who send you events from going to the top of the Contact List:** When someone sends you an event, the sender's name goes to the top of the Contact List. Uncheck the Move the Last User that Sent an Event to the Top of the Contact List check box if you want the sender's name to stay where it is.

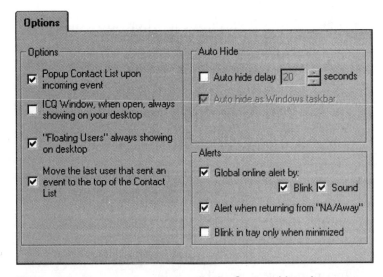

Figure 9-2. Choosing how to handle the Contact List when new events arrive.

Making Special Allowances for People on Your Contact List

ICQ offers many opportunities for giving special consideration to someone whose name is on your Contact List. Are you eager to keep someone from knowing when you are online? You can make the Away, N/A, Occupied, or DND icon appear permanently next to your name on someone else's Contact List. If someone is really bothering you, you can make the Offline icon appear next to your name at all times.

And that's not even half of it. You can accept chat requests and files from someone automatically, write a personalized status message for someone to read when he or she clicks your name and chooses the Read Message command, or make a special sound play when someone comes online.

To explore the many different ways to make special allowances for someone, start by clicking his or her name on your Contact List and choosing Alert/Accept Modes on the pop-up menu. You see the User Preferences For dialog box. Click General, as shown in Figure 9-3, to see the following four tabs. They let you set up ICQ so that you can give special treatment to someone:

- ▼ **Accept:** Receive events quickly from someone.

- ▼ **Alert:** Be informed right away when someone has connected to ICQ.

- ▼ **Message:** Write a personalized status message for someone.

- ▼ **Status:** Report your online status to someone independent of what others think your online status is.

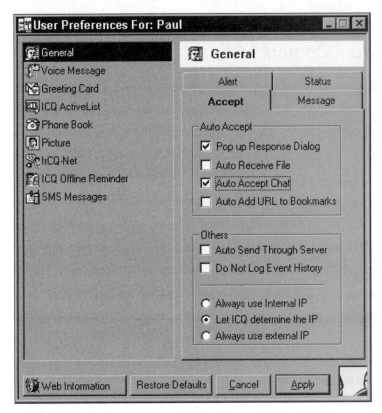

Figure 9-3. Giving someone special consideration in the User Preferences For dialog box.

Accept Tab: Receiving ICQ Events Quickly

The Accept tab in the User Preferences For dialog box (refer to Figure 9-3) gives you options for speeding the delivery of events from someone on your Contact List. Check or uncheck these options if you trust the person on your Contact List and you want to receive events quickly:

▼ **Pop up Response Dialog:** The Incoming dialog box appears right away when someone you trust sends you an event. You don't have to double-click an icon to open the dialog box.

▼ **Auto Receive File:** Files are received without the sender having to get permission to send them first.

▼ **Auto Accept Chat:** The Chat window appears immediately when you receive a chat request from someone you trust. You don't see the Incoming Chat Request dialog box.

▼ **Auto Add URL to Bookmarks:** Automatically enter all Web page addresses that the person sends you on your Incoming Bookmarks page, where Web sites you bookmark in ICQ are listed. (Click the System Notice button and choose Incoming Bookmarks to go to the Incoming Bookmarks page.)

▼ **Auto Send Through Server:** When the person is not connected to ICQ, direct all events you send him or her to the ICQ servers instead of to the OutBox. Normally, events stay in the OutBox until the other party connects to ICQ and can receive them. By sending them to the ICQ server, you make events arrive faster, because you don't have to be online for the other party to receive items.

▼ **Do Not Log Event History:** Prevent events you send and receive from being logged in the History Events Of dialog box. To open this dialog box, click a person's name on the Contact List, choose History on the pop-up menu, and choose View Messages History.

The last three options on the tab concern Internet Protocol (IP) addresses, the numerical addresses of computers on the Internet. Unless you know exactly what you are doing, make sure you select the Let ICQ Determine the IP option.

Chapter 13 explains how to bookmark your favorite Web sites in ICQ.

Chapter 3 explains the History Events Of dialog box.

Alert Tab: Being Told When Someone Has Connected to ICQ

On the Alert tab of the User Preferences For dialog box, which is shown in Figure 9-4, you can tell ICQ to notify you when someone on your Contact List connects to the network. Check the Override Global Alert check box and then consider these options when you want to know precisely when a certain someone has connected to ICQ:

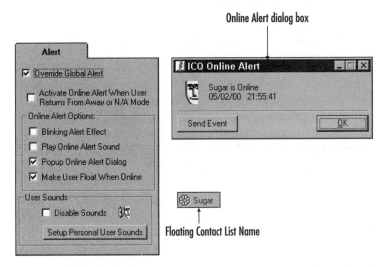

Figure 9-4. On the Alert tab, choose different ways of being alerted when someone connects to ICQ.

▼ **Activate Online Alert When User Returns from Away or N/A Mode:** You will be alerted when the person switches from N/A (Extended Away) or Away mode to Available/Connect mode. How you are alerted depends on which options you choose under Online Alert Options.

▼ **Blinking Alert Effect:** The person's name blinks and appears in different colors on the Contact List. When the ICQ window is minimized, you see a face as well as a flower where the Flower button normally is.

▼ **Play Online Alert Sound:** You hear the words, "Is online."

▼ **Popup Online Alert Dialog:** You see the Online Alert dialog box shown on the right side of Figure 9-4 when the person connects to ICQ.

▼ **Make User Float When Online:** The user's name floats when he or she connects to ICQ, as shown in Figure 9-4.

▼ **Disable Sounds:** Disable the sounds that you normally hear when the person connects to ICQ or when you receive events from him or her.

▼ **Setup Personal User Sounds:** Instead of the conventional sounds that you hear when the person comes online or sends you events, you can choose sounds of your own. After you click the Setup Personal User Sounds button, the Sound Config dialog box opens. Check the check box next to the name of a sound you want to change and then click the Select button. In the Open dialog box, select a new sound and click the Open button.

To make the same sound play whenever a person on your Contact List sends you an event or comes online, check the Use the Same Sound File for All Events check box. Then check the General check box, click the Select button, and follow the standard procedure for choosing a new sound.

Message Tab: Writing Personalized Status Messages

When you are in Free for Chat, Away, N/A (Extended Away), Occupied, or DND (Do Not Disturb) mode, anyone can click your name on his or her Contact List and choose Read Message to read an explanation of why you are in the mode you are in. However, by entering a message on the Message tab of the General section of the User Preferences For dialog box, you can write a tailor-made message for someone on your Contact List. When the special someone clicks your name and chooses Read Message, he or she sees a personalized message like the one in Figure 9-5.

Chapter 5 explains how to make a Contact List name float.

Later in this chapter, "The Answering Service: Writing Your Own Status Messages" explains how to write status messages of your own for *all* to read.

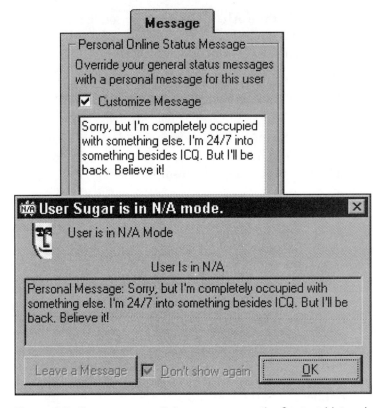

Figure 9-5. Someone can click your name on the Contact List and choose Read Message to see the words you enter on the Message tab.

On the Message tab, check the Customize Message check box and enter the message that you want the person on your Contact List to read when he or she clicks your name and chooses Read Message.

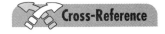

Chapter 2 explains how to choose your online status.

Status Tab: Reporting Your Online Status

As you know, an icon appears beside your name on others' Contact Lists when you click the Status button and choose a command to describe your online status. However, starting from the Status tab in the User Preferences For dialog box, you can declare your online status to one person in particular.

Declaring your online status to one person on your Contact List is a great way to protect your privacy or tell someone that you are eager to exchange events. No matter which online status others see, a person on your Contact List sees, for example, that you are disconnected from ICQ.

Click the Update Status check box on the Status tab of the General section of the User Preferences For dialog box and choose among these options to declare your online status to one person on your Contact List:

- ▼ **Away to User:** The person always thinks you are in Away mode.

- ▼ **N/A to User:** The person always thinks you are in N/A (Extended Away) mode.

- ▼ **Occupied to User:** The person always thinks you are in Occupied (Urgent Msgs) mode.

- ▼ **DND to User:** The person always thinks you are in DND (Do Not Disturb) mode.

- ▼ **Invisible to User:** The person thinks you are disconnected to ICQ, even when you are connected. Choose this command to shield yourself from bothersome people.

- ▼ **Visible to User:** The person knows that you are connected to ICQ even when you are in Privacy (Invisible) mode. Normally when you are in Privacy (Invisible) mode, others think you are disconnected from ICQ and your name appears under the Offline heading on others' Contact Lists. However, the Privacy (Invisible) icon appears next to your name under Online on the other person's Contact List when you choose the Visible to User option. As a matter of fact, if you see the Privacy (Invisible) icon under Online next to a name on your Contact List, you can be sure the person has given you special status. That person has made him- or herself invisible to most others but not to you.

Tip

When you declare a different online status to someone whose name is on your Contact List, the name appears in *italics*. Look for italicized names on the list to see who has been given special status.

Choosing How You Want to Receive Chat Requests, URLs, Files, and More

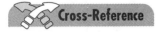

Earlier in this chapter, "Accept Tab: Receiving ICQ Events Quickly" explains how to use the Alert tab in the Alert/Accept Settings dialog box to make receiving files, chat requests, and URLs from a particular person on your Contact List easier.

ICQ offers all kinds of options for deciding how you want to receive chat requests, Web page address (URLs), files, and telephony/data/game requests. Normally, an icon appears, you double-click it, and an Incoming dialog box arrives so you can deal with the event. But you can bypass the Incoming dialog box, decline all requests automatically, or do any number of other things to make fielding events from others easier.

To explore the different ways to handle incoming events, follow these steps to open the Owner Preferences For dialog box:

1. Click the ICQ button.

2. Choose Preferences on the pop-up menu. The Owner Preferences For dialog box appears.

3. Click Events on the left side of the dialog box.

Visit the Chat, Web Page (URL), File Transfer, and Telephony/Data/Games tabs in the dialog box to tell ICQ how you want to receive chat requests, Web page addresses, files, and telephony/data/game requests. The four tabs are explained in this section. Figure 9-6 shows the Chat tab.

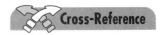

Chapter 6 explains how to chat in ICQ.

Chat Tab: Receiving or Declining Chat Requests

The Chat tab of the Owner Preferences For dialog box (refer to Figure 9-6) offers these options for handling requests to chat from people on your Contact List:

▼ **Display Incoming Chat Request Dialog Upon Receipt of a Chat Request:** You see the Incoming Chat Request dialog box right away when someone wants to chat with you. You don't have to double-click the Chat Request icon to open it.

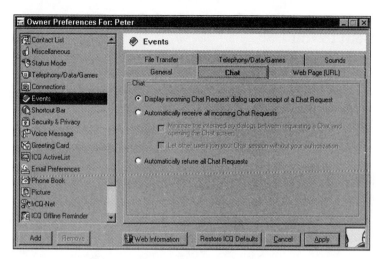

Figure 9-6. On the Chat tab of the Owner Preferences For dialog box, tell ICQ how you want to handle chat requests.

- ▼ **Automatically Receive All Incoming Chat Requests:** The Chat window opens immediately when someone wants to chat. You don't see the Incoming Chat Request dialog box.

- ▼ **Minimize the Intermediary Dialogs Between Requesting a Chat and Opening the Chat Screen:** Keeps the ICQ Chat Module message box from appearing. This message box appears briefly and offers the Abort button in case you change your mind at the last minute about accepting a chat invitation.

- ▼ **Let Others Users Join Your Chat Session Without Your Authorization:** Permits a third person to enter an ongoing chat without getting permission first. A space for the person appears instantly in the Chat window.

- ▼ **Automatically Refuse All Chat Requests:** Declines all invitations to chat automatically. The User Has Declined Your Request — No Reason Given message box appears instantly when someone asks you to chat.

Web Page (URL): Fielding Web Page Addresses Sent to You

As shown in Figure 9-7, the Web Page (URL) tab of the Owner Preferences For dialog box presents the following options for handling Web page addresses that are sent to you:

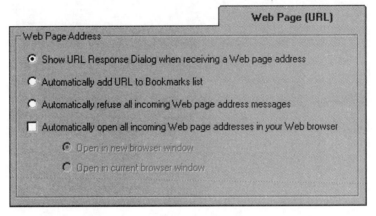

Figure 9-7. Go to the Web Page (URL) tab of the Owner Preferences For dialog box to decide the best way to handle incoming URLs.

> ▼ **Show URL Response Dialog When Receiving a Web Page Address:** The Incoming URL Message dialog box appears when someone sends you a Web page address. You can click the Go to URL button in the dialog box to visit the Web page.

> ▼ **Automatically Add URL to Bookmarks List:** All Web page addresses that are sent to you are placed automatically in your Incoming Bookmarks page, the place where Web sites you bookmark in ICQ are listed. To see the page, click the System Notice button and choose Incoming Bookmarks. The Incoming URL Message dialog box appears as well when you choose this option.

▼ **Automatically Refuse All Incoming Web Page Address Messages:** All URLs that people send you are declined. People who send them see the User Has Declined Your Request — No Reason Given message box.

▼ **Automatically Open All Incoming Web Page Addresses in Your Web Browser:** When you receive a Web page address from someone, the Web page opens in your browser or opens in a second browser window, depending on which Open option you choose.

File Transfer: Receiving or Declining Files

File transfers in ICQ can be kind of tricky. For one thing, both parties have to be connected to ICQ for the transfer to occur. And then there is the matter of whether to accept certain files. Executable files — .exe files, .bat files, and .com files — can carry viruses. The File Transfer tab in the Owner Preferences For dialog box offers these options for handling incoming files:

▼ **Show File Request Response Dialog When Receiving an Incoming File:** The Incoming File Request dialog box appears so that you can accept or reject a file that someone wants to send to you.

▼ **Accept All Incoming File Requests Automatically:** Accept files that others send without examining them first in the Incoming File Request dialog box. If you check the Minimize the File Transfer Dialog check box, the Receiving Files From dialog box is minimized as the file transfers occurs. To see the file, click the Rcvd From button on the Taskbar.

▼ **Automatically Refuse All Incoming File Requests:** Decline all requests from others to send you files. Anyone who attempts to send you a file sees the User Has Declined Your Request — No Reason Given message box.

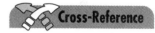

Chapter 13 explains how to send URLs to and receive URLs from others. The chapter also describes how to bookmark Web sites in ICQ.

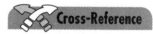

Chapter 3 explains how to trade files with people on your Contact List.

▼ **Automatically Refuse File Transfers Requests Sent by Users Not on My Contact List:** Only people whose names are on your Contact List may send you files. All others see the User Has Declined Your Request - No Reason Given message box.

▼ **Overwrite Received Files with Incoming Files by the Same Name:** When a new file arrives and it has the same name as a file in the Received Files folder (or the other folder where you keep incoming files), the new file takes the place of the old one with the same name.

▼ **Default Incoming File(s) Path:** The default location for incoming files is the `C:\Program Files\ICQ\Received Files\`*`Sender's Name`* folder, but you can click the button on the right side of this text box to tell ICQ where you want to keep incoming files.

Telephony/Data/Games: Handling Telephony Stuff

The Incoming Phone/Video/Date Request dialog box appears when someone wants to engage in an activity with you that requires an external application. Make use of these options on the Telephony/Data/Games tab in the Owner Preferences For dialog box to tell ICQ how you want to handle telephony requests:

▼ **Show Internet Telephony/Games/Chat Request Response Dialog upon Receipt of an Event:** You see the Incoming Phone/Video/Date Request dialog box so you can accept or decline the invitation.

▼ **Automatically Accept All Incoming Requests to Launch Internet Telephony/Games/Chat External Applications:** The external application launches automatically and you don't see the Incoming Phone/Video/Date Request dialog box.

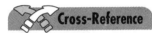

Earlier in this chapter, "Accept Tab: Receiving ICQ Events Quickly" shows how to accept files automatically from a particular person on your Contact List.

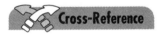

Later in this chapter, "Choosing Where to Store Incoming Files" explains how to designate a folder in which to keep the files.

- ▼ **Automatically Refuse All Incoming Requests to Launch External Applications:** Anyone who tries to engage you in a telephony activity sees the User Has Declined Your Request – No Reason Given message box.

The Answering Service: Writing Your Own Status Messages

When you are in Away, N/A, Occupied, DND, or Free for Chat mode, anyone can click your name on his or her Contact List and choose Read Message to read an explanation of why you are away or want to chat. Figure 9-8 shows the message box you see when you click the Read Message command.

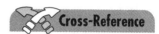

Cross-Reference

Chapter 15 explains how to use telephony applications with ICQ.

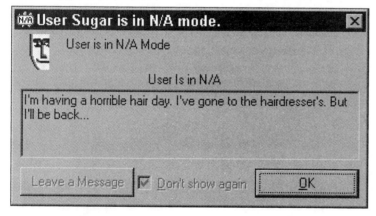

Figure 9-8. Choose Read Message on the pop-up menu to find out why someone is away.

Where do these messages come from? When you switch status modes, the Change/Confirm Message dialog box appears. From there, you can either enter your own message or click the Select Message button and choose a preset message, as shown in Figure 9-9.

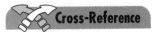

Cross-Reference

Earlier in this chapter, "Message Tab: Writing Personalized Status Messages" explains how you can write a personal status message for one person on your Contact List.

Tip

The fastest way to open the Answering Service For dialog box is to click the Answering Service button on the ICQuick shortcut bar.

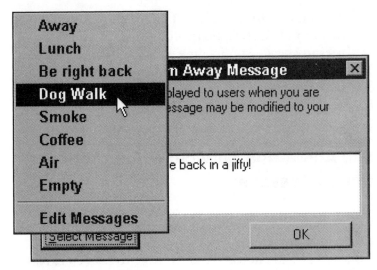

Figure 9-9. Either enter your own message or choose one when you change modes.

For each status mode for which you can leave a message — Away, N/A, Occupied, DND, and Free for Chat — ICQ offers as many as seven preset messages. You can, however, change the preset messages. For example, choosing the Dog Walk preset message, as shown in Figure 9-9, enters this message in the Change/Confirm Message dialog box: "I'm out with the dog. Be back when he's finished." Suppose you want to change that message to, "I'm out with the schnauzer, be back when he's finished chasing the cat." Change the preset messages to save yourself the trouble of typing explanations in the Change/Confirm Message dialog box or simply for the fun of it. Instead of typing an explanation, you can choose one you typed earlier.

Follow these steps to change the preset messages:

1. In Advanced mode, click the Services button.

2. Choose Answering Service on the pop-up menu. You see the ICQ Answering Service For dialog box shown in Figure 9-10.

Choose a message name

Choose a status mode

Enter the message

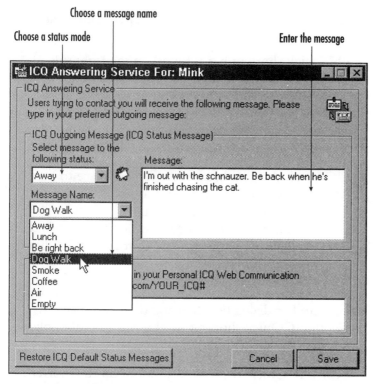

Figure 9-10. Rewriting the preset messages that you can enter when you change status modes.

3. In the Select Message to the Following Status drop-down list box, choose the status mode for which you want to change preset messages.

4. Choose the message that needs changing from the Message Name drop-down list box.

5. Type the message in the Message text box.

6. Repeat Steps 3 through 5 to change other messages.

7. Click the Save button.

Tip

You can invent your own names for preset messages. To do so, choose a message name that you need to change (or choose Empty at the bottom of the Message Name menu) and click the Rename Message Name button. In the Rename Preset dialog box, type a new name and click OK.

Customizing the ICQuick Shortcut Bar

The ICQuick shortcut bar is found on the right side of the ICQ window. By clicking the rightward–pointing arrow under the words ICQuick, you can access a popup menu for doing a task quickly — open the ICQ Answering Service For dialog box, search the White Pages, or change your self-description in the Global Directory.

The ICQuick shortcut bar is a convenient place to keep your favorite ICQ commands. And to make the shortcut bar even more useful, you can rearrange the buttons to put your favorites near the top where they are easier to find. You can even place buttons to start your favorite programs on the ICQuick shortcut bar.

Figure 9-11 shows the Shortcut Bar tab in the Owner Preferences For dialog box. Starting there, you can customize the ICQuick shortcut bar. Do either of the following to open the dialog box:

▼ Click ICQuick, the topmost button on the shortcut bar, and choose Edit on the shortcut menu.

▼ Click the ICQ button, choose Preferences, and click Shortcut Bar on the left side of the Owner Preferences For dialog box.

The buttons in the box on the right side of the Shortcut Bar tab are currently on the ICQuick shortcut bar. The buttons on the left side can be placed on the shortcut bar. Follow these instructions to customize the ICQuick shortcut bar:

▼ **Adding a button:** Click a button in the box on the left side of the dialog box and then click the Add button. The button moves to the right side.

▼ **Removing a button:** Click a button in the box on the right side of the dialog box and click the Remove button. The button appears on the left side.

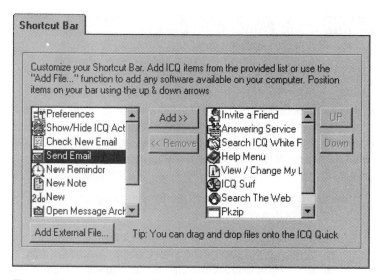

Figure 9-11. Customizing the ICQuick shortcut bar.

▼ **Rearranging the buttons:** Click a button and then click the Up or Down button as many times as necessary until the shortcut bar button is in the right place.

▼ **Putting a program button on the shortcut bar:** Click the Add External File button. In the Open dialog box that appears, locate and select the .exe file of the program whose button you want to place on the ICQuick shortcut bar. When you have selected the .exe file, click the Open button. The name of the program appears on the right side of the dialog box.

Click the Apply button in the Owner Preferences For dialog box after you have finished customizing the ICQuick shortcut bar.

Tip

In the Open dialog box, click the Details button and look for Application in the Type column to find .exe files.

Showing and Auto-Hiding the Shortcut Bar

Some people think that the ICQuick shortcut bar occupies too much space in the ICQ window. If you are one of those people, try auto-hiding the shortcut bar. After you hide the shortcut bar, you can display it again by moving the pointer over the right side of the ICQ window. When the double-arrows appear, so does the ICQuick shortcut bar. But when you move the pointer away from the window, the shortcut bar disappears.

Here are a couple of techniques for handling the ICQuick shortcut bar:

▼ **Auto-hiding it:** Click the ICQuick button — the word "ICQuick" at the top of the shortcut bar — and check the Auto Hide command on the pop-up menu. Later, if you change your mind about auto-hiding the shortcut bar, open the pop-up menu again and uncheck the Auto Hide command.

▼ **Removing it:** Click the ICQuick button and uncheck the Show command. To see the shortcut bar again, click the My ICQ button and choose Shortcut Bar (ICQuick)⇨Show.

Choosing Where to Store Incoming Files

When someone sends you a file, ICQ gives you the opportunity to decide where to store it. Click the Save As button in the Incoming File Request dialog box and choose the folder on your computer where you want the file to go.

Cross-Reference

Chapter 3 explains how to send files and receive them from others.

However, if you click the Save button in the Incoming File Request dialog box, ICQ places the incoming file in the default folder. That folder is `C:\Program Files\ICQ\Received Files\`*`Sender's Name`*. ICQ creates a new subfolder for each person from whom you received files, as shown in Figure 9-12.

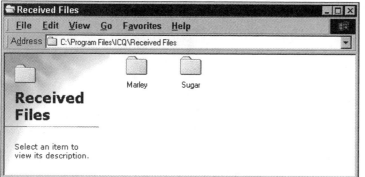

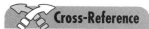

Cross-Reference

Earlier in this chapter, "File Transfer: Receiving or Declining Files" explains the other options on the File Transfer tab for handling incoming files.

Figure 9-12. By default, files sent to you are kept in the `C:\Program Files\ICQ\Received Files` folder and its subfolders.

Rather than store incoming files by default in the Received Files folder, however, you can choose a folder of your own for storing incoming files. And if you prefer to keep all the files you receive in one folder instead of several folders named after different senders, you can do that, too.

Follow these steps to designate a new folder for storing incoming files:

1. Click the ICQ button.

2. Choose Preferences on the pop-up menu. You see the Owner Preferences For dialog box.

3. Click Events on the left side of the dialog box.

4. Click the File Transfer tab. On the bottom of the tab, under Default Incoming File(s) Path, is the name of the folder where incoming files are kept, as shown in Figure 9-13.

5. Click the small folder button to the right of the folder name. The Select Directory dialog box appears (refer to Figure 9-13).

6. Select a new folder in the dialog box. To do so, double-click folder icons to open or close folders.

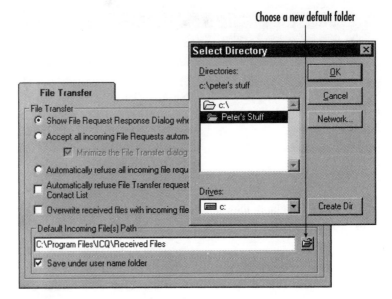

Choose a new default folder

Figure 9-13. Choosing a default folder for storing incoming files.

7. Click OK. The name of the folder you chose appears in the Default Incoming File(s) Path text box.

8. Uncheck the Save Under User Name Folder check box if you prefer to keep all incoming files in one folder, not subfolders named for each person who sends you files.

9. Click the Apply button.

Assigning Your Own Sounds to Events

As you know, most activities in ICQ are accompanied by a sound. When someone whose name is on your Contact List connects to ICQ, you hear a door knocking. When someone wants you to call them, you hear a telephone ring. Altogether, 28 different sounds come out of the ICQ program.

If you want to change the sound that plays when a message arrives or you want to laugh out loud in a chat, for example, you can do so. You can even assign your own sounds to events. For that matter, you can disable a sound to keep it from playing.

Follow these steps to decide for yourself which sound is played when an activity occurs in ICQ:

1. Click the ICQ button.

2. Choose Preferences on the pop-up menu. The Owner Preferences For dialog box appears.

3. Click Events on the left side of the dialog box.

4. Click the Sounds tab, shown in Figure 9-14.

5. From the Sound Schemes drop-down list, choose My Settings.

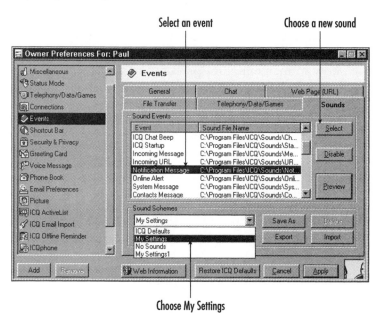

Figure 9-14. Choosing your own sounds for ICQ events.

Tip

Click the Preview button on the Sounds tab to play a sound.

6. Under Sound Events, click an event and do the following:

▲ **Change a sound:** Click the Select button, and in the Browse For dialog box, select a new sound and click the Open button.

▲ **Disable a sound:** Click the Disable button and click Yes in the confirmation box.

7. Change as many sounds as you like and then click the Apply button to close the Owner Preferences For dialog box.

Coming Up Next

Chapter 10 explains how to safeguard your privacy in ICQ. You'll learn how to ignore pesky people, choose whether others need authorization to put your name on their Contact Lists, and clamp a password on ICQ. You'll learn how to maintain your privacy and still reach into every corner of ICQ.

Chapter

10

Techniques for Safeguarding Your Privacy

Quick Look

Deciding Who Gets to Put Your Name on His or Her Contact List
page 243

Other ICQ users can either put your name on their Contact Lists immediately or obtain permission first. You decide whether others need permission by visiting the Security For dialog box.

Permanently Ignoring the ICQ Users You Don't Care to Hear From
page 245

After you put someone's name on your Ignore List, he or she will never bother you again. No matter how many events are sent to you, you never receive them.

Making Yourself Invisible to the People Who Bother You
page 247

People can send you instant messages and other events, but they never know when you are connected to ICQ because you made yourself invisible to them. The people to whom you are invisible just think that you are not connected to ICQ.

Hiding Your Online Web Status from Others
page 250

Throughout ICQ, you can view other people's online Web status — a flower icon or other indicator tells you whether an ICQ user is connected to the network. However, you can hide your online Web status from others.

Putting a Password on ICQ to Protect Your Privacy
page 252

A password can prevent others from changing your White Pages profile or even starting ICQ. ICQ offers three different levels of security. Choose the one that best suits your needs.

Chapter 10

Techniques for Safeguarding Your Privacy

This chapter explains how you can take advantage of all the wonderful features in ICQ and still maintain your privacy. You discover how to keep a close watch on who puts your name on Contact Lists, ignore people with whom you don't want to communicate, or make yourself invisible to them. You learn how to disguise your online Web status so no on knows whether you are connected to ICQ. This chapter also looks at putting a password on ICQ and keeping objectionable words from appearing in messages and the White Pages.

As with any Internet application, it is impossible to guarantee complete privacy. ICQ does its best to help you maintain privacy, but, let's face it, you're on the Internet. Privacy isn't completely guaranteed.

Authorizing (Or Not Authorizing) Your Name for Other People's Contact Lists

When you register with ICQ you make a very important decision about whether to authorize your name for others' Contact Lists. Either others need permission to put your name on their lists or others can put your name on their lists without asking you.

Maybe the best way to guard your privacy in ICQ is to be careful about who puts your name on their Contact List. People who have your name know when you are connected to ICQ. They can tell because, unless you change the default settings of ICQ, your name appears under the Online heading on their Contact Lists whenever you are online.

Follow these steps to tell ICQ whether others need permission before they put your name on their Contact Lists:

1. Click the ICQ button.

2. Choose Security & Privacy on the pop-up menu. You see the Security For dialog box.

3. Click the General tab, as shown in Figure 10-1.

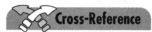

Cross-Reference

Chapter 4 describes all the details of entering names on Contact Lists.

Cross-Reference

What if somebody already has your name on his or her Contact List and you'd prefer it not be there? In that case, make yourself invisible to the nettlesome person. See "Making Yourself Invisible So Others Don't Bother You" later in this chapter.

10

Techniques for Safeguarding Your Privacy

Choose an authorization option

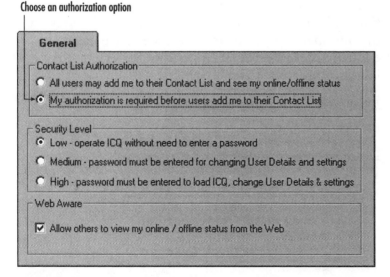

Figure 10-1. You never receive events from people on your Ignore List.

Note

You can click the More About ICQ Security button at the bottom of the Security For dialog box to learn about how ICQ handles security measures.

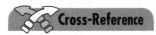

Cross-Reference

Chapter 7 explains how to search the White Pages.

Cross-Reference

Chapter 9 explains how to describe yourself in the ICQ Global Directory dialog box.

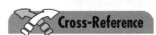

Cross-Reference

The next section in this chapter explains how, instead of ignoring people, you can make yourself invisible to them.

4. Under Contact List Authorization, choose an option:

▲ **All Users May Add Me to Their Contact List and See My Online/Offline Status:** Your name is placed automatically on others' Contact Lists. However, when your name is placed on someone's Contact List, you receive a System Notice message. It tells you who put your name on his or her Contact List and gives you the other person's name and ICQ number.

▲ **My Authorization Is Required Before Users Add Me to Their Contact List:** When someone wants to place your name on his or her list, the Incoming Request for Authorization dialog box appears on your screen. From there, you can accept or deny the request.

5. Click the Save button.

Double-Checking Your White Pages Profile

The information that you enter in the ICQ White Pages is available to all users of ICQ and to all Internet users. From time to time, be sure to open the White Pages and review the information that others can see. Be sure to enter enough information about yourself so that people whose interests are similar to yours can find you, but don't compromise your privacy. Entering your home phone number and address in the White Pages isn't necessarily a good idea, for example.

Do one of the following to review your profile in the White Pages and perhaps change it:

▼ Click the ICQ button and choose View/Change My Details on the pop-up menu.

▼ Click the View/Change My Details button on the ICQuick shortcut bar.

In the View/Change My Details dialog box, describe yourself and then click the Save button.

Ignoring Pesky People

From time to time, you get messages, Web page addresses, and EmailExpress messages from people you really don't care to hear from again. For example, you might receive one of those junk-mail advertisements that are occasionally sent to ICQ users, or you might get dogged with messages from that pesky person you prefer to ignore.

To keep from being bothered by events you don't care to receive, you can place the names of bothersome people on the Ignore List. And you can also tell ICQ that you don't want to receive certain kinds of junk-mail messages.

As shown in Figure 10-2, the Ignore List records the names of people from whom you never want to receive events of any kind. Your name still appears on these peoples' Contact Lists, and they can send you events, but the events never arrive. You never have to concern yourself with these people. To view the Ignore List, click the ICQ button, choose Security & Privacy, and click the Ignore tab in the Security For dialog box.

Follow these steps to banish someone whose name isn't on your Contact List to the Ignore List after you receive an unwelcome event:

1. Click the person's name. You will find the person's name under the Not in List heading in the ICQ window.

2. Choose Move to Ignore List from the pop-up menu that appears. The command doesn't appear on the pop-up menu if the name of the person you want to ignore is on your Contact List.

You may click the Add To Ignore List button on the Ignore tab to search for people to add to your Ignore List in the ICQ user database.

Keeping Junk Mail at Bay

The Ignore tab in the Security For dialog box (refer to Figure 10-2) offers a few options for keeping junk mail at bay. ICQ, like all public computer networks, is susceptible to junk mail, but you can prevent yourself from receiving junk mail by choosing among these options:

▼ **Accept Messages Only from Users on My Contact List:** You receive events only from people whose names are on your Contact List. All others are barred from sending you anything. The option doesn't apply to System messages (requests for authorization, for example).

▼ **Do Not Accept Multi-Recipient Messages From:** By definition, junk mail is sent to more than one person at a time, but you can prevent events that were sent to more than one person from coming your way by choosing this option. Choose All Users or Users Not on My Contact List on the drop-down list. If you choose Users Not on My Contact List, you can receive multiple-recipient messages from people on your list.

▼ **Do Not Accept WW Pager Messages:** As Chapter 14 explains, anyone can visit your Personal Communication Center and send you a WorldWide Pager message from there (click the Services button and choose My Communication Center to visit your Personal Communication Center). Click this option to prevent WW pager messages from arriving.

▼ **Do Not Accept EmailExpress Messages:** As Chapter 8 explains, you can receive e-mail messages, called EmailExpress messages, from sources outside ICQ. Click this option to prevent them from arriving.

▼ **Do Not Allow Direct Connection with Previous ICQ Software Versions:** Prevents events from arriving from ICQ users who have not upgraded to the latest version of ICQ.

Figure 10-2. You never receive events from people on your Ignore List.

To ignore someone whose name is on your Contact List, enter his or her name on the Ignore List by dragging it there: Open the Security For dialog box, place it beside the Contact List, and then click the name and drag it right to the Ignore tab.

Making Yourself Invisible So Others Don't Bother You

Another strategy for safeguarding your privacy is to make yourself invisible to the people who annoy you. Under this strategy, you can still receive events from the people in question. However, you aren't likely to receive many of them because the people to whom you are invisible think that you are disconnected from ICQ, even when you are connected.

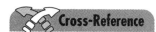

Cross-Reference

Instead of making yourself invisible to others, you can ignore them altogether. See the previous section in this chapter.

10

Techniques for Safeguarding Your Privacy

Figure 10-3 shows the Invisible List on the Invisible tab of the Security For dialog box. To view this tab, click the ICQ button, choose Security & Privacy, and click the Invisible tab.

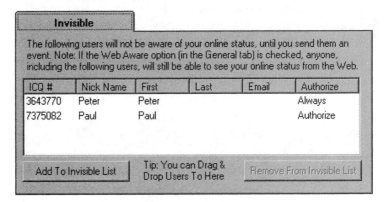

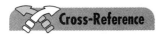

Cross-Reference

Making yourself invisible to someone doesn't mean that he or she can't tell when you're connected to ICQ. See the next section in this chapter.

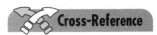

Cross-Reference

Chapter 9 explains the other options on the Status tab of the Alert/Accept Settings dialog box.

Figure 10-3. People whose names are on the Invisible List think you are permanently disconnected from ICQ.

To everyone on the Invisible List, it appears that you are disconnected from ICQ. For example, the flower icon next to your name on the person's Contact List shows that you are disconnected at all times. A person whose name is on the Invisible List can still send you events, but he or she thinks they will not arrive until you connect to ICQ. For that reason, you don't have to feel obliged to answer right away if the other party sends you an instant message or a chat request.

How you enter a name on the Invisible List depends on whether the name you want to enter is on your Contact List.

If the name of the person to whom you want to be invisible *is* on your Contact List, do either of the following to put the person's name on your Invisible List as well:

▼ Click the person's name and choose Alert/Accept modes on the pop-up menu. Then click General to view the General tabs, click the Status tab, and check the Invisible to User check box.

▼ Open the Invisible tab of the Security For dialog box. (Click the ICQ button, choose Security & Privacy, and click the Invisible.) Then drag the name of the person from your Contact List and drop it on the Invisible tab. Click Yes when ICQ asks whether to put the person's name on the Invisible List.

If the person to whom you want to be invisible *isn't* on your Contact List, your first task is to find that person's name in ICQ. Afterward, you can place his or her name on the Invisible List. Follow these steps to find someone and then make yourself invisible to him or her:

1. Click the ICQ button.

2. Choose Security & Privacy. You see the Security For dialog box.

3. Click the Invisible tab (refer to Figure 10-3).

4. Click the Add to Invisible List button. The Search for Users to Add to Your Invisible List dialog box appears.

5. On one or more tabs, enter what you know about the person:

   ▲ **Email:** The e-mail address he or she entered in the ICQ White Pages.

   ▲ **Details:** The person's nickname, first name, and/or last name.

   ▲ **ICQ#:** The person's ICQ number.

   ▲ **Interests:** The person's interests.

6. Click the Search button to search the White Pages. The person's name appears in the bottom of the dialog box, if it is found, as shown in Figure 10-4.

7. Right-click the person's name and choose Add to Invisible List from the pop-up menu.

8. Click OK in the confirmation box.

Note

The names of the people to whom you are invisible appear in *italics* on the Contact List.

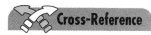

Cross-Reference

Chapter 4 explains how to search the ICQ user database.

10

Techniques for Safeguarding
Your Privacy

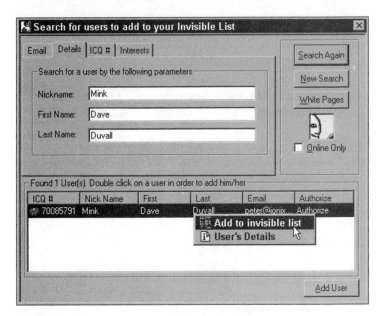

Figure 10-4. Searching for someone whose name belongs on the Invisible List.

To remove a name from the Invisible List, click it and then click the Remove from Invisible List button.

Deciding Whether to Let Others Know Your Online Web Status

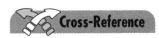

Chapter 2 explains the Status icons.

The Status icon beside your name on other people's Contact List tells them whether you are connected to ICQ, and, if you are connected, whether you want to chat or receive instant messages. However, the icon beside your name isn't the only status indicator.

Throughout ICQ, you can find status indicators that tell you whether someone is connected to the network. For example, Figure 10-5 shows the status indicator on a Personal Communication Center Page. (Click the Services button and choose My Communication Center to go to your Personal Communication Center Page.) The status indicator says "Online" so you know that this person is connected to ICQ.

Figure 10-5. A status indicator on a Personal Communication Center Page.

Figure 10-6 shows several status indicators that can come up in the results of a White Pages search. In the search results, flower icons beside people's names tell you whether they are connected to ICQ. Here are the three flower icons that appear throughout ICQ and what they mean:

▼ **A green flower:** The person is connected to ICQ.

▼ **A red flower:** The person is not connected.

▼ **A white flower:** The person has decided not to let others know his or her online Web status.

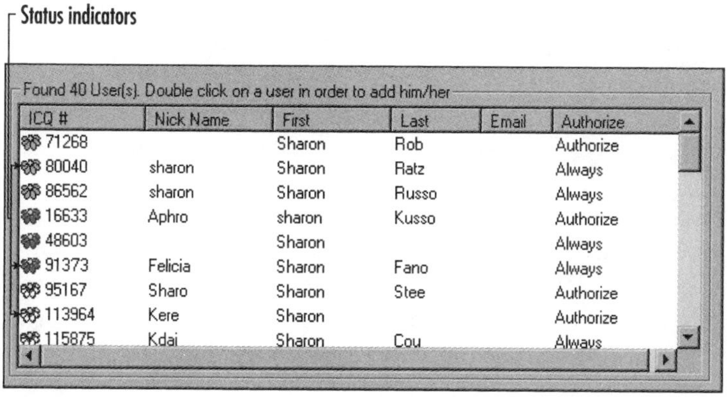

┌ Status indicators

ICQ #	Nick Name	First	Last	Email	Authorize	
Found 40 User(s). Double click on a user in order to add him/her						
71268		Sharon	Rob		Authorize	
80040	sharon	Sharon	Ratz		Always	
86562	sharon	Sharon	Russo		Always	
16633	Aphro	sharon	Kusso		Authorize	
48603		Sharon			Always	
91373	Felicia	Sharon	Fano		Always	
95167	Sharo	Sharon	Stee		Authorize	
113964	Kere	Sharon			Authorize	
115875	Kdai	Sharon	Cou		Always	

Figure 10-6. Status indicators tell you who is or isn't connected to ICQ — and even those who don't want you to know her or his online status.

Some people, for privacy's sake, prefer that others not know their online Web status. To choose whether others know your online Web status:

1. Click the ICQ button.

2. Choose Security & Privacy.

3. Click the General tab in the Security For dialog box.

4. Under Web Aware, either check or uncheck the Allow Others to View My Online/Offline Status on the Web check box.

Clamping a Password on ICQ

When you signed up with ICQ, you devised a password for getting into the network. Most people don't have to concern themselves with passwords. They simply start ICQ without having to enter one. But if you share your computer with others or you visit ICQ from the office as well as home, clamping a password on ICQ may be a good way to protect your privacy.

ICQ offers different ways to protect your privacy with passwords. Read on to learn how to clamp a password on certain areas of ICQ as well as change passwords.

Choosing a Security Level for Passwords

Depending on which security level you choose — High, Medium, or Low — a password is required to do certain tasks. Table 10-1 describes the different security levels and tells you when a password is required (indicated by an *X*). If you are operating under a High or Medium security level, the Password Verification dialog box shown in Figure 10-7 appears when you try to do the following tasks:

- ▼ **Start ICQ:** Start the ICQ program.

- ▼ **Change the password:** Change the password you use to start ICQ. To change passwords, go to the Password tab in the Security For dialog box.

- ▼ **Choose a new security level:** Choose a new security level on the General tab of the Security For dialog box, as shown in Figure 10-7.

- ▼ **Change your White Pages profile:** Change the information you entered about yourself in the ICQ White Pages. To change your profile, click the ICQ button and choose View/Change My Details.

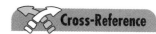 **Cross-Reference**

The next section in this chapter describes how to change passwords.

10

Techniques for Safeguarding Your Privacy

Table 10-1. Security Levels

Security Level	Start ICQ	Change Password	Change Security Level	Change White Pages Info
High	X	X	X	X
Medium		X	X	X
Low				

Follow these steps to change security levels and to require a password to do certain tasks:

1. Click the ICQ button.

2. Choose Security & Privacy on the pop-up menu that appears. The Security For dialog box opens.

3. Go to the General tab.

Choose a security level

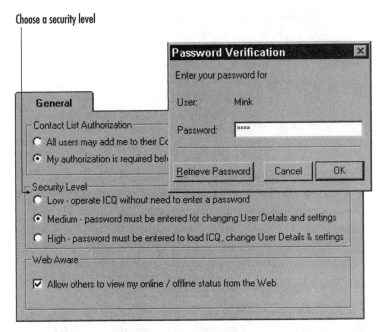

Figure 10-7. With High or Medium security, you see the Password Verification dialog box when you undertake certain tasks.

Entering Passwords When You Share a Computer

If you choose the High security level, you need to submit a password before you can start ICQ. But what if you share your computer with someone who is also an ICQ user? Does he or she also have to submit the password?

When you or your friend starts ICQ, you see the Password Verification dialog box, as usual. Click on the arrow to show the User drop-down list. Choose a name from the menu. If the person whose name is chosen doesn't need a password, he or she can start ICQ by clicking the OK button. A password isn't required.

4. Under Security Level, choose Low, Medium, or High (refer to Table 10-1).

5. Click the Save button. The Password Verification dialog box appears (refer to Figure 10-7).

6. Enter your password and click OK.

Changing Your Password

Follow these steps to change your password:

1. Click the ICQ button.

2. Choose Security & Privacy on the pop-up menu that appears. The Security For dialog box appears.

3. Click the Password tab.

4. Enter your new password in the Type Your New Password text box.

5. Enter it again in the Retype New Password text box.

6. Click the Save button. The Password Verification dialog box appears.

7. Enter your old password in the Password text box and click OK.

Keeping Profanity Out of Messages and the White Pages

No one likes to be unpleasantly surprised by profanity. To make your ICQ experiences pleasant ones, you can keep profanity from appearing in instant messages, the White Pages, find-a-friend chats, and other events that are sent back and forth in ICQ.

Tip

A fast way to enter your list on the Words List tab is to enter the words in a word-processor document. Enter one word on each line and save the file as a text-only (.txt) file. Then, in the Words List tab, click the Import List button, choose Text Files in the Files of Type drop-down list in the Open dialog box, and click the Open button.

To do so, you start by constructing a list of the words that you find objectionable. ICQ keeps the list, and when an instant message or other event arrives with an objectionable word, ICQ either places asterisks (***) where the word is or does not deliver the event. You get to decide between asterisks and not seeing events at all.

To tell ICQ which words you find objectionable:

1. Click the ICQ button and choose Security & Privacy.

2. Click the Words List tab in the Security For dialog box, as shown in Figure 10-8.

3. Click the Unlock (Enter Password) button, and, in the Password Verification dialog box, enter your password and click OK.

4. Click the Add button. The Define New Word dialog box appears.

5. Enter a word you find objectionable and click OK. You may also enter a URL.

6. Repeat Steps 4 and 5 to construct your list of words.

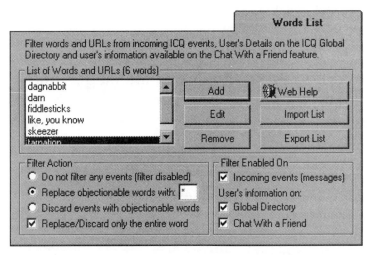

Figure 10-8. Constructing the list of objectionable words.

7. Choose among these options to tell ICQ how you want to handle events where objectionable words are found:

▲ **Replace Objectionable Words With:** Replaces objectionable words with asterisks (***) or a character you enter in the text box.

▲ **Discard Events with Objectionable Words:** Events with objectionable words are not delivered. You don't see them at all.

▲ **Replace/Discard Only the Entire Word:** The entire word is replaced by asterisks if part of the word happens to match a word on the list of objectionable words.

▲ **Incoming Events:** Instant messages, chats, Web page (URL) addresses, and other events that are sent back and forth are either suppressed or not delivered if they include objectionable words.

▲ **Global Directory:** Objectionable words in the White Pages are suppressed.

▲ **Chat with a Friend:** Objectionable words in find-a-friend chats are suppressed.

8. Click Save.

After you construct your list of objectionable words, events that include a word are either not delivered or are delivered asterisks and all, as shown in Figure 10-9.

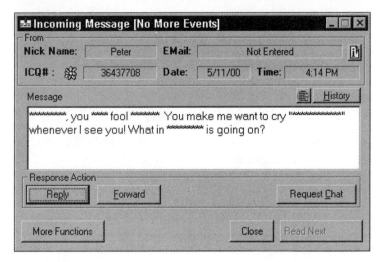

Figure 10-9. Some words in this message were deemed objectionable.

Coming Up Next

Chapter 11 explains how you can step forward and help make the ICQ community a more vibrant place. You learn what the ICQ newsletter is and how to publicize yourself in the White Pages. The chapter also describes how to manage a chat room, start your own Interest Group, and start your own ActiveList.

Chapter

11

Becoming a Pillar of the ICQ Community

Chapter 11

Becoming a Pillar of the ICQ Community

This chapter explains how to be a good citizen of ICQ and play a bigger part in the ICQ community. First, you find out how to step forward and make your presence known in ICQ by entering a detailed profile of yourself in the White Pages. You discover how to subscribe to the ICQ Newsletter and how to create a public chat room and Interest Group to help make ICQ a more interesting place to visit. Finally, this chapter explains how to own and administer an ActiveList.

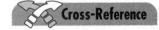

Chapter 7 explains how to search the White Pages. To see White Pages information about someone on your Contact List, click his or her name and choose User Details/Address Book.

Anyone on the Internet, not just ICQ users, may view your profile in the White Pages.

Publicizing Yourself in the White Pages

Information about all ICQ users is kept in the *White Pages*. To be a good citizen of ICQ, make sure your White Pages details are up to date, and make sure you reveal enough about yourself so that others can find you. The White Pages, for example, offer an opportunity to list where you went to high school. Enter the name of your high school, and people who attended the same high school will be able to search the White Pages and find you in ICQ.

ICQ offers several different ways to open the View/Change My Details dialog box and enter or change your profile in the White Pages. Choose one of the following methods:

- ▼ Click the View/Change My Details button on the ICQuick shortcut bar.

- ▼ Click the ICQ button and choose View/Change My Details.

- ▼ Click the My ICQ button and choose View/Change My Details.

- ▼ Click the Services button and choose ICQ White Pages⇨Publicize in ICQ White Pages.

As shown in Figure 11-1, the User Details dialog box presents ten areas for entering information about yourself. The Contact area represents a summary of information. When you are done entering or changing your profile in the White Pages, click the Save button. (Clicking the Update from Database button enters the information that ICQ has about you on its computers. Click the button when you change your profile but regret doing so. The profile that is on ICQ's computers will be entered in the dialog box and the changes you made to your profile will be erased.)

The following pages explain the ten areas in the User Details dialog box to help you portray yourself in the White Pages in the clearest possible light.

Main Area: Entering Your Name and E-Mail Address

The Main area (refer to Figure 11-1) is where you enter your nickname, first name, last name, and e-mail address or addresses. To enter an e-mail address, click the Add button and type the address in the Add Email Address dialog box. The dialog box includes a check box called Don't Publish My Email Address. If you check that box, others will not see your e-mail address anywhere in ICQ, but ICQ will be able to send you your password if you forget it. An envelope icon appears beside e-mail addresses that are published — addresses that others can see and send mail to — on the Main area.

Tip

Even if you don't want others to know your e-mail address, enter it, but click the Don't Publish My Email Address button in the Add Email Address dialog box. By entering your e-mail address, you make it possible to retrieve your password if you forget it. ICQ can mail the password to you at the address you enter.

11

Becoming a Pillar of
the ICQ Community

A published address that others can view

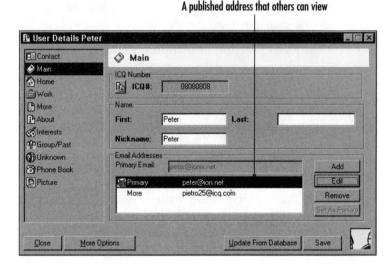

Figure 11-1: Information you enter in the User Details dialog box is stored in the White Pages.

When someone clicks your name on his or her Contact List and chooses Email⇨Send Email, the address you enter on the Main area is entered automatically in the dialog box for sending e-mail. E-mail addresses appear many places in ICQ — in Receive dialog boxes and in the White Pages, for example.

If you enter more than one e-mail address on the Main area of the User Details dialog box, select the one that you want to be your primary e-mail address and click the Set As Primary button. The primary e-mail address is the one to which ICQ sends your password to if you lose it. The word *Primary* appears beside the primary e-mail address.

Cross-Reference

Without entering phone numbers on the Home or Work area, you can let people who put your name on their Contact Lists know what your phone number is and even where to call you. See Chapter 3 for details.

Home Area: Entering Your Street Address and Home Phone Numbers

The Home area of the User Details dialog box is for entering your address and phone numbers. (Enter the phone number of your office on the Work area.) When you move the pointer over a name on the Contact List, you can view a person's home, work, and cellular phone numbers — provided he or she entered them in the White Pages.

For privacy's sake, many people don't enter their street address or phone numbers on the Home area, but be sure to enter the city, state, zip code, and country you live in to help others find you in ICQ.

Notice the Your Time listing in the lower-right corner of the Home area. If the time there isn't correct, open the GMT Offset drop-down list and select an option so that the Your Time listing is correct. ICQ notes the time that all events are sent and received. Unless the Your Time listing is correct, time notations in ICQ will not be accurate.

In case you forget where you reside, click the Display Map button on the Home area to go to a page on the Internet with a map of where you live.

Work Area: Entering a Company Address and Phone Numbers

The Work area of the User Details dialog box is for entering information about the company you work for, including your company's street address, phone number, and fax number. How much information you enter here depends on how closely you want to guard your privacy. However, be sure to fill in these boxes:

- ▼ **Position:** Enter your job title so that others who are in the same field can find you in the White Pages. Knowing others in your field can be a big help professionally.

- ▼ **Occupation:** Choose a category from the drop-down list to help others find you.

- ▼ **Home Page:** Enter your company's home page. This way, someone can go to your company's home page simply by clicking the House button beside the home page's address. (The More area offers a place to enter your personal home page.)

More Area: Entering More Information About Yourself

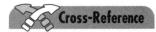
Cross-Reference

You can click the Homepage Category button on the More area to make your homepage available to ICQ search engines. Anybody who searches using the terms you use to describe your page will find your page. See Chapter 14.

As shown in Figure 11-2, the More area of the User Details dialog box is for describing yourself in more detail. If you have a homepage, be sure to enter it, because people who look you up in the White Pages will be able to click the House button beside your homepage's address to go straight to your homepage.

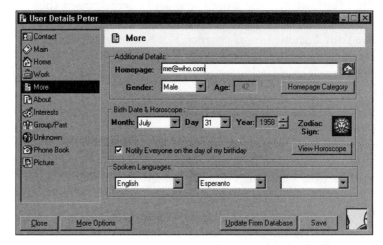

Figure 11-2. The More area of the User Details dialog box.

By entering your birth date, you not only tell ICQ users your age, you enable them to wish you happy birthday (and you can click the View Horoscope button to read your horoscope on the Internet). Don't forget to list the languages you speak as well.

About Area: Entering a Personal Message

Go to the About area to enter a personal message, describe yourself, or describe the people you would like to meet on ICQ. Anyone who clicks your name on their Contact List and chooses User's Details can read the words you enter.

Wishing — and Being Wished — a Happy Birthday

When someone on your Contact List is about to have a birthday, a red balloon icon appears beside his or her name on your Contact List so you can wish your friend a happy birthday. The balloon appears only if your friend entered his or her birth date in the White Pages. Click your friend's name and choose Greeting Card at the top of the pop-up menu to send your friend a greeting card (see Chapter 3).

When your birthday is due, the red balloon icon appears on the System Notice button. It also appears next to your name on others' Contact Lists. Expect to get a few happy birthday greetings when you see the red balloon icon.

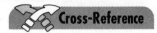

Appendix B describes the
PeopleSpace Directory.

Interests Area: Describing Your Interests

The Interests area of the User Details dialog box is for describing your interests. Actually, it is for describing your interests in such a way that other people can find out if their interests are the same as yours when they search the White Pages. You can describe four categories of interests, one for each check box on the Interests area.

To start, select a check box and then click the Edit button. You see the ICQ Interests Selection dialog box shown in Figure 11-3. Follow these steps to define an interest for the Interests area:

1. Choose a topic from the box on the left (Pets and Animals in Figure 11-3). A set of interests appears.

2. Click the plus sign beside an interest (Cats) to see a subtopic.

3. Choose a sub-interest (Burmese).

4. Click the Add button.

Within each interest, you can choose as many sub-interests as you want. However, you can't choose a new topic without clicking OK, returning to the Interests area, selecting a new check box, and clicking the Edit button beside it.

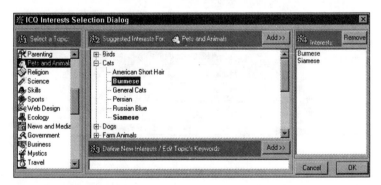

Figure 11-3: Defining your interests so that others can find you in White Pages searches.

When others search the White Pages for people with similar interests, they use the ICQ Interests Selection dialog box as well. They describe their interests the same way you do, and if your interests coincide, a match is found and you discover a new friend.

Group/Past Area: Describing Your Memberships and Past

As shown in Figure 11-4, ICQ provides the Group/Past area of the User Details dialog box so you can describe the organizations and clubs you belong to, as well as describe schools and organizations you went to or belonged to in the past. From the drop-down lists on the left, choose an option. Then enter names or keywords in the text boxes on the right.

When others search the ICQ White Pages, they choose from the same drop-down lists that you choose from on the Affiliations area. And if they enter the same names or keywords that you enter, they will find you in their searches.

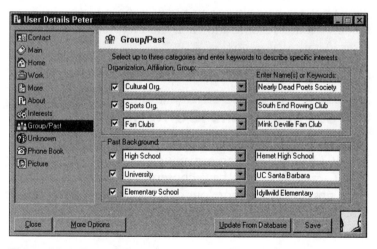

Figure 11-4. Describing your present affiliations and past associations.

Unknown Area: Seeing Which ICQ Plug-Ins Are on Your Computer

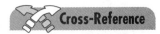

Appendix A explains plug-ins.

The Unknown area of the User Details dialog box lists the ICQ plug-ins that are loaded on your computer. Go to this dialog box to find out which plug-ins you have. By clicking the name of a plug-in, you can read its description.

Phone Book Area: Telling Others How to Reach You

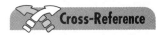

Chapter 3 explains the Phone Book area and how to make your phone numbers available.

The Phone Book area of the User Details dialog box is for handing out your phone numbers to people who have put your name on their Contact List. By way of this area, you can also tell others when you want to be reached and at which phone number you can currently be reached.

Picture Area: Making Your Photo Available to Others

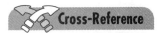

Chapter 3 explains how to view others' photos and how to let others view your photos.

Go to the Picture area in the User Details dialog box when you want to make your photo available to people who have put your name on their Contact List. To see your photo, others click your name, choose User Details/Address Book, and click the Picture area in the User Details dialog box.

To receive the ICQ Newsletter, you must have entered your e-mail address in the White Pages. See "Main Area: Entering Your Name and E-Mail Address" earlier in this chapter.

Subscribing to the ICQ Newsletter

The ICQ Newsletter, an e-mail newsletter, is sent weekly to ICQ members who have chosen to subscribe. The letter offers tips for getting more out of ICQ, points you toward ICQ features that you may not know about, and offers many hyperlinks that you can click to learn more about ICQ.

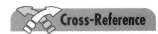

Chapter 6 explains what a public chat room is and how to join one.

Before you subscribe, look at a few back issues: Click the Services button and choose Newsletter⇨Back Issues. Your browser opens the ICQ Newsletter Web page (`www.icq.com/newsletter`). Scroll down the page and click a link to read a back issue of the ICQ Newsletter.

If you decide to subscribe, click the Services button and choose Newsletter⇨Subscribe. Click the Services button and choose Newsletter⇨Unsubscribe if you decide to no longer receive the newsletter.

Creating Your Own Public Chat Room

A public chat room works very much like a normal ICQ membership. People who want to participate in your chat room put its name on their Contact List. They know when it is up and running because its name appears under the Online area on the Contact List. When your chat room is up and running, a participant can click its name on the Contact List and choose ICQ Chat to start chatting.

Public chat rooms are registered in ICQ in the same way that memberships are. The difference, however, is that chat room names must begin with an ampersand (&). After you have created your public chat room, you can submit its name to ICQ. ICQ enters the name in the Directory of Chat Rooms so that others can find it.

To create your own public chat room, register a new account on ICQ (see Appendix A), but when you choose a nickname for the account, enter an ampersand (&) before the name. Instead of entering a first name for the account, enter the PeopleSpace subcategory in which you want it to appear in the Directory of Chat Rooms (`www.icq.com/ icqchat`). Appendix B lists the PeopleSpace categories. After you have finished registering, click the ICQ button and choose View/Change My Details. Then enter an enticing invitation to your chat room in the White Pages.

ICQ enters your chat room's name in the Directory of Chat Rooms. Your room also appears in the Newly Created ICQ Chat Rooms list. It usually takes a day or two for ICQ to list your chat room.

Starting Your Own Interest Group

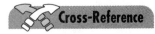
Cross-Reference

Chapter 7 explains how to join an interest group.

An *interest group* is a collection of people who share an interest in the same topic. ICQ keeps interest groups on its computers, but individuals are responsible for creating and maintaining interest groups. Follow these steps to create an interest group of your own:

1. Open your browser and go to your Service Area Web page at `groups.icq.com/service-area.asp`. The Service Area page lists the interests groups you belong to.

2. Click the Create a Group button (near the top of the page). The Create a Group In Web page appears.

3. Choose the PeopleSpace Directory category where you want your interest group to go. When others look for a group to join, they will search through the categories like the one you choose.

4. In the Create a Group page, enter a title for your interest group.

5. Click the Do It Yourself link.

6. Choose options and fill in text boxes in the Group Properties — Custom Design Options page. Be sure to enter an About Your Group and Group Description page to help others understand what the purpose of your interest group is. Don't worry — you can reverse all the choices you make later on. (You can click the Preview link at the bottom of the page to see what the color scheme you choose will look like.)

7. Click the Save Changes button at the bottom of the Web page.

When you want to change the particulars of your interest group, start by going to your Service Area page. It lists the interest group you created. Click the View button to go to the interest group, and then click the Edit Group button. You come to a Web page with hyperlinks for changing different parts of your interest group. Click a hyperlink and make your changes.

Owning an ActiveList

If you've joined an ActiveList, you may have been tempted to create one yourself. Maybe you couldn't find an ActiveList that concerns a topic or hobby that you care about. In that case, create an ActiveList of your own. No doubt other ICQ users share your interest in the topic or hobby that is your passion. This section explains how to create and administer an ActiveList.

Cross-Reference

Before you create and own an ActiveList, join a few to see what's what. See Chapter 7.

Creating an ActiveList

The first step in owning an ActiveList is to download the ActiveList server to your computer. To do that, open your Web browser and go to `www.icq.com/icqtour/advanced/activelist.html`. There you will find a link that you can click to download the ActiveList server to your computer.

After you download the ActiveList server, follow these steps to create a list:

1. Click the Start button and choose Programs⇨ ICQ⇨ICQ ActiveList⇨ICQ ActiveList Server. You see the ICQ ActiveList dialog box.

2. Make sure the first option button, Register a New ICQ ActiveList, is selected, and click Next.

3. Enter your ICQ number, enter your password, and click Next.

11

Becoming a Pillar of the ICQ Community

Cross-Reference

Earlier in this chapter,
"Interests Area: Describing
Your Interests" describes
how to choose an interest
category.

4. Enter a name for the list, a one-line description,
and, if you have created a homepage for your list,
enter its address. Then click Next.

5. In the ICQ ActiveList dialog box, click the Edit
button and choose a category for your list in the
Selected Interests dialog box. Then, as shown in
Figure 11-5, describe what you expect of your
members, choose a language or languages, and click
the Next button.

6. In the following dialog box, write a longer description of your ActiveList and click Next.

7. Describe your Internet connection and click Next.

8. Choose whether you want members to join automatically, make sure the first Directory Listings option button is selected (if it isn't selected, people will
have trouble learning about your list), enter a password, and click OK.

9. Click Next in the dialog box that says your list
was successfully created, and then click the Done
button.

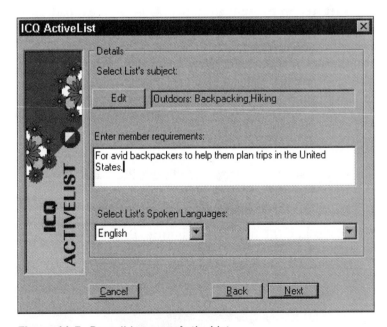

Figure 11-5. Describing your ActiveList.

You see the ActiveList Server dialog box, as shown in Figure 11-6. From this dialog box, you will administer your ActiveList.

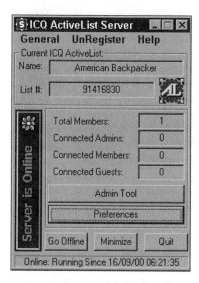

Figure 11-6. The ICQ ActiveList Server dialog box, where you administer your list.

Administering and Managing an ActiveList

ActiveLists are administered by way of the ActiveList Server dialog box (refer to Figure 11-6). Here are the three things you should know right away about this dialog box:

- ▼ To close the ActiveList Server dialog box, click the Quit button (or choose General⇨Quit).

- ▼ To open the dialog box and be able to administer your ActiveList, click the Start button and choose Programs⇨ICQ⇨ICQ ActiveList⇨ICQ ActiveList Server. Then, in the dialog box that appears, double-click the name of the ActiveList you want to open.

- ▼ To take the list on- or offline, click the Go Offline/ Go Online button (or choose General⇨Go Offline or General⇨Go Online).

Click the Preferences button in the dialog box to change the Internet connection information you entered when you created your ActiveList.

To administer your list, click the Admin Tool button. You see the Manager dialog box. By clicking the following buttons in this dialog box, you can administer your list:

- ▾ **Members:** See the names of list members. Double-click a name to learn more about the person.

- ▾ **News Board:** Post a message to members, reply to a message, or forward a message.

- ▾ **Statistics:** See you how many people are logged onto the list, how many have posted messages, and how many are chatting.

- ▾ **MOTD:** Enter the message of the day.

- ▾ **Access Groups:** Divide your membership into Active Groups. Determine what rights — for broadcasting messages, chatting, and doing other things — groups have.

- ▾ **Security:** Change the authorization setting for joining the list, as well as ban users and IP addresses from the list. You can also designate others as list administrators.

- ▾ **Properties:** Change the description and interest category that you entered when you created the list.

- ▾ **Admin Msgs:** Send messages to list administrators.

Coming Up Next

The next chapter explains how to keep track of your life with ICQ. You learn how the Notes features in ICQ can help you meet deadlines, keep appointments, and be less forgetful. The chapter also explains the Message Archive, the vast repository of all things ICQ, including events you've sent to and received from others.

Chapter

12

Keeping Track of Your
Life with ICQ

Chapter 12

Keeping Track of Your Life with ICQ

IN THIS CHAPTER

▼ Maintaining To Do notes so you know what needs doing

▼ Keeping notes on what matters in your life

▼ Being reminded by ICQ Reminder notes

▼ Revisiting and storing items in the Message Archive

▼ Finding an item in the Message Archive

▼ Printing items in the Message Archive

This chapter explains how ICQ can simplify your life — or at least make it easier to handle all the items you received. It delves into the Message Archive, the repository of events that you send and receive in ICQ. Events in the Message Archive are kept in folders, and in this chapter, you learn how to go from folder to folder and where to look for different events. This chapter explains the different kinds of reminder notes that you can write to yourself, how to replay a chat, and how to print events. You also discover how to delete events and store them in different folders in the archive.

Maintaining a List of To Do Notes

You can write To Do notes about things that need doing. After you write a To Do note or mark an event as a To Do note, the 2do icon appears in the lower-right corner of your screen to remind you that something needs doing. By double-clicking the 2do icon, you can see the first To Do note on the list in the History Event dialog box.

As shown in Figure 12-1, you can click the My ICQ button, choose ToDo on the pop-up menu, and choose Todo on the submenu to see the list. To open a To Do note on the list, click it. It appears in the History Event dialog box, as shown in Figure 12-1.

Follow one of these instructions to write a To Do note to yourself:

▼ Click the My ICQ button, choose To Do, and choose New.

▼ Click the More Functions button in an Incoming dialog box and choose Add to To Do List in the drop-down list.

You see the Add To Do Event dialog box (refer to Figure 12-1). Enter a note in the To Do Note text box and click the Add To Do button. You can also click the Select Preset To Do Note button and choose a generic note from the drop-down list.

To delete a To Do note, open it by clicking the My ICQ button, choosing ToDo, choosing Todo, and clicking the name of the note. You see the ToDo Event dialog box. Click OK, and then click Yes when ICQ asks if you want to unmark the note.

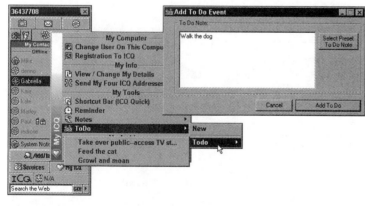

Figure 12-1. To Do notes appear on the Todo submenu.

Making Notes to Yourself

Notes resemble the yellow stick 'em notes that you sometimes see attached to manuscripts and refrigerator doors. Write a Note to mark down a deadline, for example, or to keep yourself from forgetting an appointment. The good thing about Notes is that you can make all of them appear on-screen at once, and just as quickly you can make all Notes disappear.

Follow one of these instructions to write a Note to yourself:

▼ Click the My ICQ button, choose Notes, and choose New Notes.

▼ Click the More Functions button in an Incoming dialog box and choose Create as Note on the drop-down list.

Tip

A yellow box appears, as shown in Figure 12-2. Enter your note. To make it disappear on-screen, press Ctrl+H or click the Close button (the *X*) and choose Hide on the pop-up menu, as shown in Figure 12-2.

To make a Note box only as large as it needs to be to hold the words, right-click the Note and choose Snap to Content.

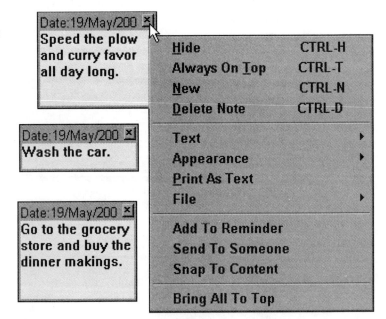

Figure 12-2. Write Notes like these to keep from forgetting.

Notes are very helpful, but they can get in the way. The easiest way to handle notes is to display them all at once, read them, and then hide them again until the next time you need them:

- ▼ **Displaying all Notes:** Click the My ICQ button, choose Notes on the pop-up menu, and choose Bring All to Front.

- ▼ **Hiding all Notes:** Click the My ICQ button, choose Notes, and choose Close All.

To delete a note, either press Ctrl+D, or click its Close button (the X) and choose Delete Note on the pop-up menu (refer to Figure 12-2).

Being Reminded of Upcoming Appointments and Meetings

Write a Reminder note to help meet a deadline or to be notified when someone on your Contact List has connected to ICQ. When a Reminder note requires your attention, you hear a beeping sound. Not only that, but an alarm clock icon appears on the System Notice button and in the lower-right corner of the screen.

Double-click the alarm clock icon and you see the ICQ Reminder dialog box shown at the top of Figure 12-3. In the dialog box, either disregard the Reminder by clicking the Dismiss button or choose an option in the Remind Again In drop-down list to be reminded later on.

To write a Reminder note, click the My ICQ button, choose Reminder, and choose New Reminder. The Add to Reminder dialog box shown on the bottom of Figure 12-3 appears. The dialog box offers two kinds of reminders:

12

Keeping Track of Your
Life with ICQ

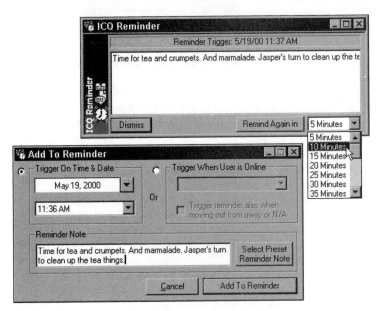

Figure 12-3. A Reminder note (top) and the Add To Reminder dialog box, where you enter Reminder notes (bottom).

▼ **Appointment or meeting reminder:** Click the Trigger on Time & Date option button and enter the date and time of the appointment or meeting by opening the drop-down lists.

▼ **Reminder when someone connects to ICQ:** Click the Trigger When User Is Online option button and choose a Contact List name from the drop-down list. You can also check the Trigger Reminder Also When Moving Out from Away or N/A check box to be alerted when the person whose name you chose leaves N/A (Extended Away) mode.

Enter your Reminder note in the text box and click the Add To Reminder button.

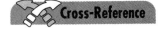

Cross-Reference

Chapter 2 describes N/A (Extended Away) mode. Chapter 10 describes other ways to be alerted to users who come online.

Introducing the Message Archive

A copy of every communication you have with someone whose name is or was on your Contact List is kept in the Message Archive. You name it, it's kept there — instant messages, Web page addresses, chats, file requests, Contact List names, telephony requests, system messages, WWPager messages, and EmailExpress messages.

Follow either of these instructions to open the Message Archive:

- ▼ Click the My ICQ button, choose Message Archive, and choose Open Message Archive. This technique takes you to the Messages folder in the Message Archive.

- ▼ Click a person's name on the Contact List, choose History on the pop-up menu, and choose Open Message Archive. The Message Archive window shows events you sent to and received from the person whose name you clicked.

As shown in Figure 12-4, you can tell what kind of event you are reviewing in the Message Archive by looking at the icon next to the event's name. As the figure also shows, you can select an event and look in the bottom half of the Message Archive window to preview what it is. For that matter, you can double-click an event to open the History Event dialog box and look very closely, as Figure 12-4 demonstrates.

The Message Archive is organized into folders and sub-folders. Table 12-1 describes the folders, all of which are found on the left side of the Message Archive window. To see what is in a folder, click its name.

Cross-Reference

Before you can open or make use of the Message Archive, you have to install it. See Appendix A.

Cross-Reference

As "Removing Names from the Contact List" in Chapter 5 explains, you can remove a name from the Contact List but still keep the name on file in the Address Book, a part of the Message Archive.

Cross-Reference

In Chapter 3, Table 3-1 explains what the icons next to events in the Message Archive mean.

Click a plus sign to open subfolders

Icons   Double-click on icon to look closely at an item

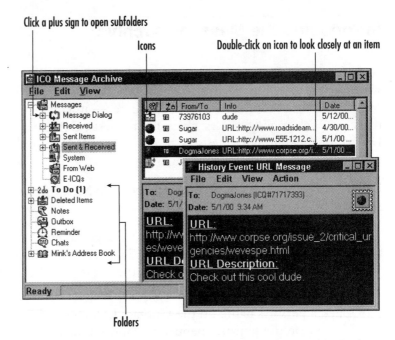

Folders

Figure 12-4. In the Message Archive window, click a folder in the panel on the left to view events on the right.

Table 12-1. Message Archive Folders

Folder	What's in It
Messages	Events that you received from others and sent to them. See "Messages Folder: Reviewing Instant Messages, URLs, and Other Communications."
To Do	Notes you write about tasks that need doing. See "Maintaining a List of To Do Notes" earlier in this chapter.
Deleted Items	Events you deleted from other folders. The events are kept in the Deleted Items folder in case you regret deleting them. See "Deleted Items Folder: Storing Events Before You Delete Them Permanently."
Notes	Notes to yourself. Displaying Notes on-screen is easy — so is hiding Notes to keep them from getting in the way. See "Making Notes to Yourself" earlier in this chapter.

Folder	What's in It
Outbox	Events that you postponed sending or that can't be sent until both parties are online. See "Outbox Folder: Holding Events Until They Are Ready to Be Sent."
Reminder	Reminder notes that you wrote. See "Being Reminded of Upcoming Appointments and Meetings" earlier in this chapter.
Chats	The text — and sound effects as well — of chats you saved. ICQ offers the Chat File Player for playing back a chat. See "Chats Folder: Reliving a Chat You Had Earlier."
Address Book	White Pages information about people whose names are or were formerly on your Contact List. See "Address Book: Storing White Pages Information."

The Message Archive works very much like those two famous Windows applications, My Computer and Windows Explorer. Where subfolders are found inside a folder, a plus sign (+) appears next to the folder's name. Click the plus sign to see the subfolders inside a folder. In Figure 12-5, the Messages folder and the Received subfolder are open. In the Received subfolder, a Contact List name has been selected, so the Message Archive window shows events that were received from the person whose name was selected.

Tip

Click the minus sign (-) next to a folder's name to hide its subfolders. The File menu offers commands for closing all folders and for opening selected folders.

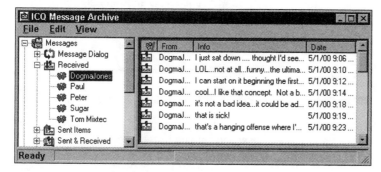

Figure 12-5. Click the plus sign (+) next to a folder name to open a folder.

By default, events in the Message Archive are arranged in ascending order by date, with the most recent event on the top of the list, but in many folders you can change the order in which events are listed by clicking the column headings (From, Info, or Date).

Exploring the Message Archive Folders

This section explains the different Message Archive folders. No matter which folder you are working with, the techniques for opening folders and subfolders are the same. Overall, the Message Archive works much like Windows Explorer, the Windows program for managing files and folders. Read on to learn about the different folders in the Message Archive and how you can use them to the best advantage.

Messages Folder: Reviewing Instant-Messages, URLs, and Other Communications

The Messages folder keeps a record of every event you sent to and received from people whose names are on your Contact List. Table 12-2 describes the subfolders inside the Messages folder.

Note

When you delete a name from your Contact List, instant messages, chats, and other events you exchanged with the person whose name you deleted are removed from the Message Archive as well.

Table 12-2. Subfolders in the Messages Folder

Subfolder	What's in It
Message Dialog	The complete history of all instant messages you traded with each person on your Contact List. Message text is shown in the window as a dialog, with your messages under your name and your partner's messages under his or her name.
Received	Events that were sent to you.
Sent Events	Events that you sent to other people.
Sent & Received	Events that you sent and received. Look in the second column to see whether you sent the event or received it.
System	Messages dealing with putting others' names on your Contact List and getting your name on others' Contact Lists.

Subfolder	What's in It
From Web	EmailExpress and WWPager messages that you received from outside the ICQ network.

Open the Message Dialog, Received, Sent Events, or Sent
& Received subfolders and you will find the names of
people on your Contact List, as shown in Figure 12-6.
Click a name and you can review events that you sent, received, or exchanged with a particular person.

By looking in the System subfolder, you can tell who put
your name on their Contact
List. In the Info column, look
for the words "The user has
added you to his/her
Contact List."

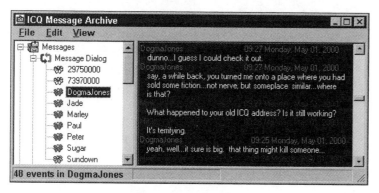

Figure 12-6. Look for names in subfolders to focus on events to or
from people on your Contact List.

Deleted Items Folder: Storing Events Before You Delete Them Permanently

The Deleted Items folder is the place where events go after you delete them. The Message Archive places events in
the folder in case you regret deleting them and you want
them back.

After you delete an event in the Deleted Items folder, it is
gone for good. You can never recover it. To delete an event
in the Deleted Items folder, select it and do one of the
following:

To remove all events from the
Deleted Items folder or one
of its subfolders, right-click
and choose Empty on the
pop-up menu. To delete several events at once, Ctrl-click
them before giving the Delete
command.

12

Keeping Track of Your
Life with ICQ

Keeping Events from Being Recorded in the Message Archive

For the sake of privacy or to keep the Message Archive from being cluttered unnecessarily, you can keep events — communications with certain people or communications from everyone — from being recorded in the Message Archive.

▼ **No events sent to or received from a certain person are recorded:** Click the person's name on your Contact List and choose Alert/Accept modes on the pop-up menu. In the User Preferences For dialog box, click General, and then click the Accept tab. Then check the Do Not Log Event History check box and click OK.

▼ **No events whatsoever are recorded:** Click the ICQ button and choose Preferences. In the Owner Preferences For dialog box, click Events. Then check the Do Not Log Event History box on the General tab.

▼ Press the Delete key.

▼ Right-click and choose Delete from the pop-up menu.

▼ Open the Edit menu and choose Delete.

To recover an event in the Deleted Items folder, right-click it and choose Restore from Deleted. The event is returned to the folder it was in before you deleted it the first time.

Outbox Folder: Holding Events Until They Are Ready to Be Sent

Chapter 3 explains how to postpone sending an event.

If you postpone sending an event, or if an event can't be sent until the recipient and sender are both online, the event is placed in the Outbox folder of the Message Archive. Go to the Outbox folder and delete the event if you change your mind about sending it.

By the way, you can see what is in the Outbox without opening the Message Archive: Double-click the System Notice button (or click it and choose History and OutBox) and then click the OutBox tab in the History of Events dialog box. You can delete events in the History of Events dialog box as easily as in the Outbox folder in the Message Archive.

Chats Folder: Reliving a Chat You Had Earlier

As long as you save a chat when you end it, the complete text of the chat is stored in the Chats folder. To relive a chat, open the Chats folder in the Message Archive and double-click the chat you want to replay. As shown in Figure 12-7, the ICQ Chat File Player appears.

Cross-Reference

Chapter 6 explains how to save a chat in the Message Archive. (Click the Close button and choose Quit - Save Chat Session.)

Figure 12-7. Reliving a chat in the ICQ Chat File Player.

The Chat File Player works much like a tape player. As the chat is played, words scroll by in the Chat window. If sounds were exchanged as part of the chat, you hear them. Use these controls to play back the chat:

- ▼ **Speed:** Drag the slider to make the chat play back faster or slower.

- ▼ **Time Line:** Drag the scroll box to move backward or forward in the chat.

- ▼ **Control:** These standard buttons — Rewind, Stop, Play, and Fast Forward — work the same as their namesakes on a tape player.

Click OK after you finish reliving the chat. The ICQ Chat File Player closes, as does the Chat window. You can print the text of a chat by clicking the Print button. Click the Export button to save the text in a format that a word processor can open.

Address Book: Storing White Pages Information

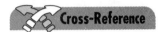

Chapter 11 describes how
the White Pages work. Click
the Retrieve button to get up-
to-date White Pages
information.

White Pages information about people whose names are
or formerly were on your Contact List is kept in the
Address Book folder of the Message Archive. Open the
folder and click a name to see the White Pages tabs —
Main, Home, Work, More Info/About, and Interests/Past.
This is the same information you get when you click a
name on your Contact List and choose User
Details/Address Book on the pop-up menu.

The icon next to the names tells you whether a person is
currently on your Contact List. A plain face means the
person is on your list, but a face with a green card beside it
means that the person was formerly on your list.

By clicking the About tab, you can write a note of your
own about a person whose name is in your Address Book
folder.

Managing Events and Folders in the Message Archive

These pages explain how to do a few housekeeping chores
in the Message Archive. To keep the archive from getting
cluttered, it pays to delete events now and then. The following pages explain how to do that. You also learn how
to create a folder of your own for storing important events
and how to move or copy events from one folder to
another.

Deleting Events from the Message Archive

Earlier in this chapter,
"Deleted Items Folder:
Storing Events Before You
Delete Them Permanently"
explains the Deleted Items
folder.

To delete an event in a folder, start by selecting it.
Ctrl+click events to select several at once. Then do one of
the following to delete the events:

▼ Right-click and choose Delete on the pop-up
   menu.

▼ Open the Edit menu and choose Delete.

Click Yes in the confirmation box to delete the event. After you delete an event, it is sent to the Deleted Items folder in case you want to recover it later on. Events deleted from the Deleted Items folder are permanently removed from the Message Archive — you can't get them back.

Creating a Folder of Your Own for the Message Archive

You can create a folder of your own for the Message Archive. Perhaps you want to move important events into a folder you create to make finding them easier. A folder you create automatically becomes a subfolder of the Messages folder, the first folder in the Message Archive.

Follow these steps to create your own folder:

1. Open the File menu in the Message Archive.

2. Choose Folder.

3. Choose New on the submenu. The Messages folder opens, and, at the bottom of the list of subfolders in the Messages folder, you see a new subfolder called New Folder.

4. Press the Backspace key to erase the words "New Folder," type a name of your own, and press the Enter key.

To delete a folder you created, right-click it and choose Delete on the pop-up menu. Rename a folder by right-clicking, choosing Rename, pressing the Backspace key, and typing a new name.

Moving or Copying Events to a Different Folder

After you have created your own folder, you can move or copy events into it. Events can be copied or moved only into folders that you created yourself. Follow these steps to move or copy an event into a folder that you created:

Cross-Reference

Earlier in this chapter, "Chats Folder: Reliving a Chat You Had Earlier" explains the ICQ Chat File Player.

12

Keeping Track of Your Life with ICQ

1. Click to select the event. To select several events at once, Ctrl+click them.

2. Open the Edit menu.

3. Choose Move To or Copy To. You see the Move To dialog box (or the Copy To dialog box if you are copying items).

4. Click the folder to which you want to move or copy the event.

5. Click OK.

Finding a Wayward Event in the Message Archive

Occasionally you lose track of an event in the Message Archive. You traded opinions about a certain something with somebody, and now you need to review the opinions that were traded. How can you find a wayward event when you don't know who sent it to you or when it was sent?

To find a wayward event, start by selecting the subfolder where you think it was located. For example, click the name of the person to whom you sent an event. Then choose Find on the Edit menu, enter a search word in the Find dialog box, and click the Find button. If ICQ can find the word, the event in which it is located is selected.

However, if the Find command doesn't get you anywhere, try out the Advanced Find command by following these steps:

1. If the Message Archive is already open, open the Edit menu and choose Advanced Find. If the Message Archive is not open, click the My ICQ button, choose Message Archive on the pop-up menu, and choose Advanced Find. You see the Advanced Find dialog box shown in Figure 12-8.

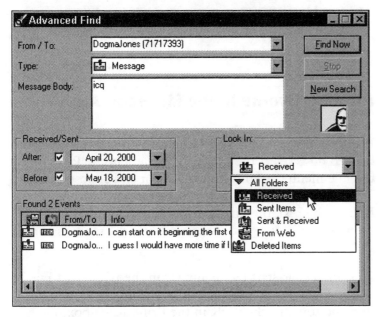

Figure 12-8. Looking for a lost event.

2. If you know who the event is from or to whom you sent it, choose a name from the From/To drop-down list.

3. If you know the type of event you are looking for, choose it from the Type drop-down list.

4. If you know a word or phrase in the event, enter it in the Message Body text box.

5. If you know roughly when the event was received or sent, check the Before and/or the After check box, and then click the down-arrow to open the calendar and select a date to enter in the After or Before text box.

6. If you know which Message Archive folder the event is likely to be in, choose it from the Look In drop-down list.

7. Click the Find Now button. If an event or events are found, they are listed at the bottom of the Advanced Find dialog box.

12

Keeping Track of Your
Life with ICQ

8. Double-click an event to open it in the History Event dialog box and view it.

Printing Events in the Message Archive

Printing an event in the Message Archive is simple. All you have to do is select the event and either choose Print on the File menu or right-click the event and choose Print. Then, in the Print dialog box, click the OK button. Besides the text, the printout lists who sent or received the event, when it was sent or received, and the sender's name and ICQ number.

To print a chat, start by opening it in the ICQ Chat File Player. Then, in the Chat File Player dialog box, click the Print button and click OK in the Print dialog box.

Coming Up Next

The next chapter explains how to make ICQ your ticket for surfing the Internet. You learn how to send and receive Web page addresses and in so doing be able to quickly visit Web pages. You also discover ICQ Surf, a means of surfing the Internet alongside other people. The chapter describes how to bookmark your favorite Web sites in ICQ and search the Internet for information.

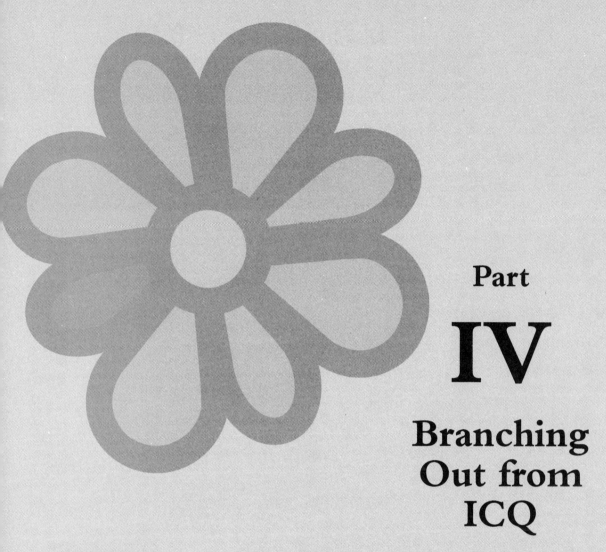

Part

IV

Branching Out from ICQ

Chapter

13

ICQ and the Internet

Quick Look

Visiting an ICQ Channel
page 296

An ICQ channel is an area of the Web, maintained by ICQ, where you can get information and insights that pertain to different topics: games, movies and TV, relationships, your finances, news, sports, music, shopping, technology, and travel.

Sending and Receiving Web Page Addresses
page 297

ICQ makes it easy to send Web page addresses (URLs) to your friends. And when a friend sends you the address of an exciting Web page, all you have to do is click a button in the Incoming URL Message dialog box to visit the Web page. You can bookmark the site very quickly as well.

Visiting the Web Pages You Bookmarked in ICQ
page 300

Bookmarking a Web page that someone sends you is easy — and so is visiting the page after you bookmark it. ICQ organizes the bookmarks under the names of the people who send you Web page addresses. You can visit a Web page you bookmarked with a couple of mouse-clicks.

Surfing the Internet — and Chatting about What You Find — with Other ICQ Users
page 302

ICQ offers a special program called ICQ Surf that makes it possible to visit Web pages and simultaneously discuss them with other surfers. You can also find the best Web sites with ICQ Surf. By going to the Hot List, you can find out where other surfers are going on the Internet.

Searching the Internet without Leaving ICQ
page 312

ICQ makes searching the Internet easy. From the ICQ window, you can search using many different search engines and make your searches as accurate as possible.

Chapter 13

ICQ and the Internet

This chapter describes the numerous ways that ICQ can make searching and using the Internet more enjoyable and productive. You learn how to send the addresses of your favorite Web pages to others, and how they can send their favorites to you. After you get a Web page address, all you have to do is click a button in a dialog box to visit the Web page. You can bookmark the Web page as well and visit it quickly starting from ICQ. This chapter also looks into ICQ Surf, a unique feature for chatting with others while you search the Internet. Finally, you discover how to search the Internet itself without leaving ICQ.

Visiting the ICQ Channels

As shown in Figure 13-1, an ICQ *channel* is an area on the Web that offers a unique insight into a certain topic. To visit a channel, click its button on the Channels bar. After you click a button, you see a window with hyperlinks that you can click to explore all that the channel offers. Channels offer all kinds of information and entertainment. Think of each channel as an online magazine — one to which you can subscribe for free.

Channels button

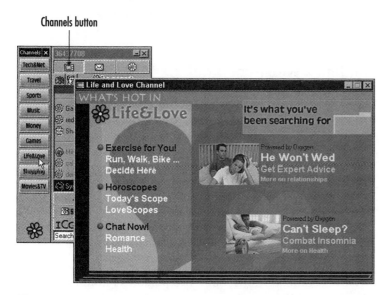

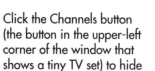

Click the Channels button (the button in the upper-left corner of the window that shows a tiny TV set) to hide or display the Channels bar.

Figure 13-1. To view a channel, click its button on the Channels bar.

Sending and Receiving Web Page Addresses (URLs)

Suppose you are surfing the Internet or you're cruising along in ICQ Surf and you come upon a Web page that you want to share with someone on your Contact List. You could send the Web page address to your friend in the form of an e-mail message, but a better way is to send a Web Page Address (URL) message. That way, after your friend receives the message, he or she can click a button to go straight to the Web page. Not only that, but your friend can click the Add to Bookmark button to bookmark the Web page as well.

Later in this chapter, "Visiting a Web Page You Bookmarked" explains how to open your browser to Web pages you bookmarked in ICQ.

Read on to learn how to send and receive Web page addresses in ICQ.

Sending a Web Page Address (URL)

Definition

A URL (uniform resource locator) is a Web page address on the Internet. Every page has its own URL. To see a page's address, open it and look in the Address box in your Web browser.

Before you can send a Web page address to someone else, you have to know what the address is. Web page addresses, of course, are difficult to remember and hard to type, but you can get around that problem. Just open your browser and go to the Web page whose address you want to send to someone else. That way, you don't have to enter the address by hand when you send it.

Follow these steps to send a Web page address (URL) to someone whose name is on your Contact List:

1. In Advanced mode, click the person's name on your Contact List.

2. Choose Web Page Address (URL) on the pop-up menu. You see the Send Online URL Message dialog box shown in Figure 13-2.

Enter an address or choose one from the drop-down menu

Send Online URL Message	_ □ ×
To	
ICQ#: 70623818 **Nick:** Marley	
EMail: Not Entered	

Select / Enter URL:

http://www.roadsideamerica.com/

Enter URL Description:

Check out this one. It's my favorite.

☐ More   Cancel   Send

Figure 13-2. Sending a Web page address to someone on your Contact List.

3. If the Web page address you want to send isn't already listed in the Select/Enter URL list box (because you aren't currently viewing the page in your default browser), either enter a Web page address by hand or choose the one you are looking for from the drop-down list.

4. Optionally, scribble a note to accompany the Web page address in the Enter URL Description text box.

5. Click the Send button.

The next section in this chapter shows what happens when you receive a Web page address.

Receiving and Bookmarking a Web Page (URL) Address

You can tell when someone has sent you a Web page address (URL) because the Web Page Address icon appears in the desktop tray and/or beside the sender's name on your Contact List, as shown in Figure 13-3. Double-click the icon and you see the Incoming URL Message dialog box, which is also shown in Figure 13-3.

Before clicking the Close button, bookmark the page, open it in your browser, or do both:

▼ **Bookmark the Web page:** Click the Add to Bookmark button, enter a descriptive name for the Web page in the Add to Favorites dialog box, and click OK. By bookmarking the Web page, you can open it quickly later on, as the next section in this chapter explains.

▼ **Visit the Web page:** Click the Go To URL button and choose Open in Current Browser window or Open in New Browser window on the drop-down list to view the Web page right away.

Definition

Bookmark means to mark a Web page in such a way that you can visit it quickly. The next section in this chapter explains how to visit a Web page you bookmarked in ICQ.

Incoming Web address

Click to bookmark the address   Click to open the Web page

Figure 13-3. Click the Go To URL button in this dialog box to visit the Web page.

Visiting a Web Site You Bookmarked

Cross-Reference

Chapter 9 describes how you can automatically bookmark all Web page addresses that are sent to you.

After you bookmark a Web page in ICQ (see the previous section in this chapter), visiting it is easy. Follow these steps to visit a Web page you bookmarked:

1. Click the System Notice button.

2. Choose Incoming Bookmarks on the pop-up menu. As shown in Figure 13-4, your browser window

opens to the ICQ Incoming Bookmarks page. In the From column are the names of each person who sent you Web page addresses (URLs) that you book-marked. Notice that each name is a hyperlink.

Note

Although the ICQ Incoming Bookmarks page appears in your browser window, it and the Incoming Bookmarks From page are actually lo-cated on your computer, as a glance at the Address box shows.

Click a hyperlink   Click a name

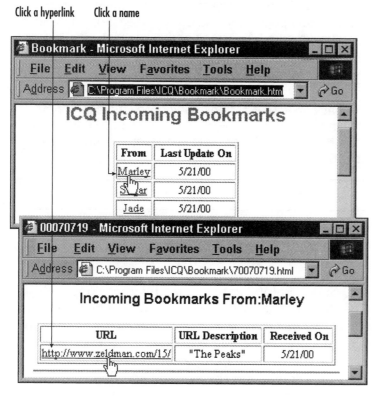

Figure 13-4. Visiting a Web page that you bookmarked.

3. Click the name of the person who sent you the ad-dress of the Web page you want to visit. Your browser window opens to the Incoming Bookmarks From page, as shown at the bottom of Figure 13-4. On the page is a hyperlink to Web pages you bookmarked.

4. Click a hyperlink to visit a Web page.

Backing Up Your ICQ Bookmarks

Lists of the Web pages that you bookmarked in ICQ are stored in the `C:\Program Files\ICQ\Bookmark` folder on your computer. The folder holds one file for each person on your Contact List from whom you received Web pages that you bookmarked. For example, if you bookmarked Web page addresses that were sent to you from ICQ member 1122334, you will find a file called 1122334 in the `C:\Program Files\ICQ\Bookmark` folder.

To back up your ICQ bookmarks, copy the appropriate file in the `C:\Program Files\ICQ\Bookmark` folder to a floppy disk. To copy all the bookmarks, copy the entire Bookmark folder.

ICQ Surf: Cruising the Internet Along with Other ICQ Members

You have to download and install ICQ Surf before you can use it. See Appendix A.

ICQ Surf is a neat way to surf the Internet along with other ICQ members. It's also a neat way to find out where other ICQ members are going on the Internet and in so doing discover interesting Web sites. Of course, you can also make new friends in ICQ Surf because you get so many opportunities to chat with others whose interests are the same as yours.

Figure 13-5 shows what your computer screen looks like when you surf the Internet with ICQ Surf. As you can see, the ICQ Surf window wraps itself around the browser window. The ICQ Surf window is composed of three parts:

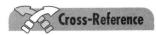

Later in this chapter, "Handling the ICQ Surf Window" offers techniques for managing the ICQ Surf window.

▼ **Users list:** The list of ICQ users who are visiting the Web site that is shown in the browser window. The list appears on the left side of the screen. Your name appears at the top of the list. By clicking a name, you can learn more about someone, engage him or her in a private chat, and even enter his or her name on your Contact List.

▼ **Public chat window:** Comments by people who are visiting the Web site shown in the browser window. The Chat window appears at the bottom of the screen. To enter a comment, type it in the text box and click the Send button.

▼ **ICQ Surf User Menu:** The number of ICQ members who are visiting the Web site. More importantly, you can click the ICQ Surf User Menu button to make the ICQ Surf window disappear or reappear. Right-click it to display more options.

Users list shows surfers currently visiting the site   Click to hide/display the ICQ Surf window

Browser window

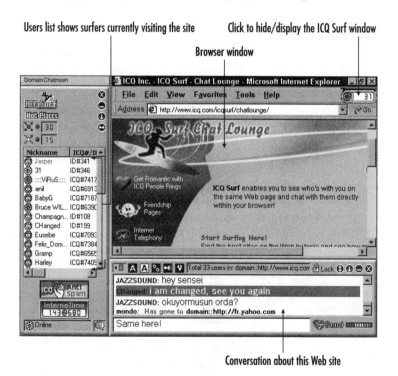

Conversation about this Web site

Figure 13-5. The ICQ Surf window wraps itself around your browser window.

Read on to learn how to log in to the ICQ Surf network. After you log on, you can find out where other surfers are congregating and thereby find out where the good Web sites are. These pages also explain how to manage the ICQ

Surf window, engage someone in a private chat, and chat along with other ICQ members who are visiting the same site on the Internet that you are visiting. This section also explains how to log off ICQ Surf.

Logging in and Entering Your Surf User Information

Tip

If you are happy with your settings and you want to log in directly to ICQ Surf without seeing the Surf Login dialog box each time you log in, check the Auto-Login to ICQ Surf without Presenting Login Dialog check box. To change your log in settings later, click the Services button, choose ICQ Surf, and choose Login Settings.

When you log in to ICQ Surf, the Surf Login dialog box shown in Figure 13-6 appears so you can decide how you want to present yourself to others who are also logged in. The options you choose determine whether others who are logged in to ICQ Surf can contact you in ICQ, whether others know your ICQ nickname and number, how ICQ Surf starts, and what others can learn about you by clicking your name.

Choose to log in with your ICQ identity or log in anonymously

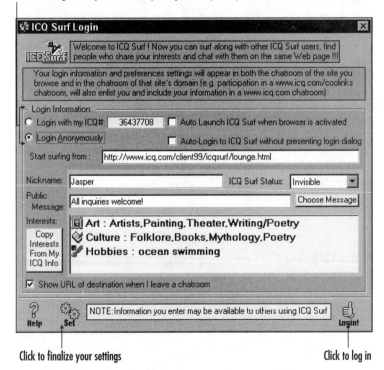

Click to finalize your settings   Click to log in

Figure 13-6. Logging in to ICQ Surf.

To log in to ICQ Surf, click the Services button, choose ICQ Surf, and choose Launch ICQ Surf. You see the ICQ Surf Login dialog box (refer to Figure 13-6). Click the Login button to start surfing right away. Otherwise, make these choices in the dialog box:

Tip

The fastest way to launch ICQ Surf is to click the ICQ Surf button on the ICQuick short-cut bar.

▼ **Surf as an ICQ member or anonymously:** If you choose Login with My ICQ#, everyone in ICQ Surf can read your ICQ number in the Users list (refer to Figure 13-5). Others can click your name on the list and send you an instant message or see your White Pages profile.

If you chose Login Anonymously, an ID number instead of an ICQ number appears beside your name in the Users list. Others can send you their ICQ numbers or request your number, but no one knows your ICQ number right off the bat.

▼ **Launch ICQ Surf when you choose or when you open your browser:** Check the Auto Launch ICQ Surf when Browser Is Activated check box to start ICQ Surf whenever your browser is open and you are connected to ICQ. This option is for fans of ICQ Surf. You can always start ICQ Surf on your own by clicking the Services button, choosing ICQ Surf, and choosing Launch ICQ Surf.

▼ **Enter a Web address to start surfing a site of your choice:** The Web address listed in the text box is that of the ICQ Surf Chat Lounge. Because most people start surfing there, you will always find plenty of people to chat with in the Chat Lounge Web page, but you can start surfing at a different Web page by entering its address in the text box.

Note

ICQ Surf offers a special command for going to the ICQ Surf Chat Lounge in your browser: Right-click the ICQ Surf User Menu button and choose Chat Lounge.

▼ **Enter a new nickname or keep your ICQ nickname:** To protect your privacy, you can enter a different nickname in the Nickname text box if you so choose. The name you enter will appear on the Users list (refer to Figure 13-5).

▼ **Choose a Surf Status:** A status icon appears next to names on the Users list (refer to Figure 13-5) to tell others whether surfers care to be contacted or don't want to be disturbed. Choose an option from the ICQ Surf Status drop-down list to describe your status. You can change your status later on by clicking your own name in the Users list.

▼ **Enter a public message:** You can click a name on the Users list and choose ICQ Surf User Info to read the public message. Either enter a message so that others who click your name will know what you are about, or click the Choose Message button and choose a generic message.

▼ **Choose whether to tell others where you are going:** When you leave one Web page to go to another, the Chat window names the Web address to which you went in case others want to follow you there (refer to Figure 13-5). However, you can keep others from following you by unchecking the Show URL of Destination When I Leave a Chatroom check box.

When you are finished with the ICQ Surf Login dialog box, be sure to click the Set button and click OK in the Preferences dialog box that appears. That way, your settings will apply next time you log in to ICQ Surf.

Now that you are ready to log in, click the Login button, in the lower-right corner of the ICQ Surf Login dialog box.

Handling the ICQ Surf Window

The ICQ Surf window can get in the way when you are surfing the Internet. However, the makers of ICQ give you many opportunities for shrinking the window or enlarging it when it needs enlarging. Table 13-1 describes the buttons you can click to handle the ICQ Surf window. Notice that the blue set of buttons is found in both the Users list and Chat window.

The descriptions in the Interests part of the ICQ Surf Login dialog box are taken from your White Pages profile. Surfers can move the pointer over icons in the Users list to find out what your interests are. See Chapter 11 to learn how to enter information about yourself and your interests in the White Pages.

Besides clicking buttons, you can hide or display parts of the ICQ window by clicking the ICQSurf button (or right-clicking the ICQ Surf User Menu), choosing Show, and choosing a sub-menu command.

Table 13-1. ICQ Surf Window Buttons

Button	Name	Click It To . . .
	ICQ Surf User Menu	Make the ICQ Surf window disappear or reappear. You can drag this button anywhere on the perimeter of your browser window. Right-click it for more options.
	Hide Surf Windows	Make the ICQ Surf window disappear. To see the window again, click the ICQ Surf User Menu button.
	Hide List Window/ Hide Chat Window	Close the Users list or the Chat window. To see the windows again, click the Open/Close Public Chat Window button or the Open/Close Users List button.
	Toggle Docking/ Floating Window Mode	Make the ICQ Surf window float in the middle of the screen. You can move a floating window around by dragging its title bar. Click the button again to dock the window to the sides of your browser window.
	Expand Window	Make the Users list or Chat window larger so you can see the information beside the names or read more text. Click the button a second time to shrink the list or window again.
	Open/Close Public Chat Window	Closes or opens the Chat window. Look for this button in the lower-right corner of the User list side of the window.
	Open/Close Users List	Closes or opens the Users list. Look for this button to the left of the Font buttons.

Hot Places: Finding Out Where Other Surfers Are

You can also right-click the ICQ Surf User Menu button and choose Hot Places to go to the ICQ Surf Most Popular Sites dialog box.

One of the best things about ICQ Surf is being able to find out where the other surfers are. It goes without saying, but people tend to hang out at the best Web sites. To find out where others who are connected to ICQ Surf are on the Internet, click the Hot Places button (look for it above the Users list). You see the ICQ Most Popular Sites dialog box shown in Figure 13-7.

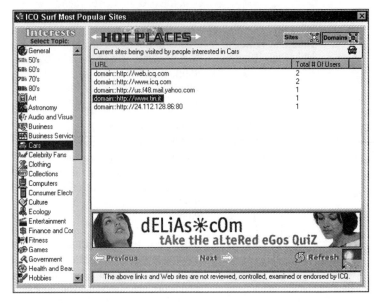

Figure 13-7. The Hot Places list tells you where people connected to ICQ Surf currently are.

Chapter 11 explains how to enter information about yourself and your interests in the White Pages. Interests you profess can be seen in the ICQ Surf Login dialog box, the dialog box you see when you start ICQ Surf (refer to Figure 13-6).

Starting from the dialog box, you can find out where people whose interests are the same as yours are surfing the Internet. Notice the Interests topics on the left side of the dialog box. Click a topic to see where people who named that topic as an interest in the White Pages are surfing at the moment. In Figure 13-7, for example, you see a list of the domains (or Web sites) where people who are interested in cars are surfing. To visit a Web site on the list, double-click its address.

Click the General topic, the first topic in the ICQ Surf Most Popular Sites dialog box, to find out where everyone who is connected to ICQ Surf is on the Internet. The Total # of Users column in the dialog box tells you how many surfers are at each domain or Web site.

Each time you go to a different Web site while you are connected to ICQ Surf, its address appears in the ICQ Surf Most Popular Sites dialog box so that others can double-click it and go to the Web page you're visiting.

Right-click a Web site name and choose Open in New Browser window to see the Web site in a new window.

Domains and Web Sites

Throughout ICQ Surf, you will find references to domains and Web sites. For example, the upper-right corner of the ICQ Surf Most Popular Sites dialog box (refer to Figure 13-7) offers a Sites button and a Domains button. Similarly, you will find a Show Domain Chat and Show Site Chat button above the Users list (along with numbers that tell how many people are on the domain and how many are on the site).

A domain is all the Web pages that are found at an address such as `www.icq.com`, whereas a Web site refers to a single Web page such as `www.icq.com/icq.com/icqsurf/hotplaces`. When you click a Domain button, you get a list of all the people viewing Web pages in the domain you are visiting, but clicking a Site button shows only the people viewing the same Web page you are viewing. Clicking a Domain button always yields more names than clicking a Site button.

A Web site crowded with many ICQ surfers can be very noisy. Click the Enable/Disable Settings button in the Chat window and choose Disable Sounds on the pop-up menu to keep sounds from playing. To hear them again, click the button and choose Enable Sounds.

Chatting in the Chat Window

To participate in a chat, click in the text box in the Chat window, type a comment, and click the Send button, as shown in Figure 13-8. Besides text, the Chat window lists, after the words "Has gone to," the Web page addresses of people who have left the chat room. When someone leaves, the address of the page he or she went to appears. If an address looks interesting, you can click it in the Chat window to open the page that the address refers to in your browser.

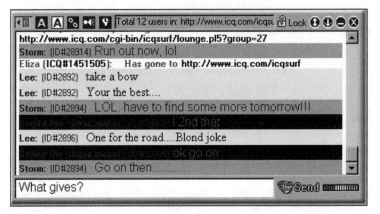

Figure 13-8. The Chat window, where you converse with others.

Note

To find out a button's name in the ICQ Surf window, move the pointer over it. A label box appears to tell you the name.

Notice the buttons along the top of the Chat window for changing fonts and background colors. Use these buttons sparingly, since unusual fonts and backgrounds make reading chats harder, as Figure 13-8 demonstrates.

The Lock/Unlock Site Chatroom button is for visiting a new page on the Internet but staying in the chat you are currently participating in. Normally, when you go to a new page, the Chat window starts recording entries from surfers who are visiting the new page, but you can click the Lock/Unlock Site Chatroom button to visit new Web sites and still linger in a chat you are enjoying. Check the button a second time to sever your connection to the old Web site and start participating in new chats.

To enter a hyperlink in the Chat window, click the Insert a Hyperlink button. Then, in the Edit Hyperlink dialog box, enter the address of the link, enter text that describes the link, and click OK. Others will not see the address in the Chat window, but they will be able to click the text you entered to go to the Web page whose address you entered in the dialog box. Enter the URL in the text description if you want others to see where they will go when they click the link.

Engaging Someone in a Private Chat

To rise above the clutter of the Chat window, you can engage someone in a private chat, as shown in Figure 13-9.
To engage someone in a chat, click their name in the
Users list and choose Personal Message on the pop-up
menu. Then, in the Personal Chat With dialog box, enter
an opening salvo and click the Send button.

Tip

Before you engage someone
in a private chat, try clicking
his or her name in the Users
list and choosing ICQ Surf
User Info or ICQ User Info.
This way, you can learn more
about him or her before you
start chatting.

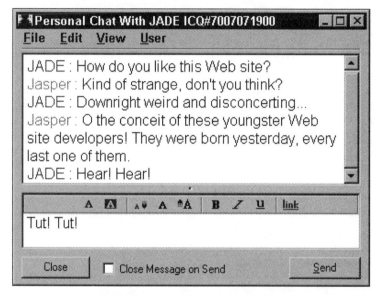

Figure 13-9. Click a person's name and choose Personal Message
to start a private chat.

You can tell when someone wants to engage you in a private chat because a chat icon starts blinking on and off beside the person's name on the Users list. Double-click the
blinking icon to open the Personal Chat With dialog box
and start chatting.

Quitting and Logging Off ICQ Surf

Here are instructions for quitting ICQ Surf and perhaps
ICQ and the Internet as well:

> ▼ **Quit ICQ Surf but stay connected to ICQ and
> the Internet:** Either click the ICQ Surf button or
> right-click the ICQ Surf User Menu button and

choose Close ICQ Surf on the pop-up menu. You will find the ICQ Surf button in the desktop tray.

▼ **Quit ICQ Surf and ICQ but stay connected to the Internet:** Close ICQ.

▼ **Quit ICQ Surf, ICQ, and the Internet:** Close your browser. (If you have a LAN or permanent connection to the Internet, you will remain online.)

Searching the Internet from Inside ICQ

After you enter a search term, move the pointer over the Go button. A label tells you what you will search for if you click Go right away. At this point, you can click Go or press Enter if you don't need to open the pop-up menu first.

You don't have to leave ICQ to search the Internet — you can do it very conveniently from the Search toolbar at the bottom of the ICQ window. Follow these steps to conduct a search of the Internet without leaving ICQ:

1. Enter a term in the Search toolbar to describe what you are searching for.

2. Click the arrow to the right of the Go button. As shown in Figure 13-10, a pop-up menu appears.

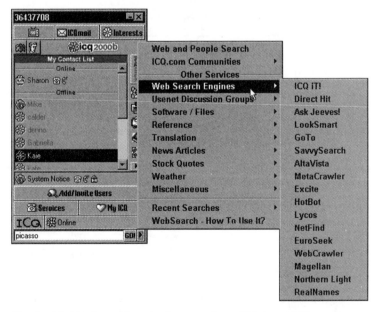

Figure 13-10. Searching the Internet from ICQ.

13

3. From the pop-up menu and its submenus, choose what you want to look for on the Internet. Table 13-2 describes the different search options.

4. Click the Go button or press the Enter key.

Table 13-2. ICQ Internet Search Options

Option	What You Get
Web and People Search	Information and people on the Internet
ICQ.com Communities	ICQ chat rooms, interest groups, user lists, and message boards (see Chapter 4)
Web Search Engines	Results obtained by the search engine you choose on the submenu
Usenet Discussion Groups	Discussion groups at AltaVista Usenet, RemarQ, DejaNews, or HotBot Usenet
Software/Files	Sites where you can download software programs
Reference	Various reference works, including the Merriam-Webster Online Dictionary and Roget's Thesaurus
Translation	Online translation services (choose one from the submenu)
News Articles	Articles from various news services
Stock Quotes	Stock quotes from different financial reporting services
Weather	Weather from different weather reporting services
Miscellaneous	People finder and movie databases

An ICQ Web page appears with the results of the search. Click a link on the page to go to a site on the Internet.

Tip

Choose Recent Searches, the second-to-last option on the pop-up menu, to repeat a search you made since the last time you started ICQ.

Coming Up Next

The next chapter explains how to make a home for yourself on the Internet, as you learn how to create and design an ICQ homepage that others can visit. You also learn about the free Web hosting service that ICQ offers.

Chapter

14

Making an ICQ Home on the Web

Quick Look

Chapter 14

Making an ICQ Home on the Web

This chapter explains how to claim a corner of the World Wide Web with ICQ. You'll learn all the different "homes" you can make on the Web with the help of ICQ. This chapter explains how to create an ICQ Web Front and a free ICQ Homepage with the convenient tools that ICQ offers.

Your ICQ "Homes" on the Web

ICQ gives you several opportunities to make your presence known on the Internet. And you don't have to pay a dime for any of them. Every ICQ member can take advantage of the following Web services:

▼ **Personal Communication Center:** To visit your Personal Communication Center, click the Services button and choose My Communication Center on the pop-up menu. Visitors can contact you, learn more about you, chat with you, or send you a WWPager message from your Personal Communication Center. Anyone, ICQ member or not, can visit the place by going to this address: `wwp.icq.com/your ICQ number`. See "Exploring Your Personal Communication Center" for details.

▼ **Free Web Page:** ICQ members can post a page, called the ICQ homepage, on the Web for free. And, with templates and other tools, ICQ makes creating the page fairly easy. Your ICQ Homepage is hosted by computers at ICQ and is available to surfers at all times. See "Taking Advantage of the Free ICQ Homepage."

▼ **ICQ Web Front:** The 2Way Web Communication Center is a Web site, hosted from your computer, that others can visit while you are online and connected to ICQ. ICQ offers special tools for constructing the Web site. See "Creating and Activating Your ICQ Web Front."

▼ **White Pages Homepage listing:** You can enter the address of a Web site you maintain or are affiliated with in the White Pages so that others can visit the site. Starting from the More tab of the User Details For dialog box, someone can click the Homepage button to open your site. See Chapter 11 for more information.

Exploring Your Personal Communication Center

As soon as you register with ICQ, you are given a Web page on the Internet at this address: `wwp.icq.com/your ICQ number`. The Web page is called your *Personal Communication Center,* as shown in Figure 14-1. To see what yours looks like, either go to it in your browser or click the Services button and choose My Communication Center on the pop-up menu.

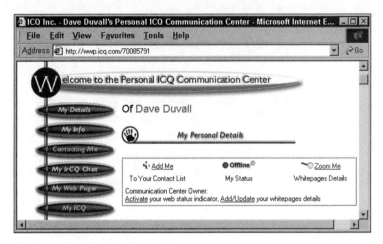

Figure 14-1. Every ICQ member gets a Personal Communication Center on the Internet.

Cross-Reference

Chapter 4 describes a special "four addresses" command for sending your Personal Communication Center address to others.

Tell others about your Personal Communication Center on the Internet. People can visit it on the Internet and communicate with you whether or not they are users of ICQ. They can communicate with you as well from the Personal Communication Center whether or not they are ICQ users. Table 14-1 describes all the features on a Personal Communication Center page. Click the links on the left side of the page to get from place to place.

Table 14-1. Personal Communication Center Features

Link	Feature
My Details	My Personal Details: Links for a viewer to either check out the profile you entered in the White Pages or add your name to his or her Contact List. The online Web status indicator tells whether you are connected to ICQ.
My Info	My Answering Machine/Info/About/ NetPhone: The self-description you entered on the Info/About tab in the White Pages appears here. (Click the ICQ button, choose View/Change My Details, and click the About tab to edit any information stored there.)

Contacting Me	My ICQ Contact Addresses: Instructions for contacting you by ICQ, by EmailExpress, and by visiting your ICQ Homepage (if you have one).
My IrCQ Chat	Personal IrCQ Chat Room: An IrCQ chat room. You can engage people who are not ICQ members in chats from this room.
My Web Pager	Contact Me by Web pager: The WorldWide Pager form. Someone can fill out this form and send you a message. The message is delivered by ICQ as a WWPager message.
My ICQ	Contact Me by ICQ: If you are connected to ICQ, other ICQ members can click links here to put your name on their Contact Lists, engage you in a chat, or send you a message. The online Web status indicator tells whether you are connected.
My Web Front	My Homepage: A link to the homepage whose address you entered in the White Pages (click the ICQ button, choose View/Change My Details, and click the Work tab to enter the address).
My EmailExpress	Contact Me by My EmailExpress: A viewer can click a link here to open his or her default e-mail program and send you an e-mail message. The message is delivered by ICQ.
Phone Callback	Phone Callback: A form for entering phone numbers and sending them to you. The phone numbers are delivered by ICQ as a WWPager message.
Your Own Center	Have Your Own Personal Communication Center: An invitation for the viewer to receive his or her own Personal Communication Center by downloading ICQ.

continued

14

Making an ICQ Home on the Web

Table 14-1. *continued*

Link	Feature
Finding You	Enable Other People to Contact You: A link you can click to get instructions for publicizing your Personal Communication Center Web page on popular search engines.
Install on Your Site	Install This Communication Center on Your Site: Instructions for placing your Personal Communication Center page on your Web site, if you have one, building a Web site, and finding Web space.
Empower Your Site	Empower Your Website with Online Communication: Links you can click to learn how to place an ICQ Communication Panel on your Web site, if you have one.
Find Friends	Find an Old Friend, Make a New One: A link to a page where you can learn how to meet people on ICQ, visit a random ICQ member's Personal Communication Center, go to the PeopleSpace Directory, or look up a friend's ICQ number.

Taking Advantage of the Free ICQ Homepage

ICQ offers its members the opportunity to post a page on the Web — for free. Each page includes a banner ad at the top and an ICQ communication panel and counter at the bottom. In between, you are free to exercise your imagination and put whatever you want on your homepage. To help you along, ICQ offers templates and other tools that make fashioning a homepage easy.

Unlike an ICQ Web Front (explained later in this chapter), an ICQ Homepage resides on the ICQ computers, so it is available to Internet surfers at all times. And one of the nicest things about ICQ Homepages is not having to worry about uploading them to an Internet Service Provider (ISP). If you have any experience with Web pages, you know that uploading them can be a hassle. ICQ Homepages, however, are stored on computers at ICQ, so you don't have to concern yourself with transferring your homepage to an ISP.

To see examples of ICQ Homepages before you create one, go to www.icq. com/hp, click a category under Browse the Homepages, and click a homepage name to open a homepage.

14

Making an ICQ Home on the Web

Signing Up for an ICQ Homepage

Follow these steps to sign up for a free ICQ Homepage:

1. Open your browser and go to this address: www.icq.com/hp.

2. Click the Get a Homepage hyperlink. You see a form for entering information.

3. Enter your ICQ number, enter your ICQ password, and click the Go button. Then read the Terms of Use and click the I Agree button. People browsing homepages in ICQ will be able to find your ICQ Homepage by looking under the category you chose.

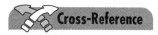

Appendix B lists the PeopleSpace categories.

4. Enter a shortcut name in the text box and click OK. The name you enter will determine the address of your homepage.

Now that you've signed up, you can begin creating your homepage.

Tell your friends that they can access your new homepage at either of these addresses:

▼ *Your Shortcut*.home.icq.com

▼ *Your ICQ number*.home.icq.com

Creating Your ICQ Homepage

If you just signed up for an ICQ Homepage, click the New to Making Home Pages, Start Here hyperlink. Otherwise, go to this address: *Your ICQ number.* *home.icq.com/hp.* And after you arrive, click the Make a New Page hyperlink.

You come to page called Make a New Page. From here, choose a template for creating your page. To do so, click a template name. As shown in Figure 14-2, a page appears so that you can choose a color scheme and enter a title for your homepage. The picture shows roughly what your homepage will look like. If you don't like the page, click the Back button in your browser and choose another template.

Definition

A template is a special file that is used as the starting point for creating Web pages. Each template comes with predefined styles and formats, so most of the layout work is already taken care of.

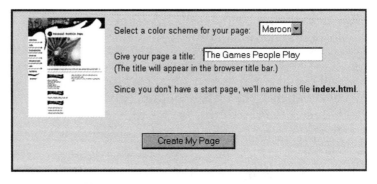

Figure 14-2. Choosing a color scheme and title for the homepage.

Click the Create My Page button. Now you're getting somewhere. You see a facsimile of your homepage. Notice the Change buttons and Add buttons throughout the page. Click one of those buttons and you get a dialog box for entering text, entering graphics, entering hyperlinks, or doing any number of things to fashion your homepage into an interesting and exciting one.

Click the Save Page button (you'll find it near the top of the page) when you are done creating your homepage.

The first time you click the Save Page button, a dialog box asks you to enter a title and description of your homepage. The title and description you enter will appear in the search results when others search the Internet for the kind of information that is found on your homepage. Be sure to enter a descriptive title and a vivid but to-the-point description. Then click the Set Title & Description button.

Editing and Changing Your Homepage

To edit or change your homepage, start by opening your browser and going to this address: `Your ICQ number.home.icq.com/hp`. Then click the Change a Page hyperlink. You go to a page called Change a Page. Here, you will find a list of hyperlinks, one for every page on your homepage.

Click a hyperlink (click `<index.html>` to go to your first page) to open a page and start editing it. You see the same page you used to create your homepage. Make your edits and changes here. Don't forget to click the Save Page button after you are finished.

Creating and Activating Your ICQ Web Front

Every ICQ member gets the opportunity to create an ICQ Web Front, also known as a Personal ICQ Homepage. Figure 14-3 shows an example of an ICQ Web Front. After you create and activate the page, a small House icon appears beside your name on others' Contact Lists. Anyone can click the icon and choose User's 2Way Web Communication Page to open the page in their browser window. People who are not ICQ members or don't have your name on their Contact Lists can also open your ICQ Web Front by going to this address: `members.icq.com/Your ICQ Number`.

Note

The ICQ Web Front is a plug-in that must be downloaded separately from ICQ. See Appendix A.

While viewing your ICQ Web Front, others can obtain your IP (Internet protocol) address merely by glancing at the title bar of their browser windows. (For that matter, others can see your IP address while you view their Web pages.) A hacker can invade your computer while you are online if he or she knows your IP address. Not that you should be overly concerned about it, but it can happen.

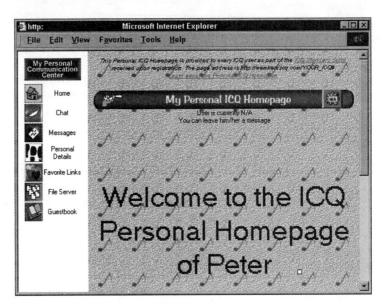

Figure 14-3. To visit an ICQ Web Front, click the House icon and select User's 2Way Web Communication Page.

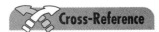

Earlier in this chapter, "Exploring Your Personal Communications Center" explains the Personal Communication Center.

In every respect except one, an ICQ Web Front works like a Web site. The difference between it and a Web site, however, is that your ICQ Web Front is kept on your computer, not on a computer at an Internet Service Provider (ISP). To view your ICQ Web Front, others download it directly from your computer to their Web browsers. Therefore, you have to be online and connected to ICQ before others can visit your ICQ Web Front.

When you're not online, the House icon does not appear beside your name (unless you've created an ICQ homepage, in which case others can click the House icon to visit it). Anyone who chooses the User's 2Way Web Communication Page command while you are offline goes either to your Personal Communication Center or your ICQ Homepage, if you have one. For the sake of privacy, you can keep others from downloading your ICQ Web Front when you *are* connected to ICQ (by clicking the Services button, choosing My ICQ Web Front, and unchecking the Activate My ICQ Web Front command).

Visitors to your ICQ Web Front can click links on the left side of the pages to go from page to page. They can engage you in a chat, send you a message, view your White Pages profile, see a list of links to your favorite Web sites, download files, or sign your guestbook.

To help you make your ICQ Web Front your own, ICQ offers tools for customizing it. You can add pages or remove the generic pages that you get to begin with. You can change page backgrounds, fonts, and the banners that appear at the top of pages.

Starting Work on Your ICQ Web Front

Before you can start building an ICQ Web Front, you have to activate it. To do so, click the Services button, choose My ICQ Web Front on the pop-up menu, and check the Activate My ICQ Web Front command.

Now that your ICQ Web Front has been activated, you can view it: Click the Services button, choose My ICQ Web Front on the pop-up menu, and choose View My 2Way Web Communication Page. You hear a doorbell chime and the page appears. Notice how many visitors have come to the page — just one. Congratulations — you are the first visitor. As of this moment, the House icon appears beside your name on others' Contact Lists.

You will hear the doorbell chime whenever someone visits your ICQ Web Front. The icons on the left side — Home, Chat, Messages, Personal Details, Favorite Links, File Server, and Guestbook — are hyperlinks. Click a link and you go to a new page, just as visitors to your ICQ Web Front will do.

Your next task is to customize the ICQ Web Front to make it your own. ICQ offers a very convenient command for doing that, as the next section explains.

Note

Happily, you don't have to know HTML coding to customize an ICQ Web Front.

Cross-Reference

See "Adding and Removing Pages" later in this chapter to learn how to remove a page or include one of your own in your ICQ Web Front.

Customizing Your ICQ Web Front

To start customizing your ICQ Web Front, click the Services button, choose My ICQ Web Front on the pop-up menu, and click the Customize My ICQ Web Front command. You see the Main tab of the ICQ Web Front dialog box, as shown in Figure 14-4.

Click to customize different pages

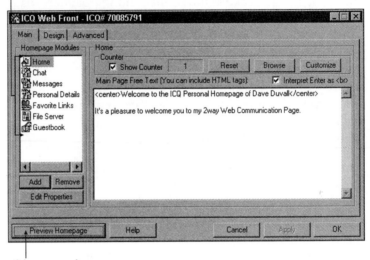

Click to see your changes

Figure 14-4. Customize your ICQ Web Front in the ICQ Web Front dialog box.

Look under Homepage Modules in the dialog box and you will see that the module names correspond to the pages on your ICQ Web Front. By clicking a module name, you can customize a page. In Figure 14-4, for example, the Home module is selected, so the dialog box offers opportunities for customizing the homepage.

Table 14-2 describes the different pages in the ICQ Web Front. As you customize, click the Apply button. Click the Preview Homepage button from time to time to see what effect your changes have. Read on to learn how to customize the different pages and customize all the pages at once. To customize all the pages at once and give them a uniform appearance, start at the Design tab of the ICQ Web Front dialog box.

Table 14-2. ICQ Web Front Pages

Page	What's on It
Home	A Welcome notice and a counter that tells how many people have visited.
Chat	A Chat window so visitors can engage you in a chat, as well as a form for sending a chat invitation.
Messages	A form for sending you a message.
Personal Details	Information about you from the White Pages.
Favorite Links	Links to ICQ Web pages. You can also put your favorite links here.
File Server	A means for visitors to download files from your computer.
Guestbook	Comments from visitors as well as a form for entering comments.

Design Tab: Giving Your ICQ Web Front a Uniform Look

Starting from the Design tab of the ICQ Web Front dialog box, you can give commands that apply to all the pages — Home, Chat, Messages, and so on. As shown in Figure 14-5, the Design tab offers commands for changing the heading, online status icon, background color, text color, font, and font size throughout your ICQ Web Front Web site. You can also choose a *scheme*, a predesigned appearance for all the pages, from the Scheme drop-down list.

Definition

A frame is the area along the side of a Web page and the ICQ Web Front where you find links that you can click to go from page to page.

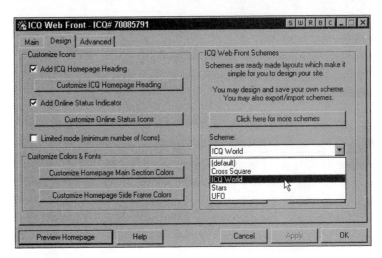

Figure 14-5. Choices on the Design tab apply throughout your ICQ Web Front.

To completely overhaul all areas of the ICQ Web Front, choose a scheme from the Scheme drop-down list (refer to Figure 14-5). Otherwise, follow these instructions to make the changes yourself:

Schemes can be very advantageous. Not only do you save time designing your ICQ Web Front, but you also make sure that the pages look consistent with one another.

▼ **Customize ICQ Homepage Heading:** The *homepage heading* is the banner on the top of pages that reads, "My Personal ICQ Homepage," as shown in Figure 14-6. Click the Customize ICQ Homepage Heading button and, in the Select Homepage Heading dialog box, either click the Browse Pictures button to choose a new heading from a Web page or click the Select from Disk button to choose a new heading. To keep a heading from appearing, uncheck the Add ICQ Homepage Heading check box.

Heading   Status icon

Figure 14-6. A heading and Status icon are at the top of all the pages.

▼ **Customize Online Status Icons:** The *Online Status icon* appears to the right of the homepage heading (refer to Figure 14-6) and is on all the pages. Click the Customize Online Status Icons button to choose a different Status icon.

▼ **Customize Homepage Main Section Colors:** Click this button to bring up the Set Homepage Common Colors dialog box. From there, click a color button to open the Color dialog box and choose a new color for text, table text, the page background, or links. You can also choose a font, a font size, and a font style for text.

▼ **Customize Homepage Side Frame Colors:** Click this button to bring up the Customize Colors for Left Frame dialog box. It looks and works exactly like the Set Homepage Common Colors dialog box. The choices you make here, however, apply to the frame — the area on the left side of pages where the icons and text labels are.

The Set Homepage Common Colors and Customize Colors for Left Frame dialog boxes offer a means of putting background images on pages. Select the Add Background Picture check box and then click the Select File from Disk or Browse Image Catalog button to choose an image.

Entering Headings and Choosing Fonts on Different Pages

No matter which page — Home, Chat, Messages, and so on — you are working on, the techniques for changing fonts, font sizes, and backgrounds are the same. The technique for entering a heading that goes across the top of the page is the same, too.

Under the Homepage Modules area on the Main tab of the ICQ Web Front dialog box (refer to Figure 14-4), click the page that needs changing. Then click the Edit Properties button. You see the Edit Homepage Module dialog box shown in Figure 14-7. From there, follow these instructions to customize the page:

14

Making an ICQ Home on the Web

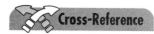
Cross-Reference

The previous section in this chapter describes how to apply new backgrounds, fonts, and font sizes to all the pages at once.

Saving and Applying Schemes You Created

Feel free to experiment with different background colors, text colors, fonts, and headings in your ICQ Web Front. And if you hit upon a scheme you like, be sure to save it as a scheme That way, you can apply it again without having to go to the work of changing background colors, text colors, and so on all over again. All you have to do is choose a scheme from the Scheme drop-down list on the Design tab (refer to Figure 14-5) to change all the settings at once.

To save a scheme so you can apply it later, click the Save As button on the Design tab. Then, in the Save Scheme dialog box, enter a descriptive name and click OK. To apply the scheme, choose its name from the Scheme drop-down list.

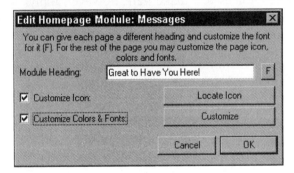

Figure 14-7. Changing the appearance of an individual page.

▼ **Enter a heading:** Type a heading in the Module Heading text box. To choose a font and font size for the heading, click the F button and choose options in the Select Font dialog box.

▼ **Choose an icon:** Icons appear in the frame on the left side of the ICQ Web Front. To choose a new icon for a page, select the Customize Icon box, click the Locate Icon button, and choose a new icon.

▼ **Change the background, font, and font size:** Select the Customize Colors & Fonts box and click

the Customize button. Then, in the Customize
Colors For dialog box, choose new colors for text,
the page background, and hyperlinks. You can also
choose a new font and font size.

Homepage: Welcoming Visitors

Under Homepage Modules in the ICQ Web Front dialog
box (refer to Figure 14-4), click Home to customize your
homepage. The Homepage is a good place to enter a message of some kind. To change the appearance of the
counter, click the Browse button and choose a new
counter. Or else click the Customize button and choose a
new style of counter from the drop-down list. The *counter*
is the number at the bottom of the page that tells how
many people have visited.

Chat Page: Inviting Others to Chat

Click Chat under Homepage Modules in the ICQ Web
Front dialog box (refer to Figure 14-4) to change the note
that appears on the top of the Chat page.

Messages Page: Inviting Others to Send You a Message

Click Messages under Homepage Modules in the ICQ
Web Front dialog box (refer to Figure 14-4) to write a
note about messages or perhaps change the instructions for
sending a message on the Message page.

Personal Details Page: Telling Others about Yourself

In the ICQ Web Front dialog box (refer to Figure 14-4),
click Personal Details under Homepage Modules to put a
heading or a self-description on the Personal Details page.
You can also click the Select Picture button to put a picture of yourself on this page, as long as the file from which
you get the picture is a .gif, .jpg, or .jpeg file. The picture
appears between the heading and the details.

Details on the Personal Details page come from your profile in the White Pages. To change your profile, click the
View/Change My Details button. You'll find it on the
right side of the dialog box. (Even if you didn't enter any

Tip

To enter blank lines on a
page, enter the HTML code
`<br>` where you want the
blank line to go. Don't enter
any other text on the line
where the `<br>` code is.

14

Making an ICQ Home on the Web

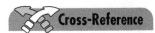

Cross-Reference

Chapter 11 explains how to enter your profile in the White Pages.

details in the White Pages, your ICQ number, Personal Communication Center address, and EmailExpress address appear on this page.)

Favorite Links Page: Entering Links to Your Favorite Web Pages

A visitor to your ICQ Web Front can click a link on the Favorite Links page and go to a page on the Internet. To begin with, the best and most interesting sites at ICQ appear on the page, and you can place links to your favorite sites as well.

To place a link of your own on the page, start by clicking Favorite Links in the Homepage Modules area of the ICQ Web Front dialog box, as shown in Figure 14-8. Then follow these steps to enter a link to one of your favorite Web sites:

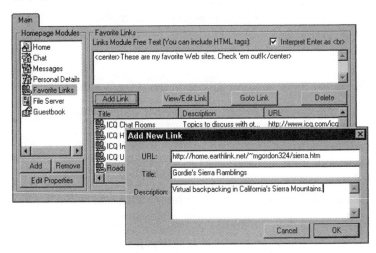

Figure 14-8. Placing a link to a Web site on the Favorite Links page.

Tip

The fastest way and most accurate way to enter an address in the URL box is to go to the Web site and copy the address from the Address box in your browser. Then right-click in the URL box and choose Paste.

1. Click the Add Link button. As shown in Figure 14-8, the Add New Link dialog box appears.

2. Enter the address of the Web site in the URL box.

3. Enter the title of the Web site in the Title box.

4. Write a description of the site in the Description box.

5. Click OK.

To test the link, select it in the Favorite Links tab and click the Goto Link button. If you entered the address correctly, the Web site page appears in your browser window. Select a link in the list and click the View/Edit Link button to correct its address, change its title, or rewrite its description. The Delete button, of course, is for deleting links on the Favorite Links page.

File Server Page: Offering Files for Visitors to Download

Under Homepage Modules in the ICQ Web Front dialog box, as shown in Figure 14-9, click File Server to make files available for others to download from your ICQ Web Front. Follow these steps to add each file you want others to be able to download:

Definition

Download means to copy a file over the Internet from one computer or server to another.

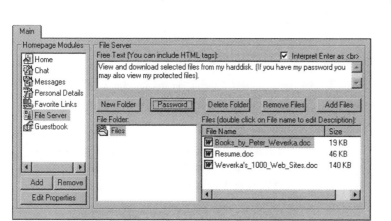

Figure 14-9. Making files available for downloading.

1. Click the Add Files button. The Open dialog box appears.

2. Locate the file, select it, and click the Open button. The name of the file appears in the File Name list.

To remove a file from the list, select it, click the Remove Files button, and click Yes in the confirmation box. Deleting a file this way does not delete the file on your computer. It merely removes a copy of the file from the `C:\Program Files\ICQ\Root\`*`Your ICQ Number`*`\personal\files` folder. When you make a file available for downloading, ICQ places a copy of the file in that folder.

Guestbook Page: Viewing Your Guestbook

Click Messages under Homepage Modules in the ICQ Web Front dialog box (refer to Figure 14-4) to write an introduction to your guestbook. Many Web sites have a guestbook, a place where visitors can leave their names and a comment or two. The names of people who have entered comments in the guestbook appear in the dialog box. Select a name and then click the View Guest Record button to read the entire entry. To delete an entry, select it and click the Delete Guest Record button.

Adding and Removing Pages

Perhaps you don't need all the pages in the ICQ Web Front, or perhaps you want to create a new page. Follow these steps to remove a page:

1. Under Homepage Modules on the Main tab of the ICQ Web Front dialog box, click the page you want to remove. (You can't remove the homepage.)

2. Click the Remove button. A dialog box asks if you really want to remove the page.

3. Click the Yes button. A dialog box asks if you want to store the page in case you need it in the future. If you click Yes, you will be able to get the page back by clicking the Add button and choosing its name on the pop-up menu.

4. Click Yes or No.

Choose a module from the Select/Enter Module Name drop-down list to get a pre-designed page that spares you the trouble of designing the page yourself.

To add a new page to your ICQ Web Front, start from the Main tab of the ICQ Web Front dialog box, click the Add button, and choose Custom Module on the pop-up menu. You see the Create/Edit Web Page Module dialog box. The options in this dialog box — for entering a heading, choosing an icon, and choosing fonts and colors — are familiar to you if you have spent any time creating an ICQ Web Front. Be sure to click the Apply button after making a change. If you click OK, you close the ICQ Web Front dialog box.

The module name and icon you choose will appear in the frame on the left side of the page.

Activating and Deactivating Your ICQ Web Front

As I mentioned earlier in this chapter, your ICQ Web Front doesn't have to be available all the time. While you're connected to ICQ, you can decide whether others can visit it. To activate or deactivate your ICQ Web Front, click the Services button, choose My ICQ Web Front, and uncheck or check the Activate My ICQ Web Front command on the submenu.

Many ICQ users deactivate their ICQ Web Fronts from time to time for privacy's sake or to take down the page while they are redesigning it.

Visiting Someone Else's ICQ Web Front

You can tell when someone has activated an ICQ Web Front (or an ICQ homepage) because a small House icon appears beside his or her name on your Contact List. When you spy the House icon, do either of the following to view the ICQ Web Front:

▼ Click the House icon and choose User's 2Way Web Communication Page on the pop-up menu.

14

Making an ICQ Home on the Web

Note

A House icon also appears when someone has created an ICQ Homepage. (See "Taking Advantage of the Free ICQ Homepage" earlier in this chapter.)

▼ Click the person's name, choose Homepages on the pop-up menu, and choose User's 2Way Web Communication Page on the submenu.

If you try going to the ICQ Web Front of someone who isn't online or hasn't activated the page, you go to the person's Personal Communication Center instead.

Coming Up Next

The next chapter explains how to call on the ICQphone, send SMS messages, and send Wireless Pager messages. You also discover how you can play games and use telephony applications with ICQ. And you learn how to find other gamers and people who use the same telephony applications as you on the network.

Chapter

15

ICQ with Telephony and Games

Quick Look

Calling on the ICQphone   page 345

ICQphone may be the least expensive way to make long-distance telephone calls. The calls are carried over the Internet. You can call other ICQ users or conventional phone numbers. If you have an ICQphone account, you can even use ICQphone to dial from a conventional telephone to another conventional telephone.

Trading SMS Text Message with Cellular Phone Users   page 348

You can trade SMS (*short messaging service*) text messages with cellular phone users whose telephones employ SMS technology. The other party doesn't have to be an ICQ user.

Sending Wireless Pager Messages   page 351

Whether or not the recipient is an ICQ user, you can send wireless pager messages to others from ICQ. After you have entered the recipient's wireless pager address, all you have to do is click his or her name on the Contact List, choose Wireless Pager Message on the pop-up menu, and enter your message.

Sending Out an Invitation for a Telephony Chat or Game   page 352

You can send invitations to chat with a telephony application or play an online game to anyone on your Contact List. If the other person accepts and he or she has also installed the application or game, the telephony or game application opens right away so you can start chatting or playing.

Sending and Receiving Voice-Messages
and Wave Sound Files   page 360

ICQ offers a special dialog box for recording voice-messages — and you can send them right away to people whose names are on your Contact List. You can send and receive wave (.WAV) sound files as well.

Chapter 15

ICQ with Telephony and Games

This chapter takes on what is a pretty amazing little device — the ICQphone. As long as you have a microphone and sound on your computer, you can use it to place Internet telephone calls all around the world. You will also find instructions for trading SMS (short messaging service) text messages with cellular phone users and sending messages to people who have wireless pagers. This chapter explores how to launch telephony and game applications in ICQ and describes ICQ resources for gamers. Finally, you find instructions here for trading voice-mail messages.

Talking on ICQphone

ICQphone is a great way to lower your telephone bill. In fact, it wouldn't be a stretch to say that ICQphone is an innovative way to make telephone calls. The calls are live. They are conducted in real time, just like telephone conversations. Instead of being carried by conventional means, however, the calls are carried less expensively over the Internet.

Table 15-1 describes the different ways to call with ICQphone. The following must be installed on your computer to use ICQphone:

▼ A sound card

▼ A 28.8 kbps or faster modem (the faster, the better)

▼ A microphone and speakers or a microphone and headphones

Note

To see what the calling rates for using ICQphone are, go to this address on the Internet and click the USA Rates or International Rates hyperlink: `icqphone.icq.com/pc/rates.html`

Table 15-1. Types of ICQphone Calls

Type of Call	Fees?	Description
PC-to-PC	No	A call between two ICQ users conducted over their computers.
PC-to-phone	Yes	A call from an ICQ user made over his or her computer to a regular telephone. You need an ICQphone account to make this call. Your account is billed. The recipient of the call need not be an ICQ user.
Phone-to-PC*	Yes	A call from a regular telephone to an ICQ user that the user receives over his or her computer. Both parties must be ICQ users. The receiving party must be online and connected to ICQ. You need an ICQphone account to make this call. The call is billed to the account held by the person who initiates the call.
Phone-to-phone*	Yes	A call from a regular telephone to a regular telephone. The person who initiates the call must be an ICQ user. You need an ICQphone account to initiate this call, and your account is billed.

*As of this writing, calls must be initiated in these countries: United States, Canada, Australia, Brazil, China, Denmark, France, Germany, Hong Kong, Israel, Italy, Japan, Malaysia, New Zealand, Philippines, Russia, Spain, Sweden, The Netherlands, and United Kingdom.

15

ICQ with Telephony and Games

Doing the Setup Work

Before you can start talking on ICQphone, you have to do a bit of setup work. To wit, you have to test the microphone and sound capabilities on your computer, configure your computer to run ICQphone, set up an ICQphone account, and test to see whether your computer is locked behind a firewall. You can do all that starting from the ICQphone section of the Owner Preferences For dialog box. Follow these steps to get there:

1. Click the ICQ button.

2. Choose Preferences.

3. Click ICQphone on the left side of the Owner Preferences For dialog box.

Making Sure Your Microphone and Sound Are Adequate

As shown in Figure 15-1, go to the Settings tab in the ICQphone section of the Owner Preferences For dialog box to test your microphone and sound capabilities. Choose options under Preferred Devices to test your sound and microphone:

▼ **Testing the sound:** From the Playback drop-down list, choose which sound card you want to test and click the Test button. You should hear the words "Welcome to ICQphone." If the sound you hear isn't loud enough, double-click the Volume icon in the tray (or click the Audio Settings button and then click the Playback icon — the icon below the words "Playback" in the Multimedia Properties dialog box). Then, in the Volume Control dialog box, drag the Volume Control and Wave sliders to maximum volume.

▼ **Testing your microphone:** From the Playback drop-down list, choose which device to test, click the Test button, and speak for two seconds into your microphone. The words you speak are automatically played back for you. If the sound isn't loud enough,

click the Audio Settings button. Then, in the
Multimedia Properties dialog box, click the
Recording icon — the icon right below the word
"Recording." You see the Recording Control dialog
box. Drag the Microphone Balance and Line In
Balance to maximum volume.

Choose options under Voice Settings to control how your
computer records and sends sound:

▼ **Suppress Silence:** Silence is not recorded.
Choosing this option reduces the size of the sound
files that are sent across the Internet, which makes
sound travel faster. However, voice recordings can
sound choppy when this option is turned on.

▼ **Voice Activity Detection:** Recording does not
commence until a voice is heard. This option also
reduces the size of sound files but can cause choppi-
ness in sound.

▼ **Automatic Frame Rate:** Uncheck this option to
choose a new Frames/Packet and Jitter Buffers rate.

15

ICQ with Telephony and Games

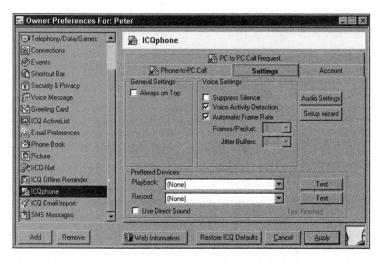

Figure 15-1. Get set up to use ICQphone in the ICQphone section
of the Owner Preferences For dialog box.

Seeing Whether Your Computer Is Behind a Firewall and Can't Use ICQphone

ICQphone may not work if your ISP or network administrator has set up a firewall or proxy server, two mechanisms
designed to protect networks from intruders. Before you
try out ICQphone, you may as well test to see if you can
use it by following these steps:

1. Starting from the Settings tab in the ICQphone
   section of the Owner Preferences For dialog box
   (refer to Figure 15-1), click the Setup Wizard
   button.

2. Click Next twice to come to the firewall test
   dialog box.

3. Click the Test button. The dialog box tells you
   whether you can use ICQphone.

Setting Up an ICQphone Account

Cross-Reference

Earlier in this chapter, Table
15-1 explains the different
types of phone calls you can
make with ICQphone.

If you intend to make PC-to-phone, phone-to-PC, or
phone-to-phone telephone calls with ICQphone, you
must set up an ICQphone account. Starting from the
ICQphone section of the Owner Preferences For dialog
box (refer to Figure 15-1), go to the Account tab. Then
click the Create New Account button. You go to a page
on the Internet for registering with ICQ phone, where
you are asked to supply your ICQ screen name, first and
last name, e-mail address, country of residence, as well as a
Personal Identification Number (PIN). For an account
number, you get your ICQ number (although you can
create more than one account, and additional accounts are
given a random 12-digit number).

You start with an account balance of $1. To find out what
your account balance is, return to the Account tab and
click the Obtain Balance button. To deposit money in
your account, click the Add Funds button. You go to a
Web page where you enter your ICQ number and PIN to
log in. After that, you come to a page where you can
recharge your account and do a number of other things,
including examine your billing history or see a list of
phone calls you made in the past.

Opening and Handling the ICQphone Window

Before you learn your way around the ICQphone window, as shown in Figure 15-2, you should first find out how to open the window. You can do either of the following:

- ▼ Click the name of the person you want to dial on your Contact List and either choose ICQphone⇨ Launch ICQphone Client or, if phone numbers appear on the submenu, choose the number you want to dial.

- ▼ Click the Services button and choose ICQphone⇨Launch ICQphone Client.

Tip

The fastest way to open ICQphone is to click the Phone Client icon on the ICQuick shortcut bar.

Click to call or hang up

Enter phone number   Control the volume

Figure 15-2. The ICQphone window.

15

ICQ with Telephony and Games

Following are the different ways to enter the phone number you want to dial. After you have entered the number, click the Call button.

▼ Click a name on your Contact List, choose ICQphone, and choose a number from the shortcut menu. You can go this route only if the person in question has made his or her phone numbers available. (If you accidentally choose the wrong number, click the down arrow in the phone number text box in the ICQphone window and choose the correct number from the drop-down list.)

▼ Either type the phone number or enter it by clicking the number buttons. As Figure 15-3 shows, you have to enter phone numbers a certain way when you enter them yourself. (ICQ enters numbers correctly when you choose them from a submenu.) In the United States, for example, enter 1, the area code, and then the phone number.

Tip

Click the Help button and choose Dialing Instructions if you have trouble remembering how to enter telephone numbers.

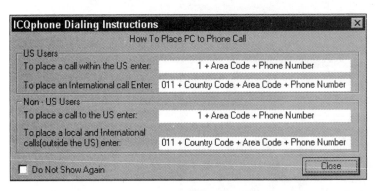

Figure 15-3. Be sure to observe the rules for entering phone numbers.

The ICQphone window (refer to Figure 15-2) offers these amenities:

▼ **Clock:** Shows the length of the call.

▼ **Phone number text box:** Either type a phone number here or click the number buttons to enter a phone number.

▼ **Call/Hang Up button:** Starts and ends telephone calls.

▼ **Volume slider:** Move the flower icon up or down to turn the volume up or down.

▼ **Menu button:** Opens a submenu. Choose Preferences to quickly go to the Owner Preferences For dialog box and change settings (see "Doing the Setup Work" earlier in this chapter). Choose Always on Top if you want the ICQphone window to appear before any other open window. Chose Exit to close ICQphone.

▼ **Account button:** Takes you to the Account tab in the Owner Preferences For dialog box and obtain your account balance or make a deposit in your account (see "Doing the Setup Work" earlier in this chapter.

▼ **Help button:** Opens a submenu with options for getting help using ICQphone.

▼ **Mute button:** Mutes your side of the conversation.

▼ **Voice Mail button:** Opens the ICQ Email dialog box so that you can send an EmailExpress message or voice mail message.

▼ **My Contacts button:** Displays a list of people on your Contact List who are connected to ICQ. Select a name on the list to open the Send Online PC to PC Request dialog box.

▼ **ICQphone Status button:** Opens a drop-down list so that you can broadcast your ICQphone status to others (see "Broadcasting Your ICQphone Status" later in this chapter).

Calling by ICQphone

As Table 15-1 pointed out earlier in this chapter, you can make four different kinds of phone calls with ICQphone. This section provides detailed instructions for initiating and receiving the different phone calls.

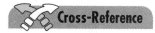

Cross-Reference

Later in this chapter, "Sending and Receiving Voice-Messages" explains voice mail. See Chapter 8 for advice about sending e-mail in ICQ.

The previous section in this chapter explains how to open the ICQphone window, enter a phone number correctly, and initiate a phone call (click the Call button).

If the ICQphone window is already open, click the My Contacts button and choose the name of an online user from the drop-down list to initiate a PC-to-PC call.

Chapter 9 explains how you can automatically accept or decline ICQphone calls and other events.

Click the Help button in the ICQphone window and choose Access Numbers to go on the Internet and find out which access number to call.

PC-to-PC Calls

On your Contact List, select the name of an online ICQ user and choose ICQphone⇨Send PC to PC Call. You see the Send Online PC to PC Call Request dialog box. Enter an invitation to chat on the phone and click the Send button. If the other party accepts your invitation, the call begins.

To receive a PC-to-PC call, double-click the ICQphone icon in the system tray, or, if the call is coming from someone whose name is on your Contact List, double-click the icon beside the person's name. Click the Accept button to accept the call or the Decline button to decline it.

PC-to-Phone Calls

Enter the phone number you want to call in the phone number text box and click the Call button. Then, in the dialog box that appears, enter your ICQphone account number (that is, your ICQ number unless you have more than one ICQphone account), enter your PIN, and click OK.

Phone-to-PC Calls

As long as the person you want to call is an ICQ user and is online, you can call him or her. In the ICQphone window, click the Help button and choose Access Numbers from the drop-down list. You go to a page on the Internet where you can obtain a telephone number to call. Call the telephone number using your telephone. You will be asked to enter your ICQ number, your PIN number, and the ICQ number of the person you want to speak to. After you have entered the numbers, the other party comes online — provided he or she accepts your call.

When you receive a phone-to-PC call, the ICQphone icon appears in the system tray and on your Contact List as well if the call is coming from someone whose name is on your Contact List. Double-click the icon to open the Incoming Phone-to-PC Call Request dialog box. Click the Accept button to accept the call or the Decline button to decline it.

Broadcasting Your ICQphone Status

Your ICQphone status tells others whether you will receive ICQphone calls. To change your ICQphone status, click the down-arrow under My ICQphone Status in the ICQphone window to open the My ICQphone Status menu and choose Show. After you choose Show, the ICQphone symbol — a tiny telephone receiver — appears next to your name on others' Contact Lists so they know you are taking calls. The symbol appears as well on the System Notice button so you know what your ICQphone status is.

Change your status   ICQ phone status icons

15

ICQ with Telephony and Games

Phone-to-Phone Calls

To send a phone-to-phone call, you need the access number for initiating the call, your ICQ number, your PIN number, and the telephone number of the party you want to call. With that information in hand, call the access number using your telephone, enter your ICQ number, enter your PIN, and enter the number you want to call. You must enter the telephone number in the correct format. In the United States, for example, enter 1, the area code, and the telephone number, even if your call is local. (Click the Help button and choose Dialing Instructions or refer to Figure 15-3.)

SMS: Trading Text Messages with Cellular Phone Users

SMS (short messaging service) is a technology whereby cellular phone users can trade text messages with one another. As an ICQ user, you can also get into the game. You can send SMS messages to cellular phone users whose telephones employ SMS technology. And you can receive SMS messages from others as well. Read on to discover how to enter cellular phone numbers so that you can trade SMS text messages.

Entering Cellular Phone Numbers

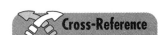
Cross-Reference

If the person with whom you want to trade SMS messages is not an ICQ user, add the person's name to the Contact List as a non-ICQ user. See Chapter 4.

SMS messages can be sent to anyone, but they can be sent faster when recipients' names are on the Contact List. To send an SMS message to someone on your Contact List, his or her cellular telephone number must be on file in the User Details dialog box. What's more, the number must be "SMS available." You can tell who on your Contact List has a cell phone that is SMS available because the SMS icon appears next to those peoples' names, as shown in Figure 15-4.

Follow these steps to be able to trade SMS messages with someone on your Contact List:

1. Select the name of the person.

2. Choose User Details/Address Book.

3. Click Phone Book to open the Phone Book section of the User Details dialog box, as shown in Figure 15-4.

SMS icons

Cross-Reference

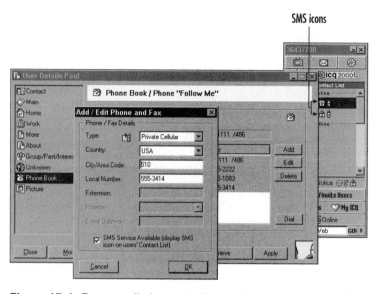

Chapter 3 explains the details of entering phone numbers, cellular and otherwise, in the User Details dialog box. People on your Contact List can make the numbers available to you.

Figure 15-4. Enter a cell phone number so that you can trade SMS messages.

4. Enter a cellular phone number or edit a phone number so that you can trade SMS messages:

   ▲ **Add new number:** Click the Add button to open the Add/Edit Phone and Fax dialog box (refer to Figure 15-4). From the Type drop-down list choose a Cellular phone option. Then enter the number and check the SMS Service Available check box.

   ▲ **Edit a number:** Select the number and click the Edit button to open the Add/Edit Phone and Fax dialog box (refer to Figure 15-4). Make sure a cellular phone number is chosen from the Type drop-down list. Then check the SMS Service Available check box.

5. Click Apply and then click Close in the User Details dialog box.

Tip

To permanently change the signature at the bottom of SMS messages, click the ICQ button and choose Preferences. Then click SMS in the Owner Preferences For dialog box, and select the General tab. There, you can enter a signature or uncheck the Add Signature to Outgoing SMS Messages check box to keep signatures from appearing.

15

ICQ with Telephony and Games

Trading SMS Messages with Others

Follow these instructions to send an SMS message:

▼ **If a person's name is on your Contact List:**
Click the name of the person and choose SMS
Message on the pop-up menu. You see the Send
SMS Message dialog box shown in Figure 15-5.
Enter your message and click the Send button.

▼ **If a person's name is not on your Contact List:**
Click the Services button and choose SMS message.
Then enter a cellular phone number in the Add/Edit
Phone and Fax dialog box and click OK. In the Send
SMS Message dialog box (see Figure 15-5), enter
your message and click the Send button.

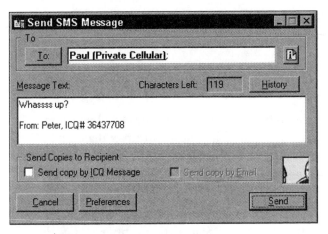

Figure 15-5. Sending an SMS message.

After an SMS message is sent, you receive a message from
ICQ that says whether the SMS message was transmitted
successfully.

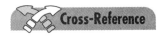
Cross-Reference

Chapter 9 explains how you
can automatically accept or
decline SMS messages and
other events.

To receive an SMS message, double-click the SMS message icon. It appears on the System Notice button and, if
the sender's name is on your Contact List, next to the
sender's name as well. In the Incoming SMS Message dialog box, click the Accept button if you want to read the
message.

Sending Wireless Pager Messages

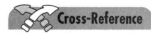

Yes, it can be done — you can send wireless pager messages to wireless pager users from inside ICQ. To send a message, however, the recipient's name must be on your Contact List. What's more, you must have entered a wireless pager address in the User Details dialog box.

Follow these steps to enter a wireless pager address for someone whose name is on your Contact List:

1. Select the person's name.

2. Choose User Details/Address Book to open the User Details dialog box.

3. Click Phone Book to open the Phone Book section of the dialog box.

4. Click the Add button. You see the Add/Edit Phone and Fax dialog box.

5. From the Type drop-down list, choose Wireless Pager.

6. Enter the country, city/area code, and local number.

7. From the Provider drop-down list, choose a provider name.

8. Enter a subscriber name in the Subscriber text box.

9. Click OK in the Add/Edit Phone and Fax dialog box.

10. Click the Apply button and then the Close button.

Now that you've done the preliminary work, you will be glad to know that sending a wireless pager message is easy: Click the recipient's name on your Contact List, choose Wireless Pager Message on the pop-up menu, enter your message in the Send a Wireless Pager Message dialog box, and click the Send Pager Message button.

Cross-Reference

If the person to whom you want to send a wireless pager message is not an ICQ user, add the person's name to the Contact List as a non-ICQ user. See Chapter 4.

15

ICQ with Telephony and Games

Using Telephony Applications and Playing Games

ICQ offers several very useful commands for finding and connecting with others in order to use telephony applications or play online games. After you tell ICQ which telephony and game applications are installed on your computer, you can start the applications whenever someone invites you to use them or when someone accepts an invitation from you to use them. You don't have to fumble around on your machine to start the applications every time you receive an invitation — you only have to click a button in ICQ.

ICQ can be configured to launch almost any external application utilizing direct user connection. This section explains how to configure ICQ so that ICQ can launch any number of telephony/game applications (even the ones that it doesn't recognize). You discover how to send and receive invitations to voice-chat, video-conference, and play games. Finally, this section points the way to resources on ICQ for telephony chatters and gamers.

Configuring ICQ to Launch a Telephony or Game Application

ICQ recognizes a core set of telephony/game applications. You can tell which ones they are by clicking any name on your Contact List and moving the pointer over the Other, Other IP Phones/Voice Chat, or Games options on the pop-up menu. Under the word "Installed" on the submenus that appear, you see the names of telephony/games applications that are installed on your computer. If someone invites you to run one of these applications, you are ready to go.

Suppose, however, that you favor a telephony/game application that ICQ doesn't recognize and you want to be able to run the application with other ICQ users. In that case, you have to configure ICQ to launch the telephony/game application. Specifically, ICQ needs to know where the executable file (a file with an **exe** extension) that launches the program is located on your computer. ICQ also needs to know if command-line variables are required. A *command-line variable* is a command that you type to start or configure a program.

Follow these steps to configure ICQ so that you can use a telephony application or play a game with someone else:

1. Click the ICQ button.

2. Choose Preferences on the pop-up menu. You see the Owner Preferences For dialog box.

3. Click Telephony/Data/Games on the left side of the dialog box to open the Telephony/Data/Games tab, as shown in Figure 15-6. It lists telephony/data/ game applications that ICQ recognizes or that you configured yourself. An icon appears beside the names of applications that have already been downloaded to your computer and are configured to be run under ICQ. Applications without an icon next to them have not yet been downloaded to your computer.

Note

For two ICQ users to launch an external application utilizing direct user connection, both must have the external application installed on their computer.

Icons mean that an application is ready to be run.

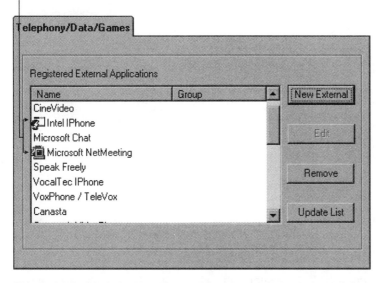

Figure 15-6. Click the New External button to configure an application to run under ICQ.

4. Click the New External button. You see the Define New External Application dialog box shown in Figure 15-7.

5. On the Externals Group drop-down list, decide how you want to choose the application's name when you invite someone else to use it with you:

▲ **General:** You click the person's name on your Contact List, choose Other, and click the application name.

▲ **Internet Telephony/Voice Chat:** You click the person's name, choose Other IP Phones/ Voice Chat, and click the application name.

▲ **Games:** You click the person's name, choose Games, and click the application name.

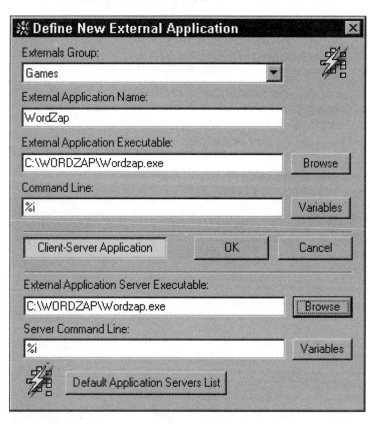

Figure 15-7. Configuring an application so that you can launch it from ICQ.

6. In the External Application Name text box, enter the name of the application. The name you enter will appear on the pop-up menu when you invite someone to use the application. It will also appear in the Incoming Phone/Video/Data Request dialog box when you send the invitation to someone else.

7. Click the Browse button and, in the Open dialog box, find and select the executable (**exe**) file of the application you are configuring for ICQ. Then click the Open button. The path to the file appears in the External Application Executable text box.

8. If command-line variables are required for running the application, click the Variables button and choose an option from the drop-down list. Go to the application's Web site or check the help files or documentation that came with the application to find out whether entering a command-line variable is necessary.

9. If the application is a client-server application, click the Client-Server Application button and then complete the following information:

▼ **External Application Server Executable:** Enter the path to the server (consult the documentation).

▼ **Server Command Line:** Enter or choose a command line (consult the documentation).

▼ **Default Application Servers List:** Click this button and, if possible, enter a default server for the application.

10. Click the OK button.

11. Click the Apply button in the Owner Preferences For dialog box.

12. Close and reopen ICQ so that ICQ can recognize the application you configured.

Caution

If you are configuring an application that ICQ recognizes, be sure to enter the name as it appears on the Telephony/Data/Games tab. That way, when you invite others to use the application, they will know which application you are referring to.

Tip

To help find executable (exe) files in the Open dialog box, click the Details button or Details option on the View menu and look for the word *Application* in the Type column.

15

ICQ with Telephony and Games

If you enter information incorrectly in the Define New External Application dialog box, go to the Telephony/Data/Games tab of the Owner Preferences For dialog box (refer to Figure 15-6), click the name of the application whose information you entered incorrectly, and click the Edit button. Then enter the correct information.

To remove an application name from the Other, Other IP Phones/Voice Chat, or Games menu (which you see when you click a person's name on your Contact List), go to the Telephony/Data/Games tab of the Owner Preferences For dialog box (refer to Figure 15-6), select the application name, and click the Remove button.

Sending a Telephony/Game Invitation

In order to engage in a voice-chat, a video-conference, or a game with someone else, the other party must install the telephony/game application on his or her computer. Also, the other person must configure the application to launch under ICQ. If you send somebody an invitation and he or she doesn't have the telephony application or game, you get a message that reads, `User doesn't have that program`.

Follow these steps to send someone on your Contact List an invitation to voice-chat, video-conference, or play an online game:

1. Click the person's name on your Contact List.

2. Choose Other, Other IP Phones/Voice Chat, or Games on the pop-up menu.

3. Choose the name of the telephony or game application that you want to use from the submenu. You see the Send Online Phone/Video/Data Request dialog box shown in Figure 15-8.

Downloading a Telephony/Game Application

Here are a couple ways to download telephony/game applications that you can use with other ICQ users:

▼ Click any name on the Contact List, choose Other, Other IP Phones/Voice Chat, or Games, choose View List - Download, and choose the application name from the pop-up menu. The External Application Not Available dialog box appears. Click the Go to Product Home Page button to open your browser to a Web page where you can download the application.

▼ Open your browser and go to www.cnet.com or www.download.com. To find the application you want to download, enter its name in the Search box and click the Go button.

Figure 15-8. Sending an invitation to engage in a voice-chat, video-conference, or game.

4. If the telephony or game application requires choosing more options to launch the application, you fill out other dialog boxes.

5. Optionally, type an invitation in the text box.

6. Click the Send button.

At this point, a wizard may appear if you have to enter additional information. If the other party accepts your invitation, ICQ launches the application you chose. Otherwise, you get a denial notice of some kind.

Fielding a Telephony/Game Invitation

When someone wants to engage you in a voice-chat, video-conference, or game, the Phone/Video/Data Request icon appears in the system tray (lower-right corner of the screen) and beside a name on the Contact List as well, if the name of the person who sent the invitation is on your Contact List. As shown in Figure 15-9, you see the Incoming Phone/Video/Data Request dialog box when you open the invitation.

Do one of the following to handle the invitation:

▼ **Accept it:** Click the Accept button. The application is launched on your computer and on the other party's computer.

▼ **Decline it:** Click the Do Not Accept button and choose a Decline option from the pop-up menu.

▼ **Tell the other party that you don't have the application:** Click the I Don't Have It button. The other party gets a message that reads, `User doesn't have that program`.

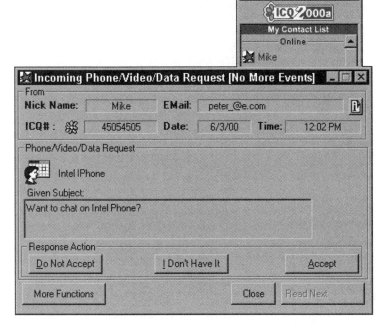

Figure 15-9. Receiving an invitation to voice-chat, video-conference, or play a game.

ICQ Resources for Telephony Chatters and Gamers

Table 15-2 lists ICQ resources for telephony chatters and gamers. With the number of chatters and gamers on ICQ, you are sure to find someone with whom to gab or test your skills.

Table 15-2. ICQ Telephony and Gaming Resources

Resource	*Description*
Chat Request page	A way to find others who want to chat with a telephony application. Look in the Telephone column. After you click the View button, look in the Internet-Telephony column to find out which applications others want to chat on. (Chapter 6 explains the Chat Request page.) Go to this address in your browser: `www.icq.com/chatrequest`

continued

Table 15-2. *continued*

Resource	Description
Games channel	Hyperlinks you can click to play games online with others or by yourself. Click the Services button and choose ICQ Channels⇨Games.
Games network	A means to search for user lists, interest groups, chat rooms, and message boards for gamers. Open your browser to this address: `www.icq.com/networks/Games`
Games Request page	Amenities for gamers. Open your browser to this address: `www.icq.com/gamerequest`. Then click the Now Playing link to join a game in progress, click the Available Games link to post an invitation to others to play, or click the User to User Help link to get advice for configuring games.
Voice, Video, and Conferencing est groups	Interest groups devoted to telephony Data-applications (Chapter 6 explains interest inter-groups). Go to `groups.icq.com/InternetTelephonya`
Voice, Video, and Data-Conferencing chat rooms	ICQ chat rooms where chats are conducted on telephony applications (Chapter 6 public describes chat rooms). Go to this address: `www.icq.com/icqchat/VoiceVideoDataC`
Voice, Video, Data-Conferencing user lists	User lists that pertain to telephony applications (Chapter 6 describes user lists). Go to this address: `www.icq.com/icqlist/VoiceVideoDataC`

Sending and Receiving Voice-Messages

As long as both parties are online, ICQ users can send and receive voice-messages and save (.WAV) sound files. To record a voice-message, your computer must be equipped with a microphone. Make sure that your microphone is ready to record and then follow these steps to send a voice-message or sound file to someone from your Contact List who is currently connected to ICQ:

1. Click the person's name on your Contact List.

2. Choose Voice Message on the pop-up menu. The Send Online Voice Message dialog box shown in Figure 5-10 appears.

3. Send a voice-message or a wave file. Voice-messages cannot be longer than 120 KB (roughly 15 seconds):

▲ **Send a voice-message:** Click the Send:Voice Message option. Then click the Record button (or press Ctrl+R) and start talking into your microphone. When you are finished recording, click the Stop button (or press Ctrl+S). Table 15-3 describes the different recording and playback buttons.

Note

A better way to handle voice-messages is to send them by way of ICQphone. See the start of this chapter.

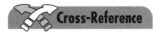

Cross-Reference

You must download a plug-in to send voice-messages. See Appendix A.

Tip

In the Send Online Voice Message dialog box, you can click the Incoming Folder button to open the folder where voice-messages sent to you are stored. Or click the Outgoing Folder button to open a folder where voice-messages you sent to others are stored.

15

ICQ with Telephony and Games

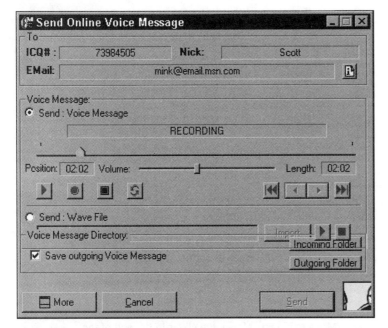

Figure 15-10. You can record a message or send a wave file in the Send Online Voice Message dialog box.

▲ **Send a wave file:** Click the Send: Wave File option. Then click the Import button, find and select the file you want to send in the Open dialog box, and click the Open button. Enter a word or two to describe the sound file in the Additional Text box. (You can click the Play button to hear the file before you send it.)

4. Click the Send button.

The Send Online Voice Message dialog box remains on-screen until the recipient either accepts or declines the voice-message or wave file. If the event is accepted, the dialog box tells you the transfer rate and shows you how much of the file has been transmitted.

Table 15-3. Buttons for Recording and Playing Voice-Messages

Button	Name	What It Does
▶	Play	Plays back a message you recorded (you can also press Ctrl+P.)
●	Record	Records your message. Click the button (or press Ctrl+R) before recording.
■	Stop	Stops playing or recording a message (You can also press Ctrl+S.)
↻	LoopPlay	Plays the voice-message continuously.
◀◀	Back to Start	Moves the slider to the start of the message.
◀	Forward	Moves forward through the message two seconds at a time.
▶	Backward	Moves backward through the message two seconds at a time.
▶▶	Move to Finish	Moves the slider to the end of the message.

When you receive a voice-message or sound file, the voice-message appears in the system tray and beside a name on your Contact List. After you open the message, you see the Incoming Voice Message dialog box. Click the Accept button there and the Voice Message dialog box appears, as shown in Figure 15-11. After arriving on your computer, the voice-message or sound file plays right away.

Table 15-3 describes the buttons you can click to replay the voice-message or file. Voice-messages and sound files that you receive are kept in C:\ProgramFiles\ICQ\Plugins\VoiceMessage\Incoming*Sender's Name* folder. But you can store a voice-message or file wherever you please by clicking the Save To File button.

Figure 15-11. You can replay a voice-message or sound file in the Voice Message dialog box.

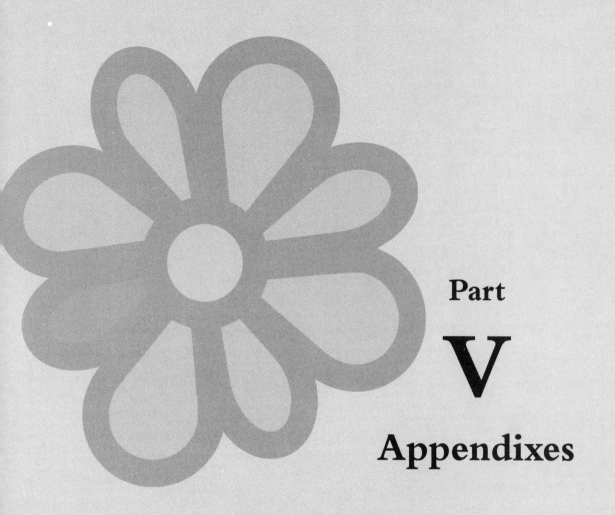

Part

V

Appendixes

Appendix A

Installing and Registering with ICQ

This appendix explains how to download ICQ from the Internet, install ICQ on your computer, and register with the ICQ network. You also learn how to register on more than one computer, find out if you have the latest version of ICQ, back up important files, install the Message Archive, and install ICQ Surf. You will also find instructions here for running ICQ if you share your computer with another ICQ user.

Installing ICQ on Your Computer

ICQ is free. You don't have to pay a dime to acquire the software or run it on your computer. All you have to do is download the software, install it on your computer, and register to become a user of ICQ.

The next section in this appendix explains how to register with ICQ.

Downloading and installing ICQ takes between 5 and 20 minutes, depending on the speed of your computer and the speed of your Internet connection. The ICQ file that you download is about 6 megabytes (MB).

Following are instructions for downloading the ICQ software from the Internet and then loading the software on your computer.

Downloading ICQ 2000b

Follow these steps to download ICQ so that you can load the software on your computer:

Tip

Want to download a foreign-language version of ICQ? Click the Services button and choose Translation⬄ Download ICQ in Your Own Language.

1. In your browser, go to the ICQ Web site at this address: `www.icq.com`.

2. Click the ICQ 2000b hyperlink. You can find this hyperlink on the left side of the Web page under "Free ICQ Software." You come to a Web page with news about downloading ICQ.

3. Look for and click the link that describes which version of ICQ you want to install. You most likely want the link for downloading ICQ for Windows 95/98/2000/NT4, but ICQ also offers software for Macintosh users, PowerPC users, and others. After you click the link, you come to the ICQ 2000 download page with instructions for downloading.

4. Look for and click the Download ICQ 2000b link. You come to a page at Cnet.com for downloading software.

5. Click the Download Now link. The File Download dialog box appears, as shown in Figure A-1.

6. In the File Download dialog box, select the Save This Program to Disk option button.

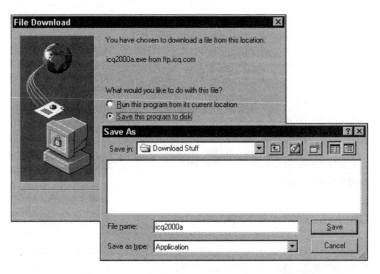

Figure A-1. Click Save This Program to Disk to download software to your computer.

7. Click the OK button. You see the Save As dialog box. Which folder you save the installation file in doesn't matter as much as remembering where you save the file. Later, after you download the file, you will have to find it on your computer to start the installation procedure.

8. Find and select the folder in your computer where you want the file to be after you download it.

9. Click the Save button. The Copied dialog box appears as the file is sent over the Internet to your computer. How long the file takes to arrive depends on the speed of your computer and the speed of your Internet connection. When the file has finished downloading, the Copied dialog box disappears.

Loading the ICQ Software on Your Computer

After you have downloaded the ICQ 2000b software on your computer, follow these steps to install the software:

1. Start Windows Explorer or My Computer and open the folder where you saved the ICQ 2000b installation file. The file is called `icq2000b`.

2. Double-click the `icq2000b` file. You see the Welcome screen.

3. Click the Next button.

4. Read the license agreement and click the Next button. The ICQ files are copied to your computer. Soon a dialog box tells you that the installation is complete and that you need to reboot your computer. *Reboot* means to restart your computer.

5. Click OK in the Installation Complete dialog box.

6. Click OK in the Install dialog box to restart your computer.

When your computer restarts, you see the first ICQ Registration dialog box. Keep reading to find out how to register with ICQ.

Caution

Always close all open programs before you install new software.

To register with ICQ, your computer must be connected to the Internet.

Registering Yourself with ICQ

When you register, you describe yourself and your Internet connection to ICQ. After you register, you get an ICQ number. Other ICQ users will know you by the nickname you choose for yourself and the ICQ number that is assigned to you. All the information you enter will be available to other ICQ users, so be careful what you enter. You can, however, change any piece of information you enter about yourself later on. Only the ICQ number that is assigned to you is permanent and cannot be changed.

After you install ICQ (the previous section in this chapter explains how), follow these steps to register with ICQ:

1. Under Connection Type in the ICQ Registration dialog box, choose which type of Internet connection you have, Modem or Permanent, and then click the New ICQ# Click Here button. Most people have a modem connection to the Internet, but if your computer is connected to the Internet by way of a network or cable modem, choose Permanent.

2. In the ICQ Registration dialog box, as shown in Figure A-2, enter your particulars and a password:

Don't forget your ICQ password. You need it to take advantage of many ICQ features. In fact, you might write it down and store it in a safe place.

▲ **Details:** Enter your first name, last name, and a nickname. Only the nickname is required. You can leave the First Name and Last Name boxes empty.

▲ **E-mail address:** Enter your e-mail address. If you want to keep other ICQ users from knowing your e-mail address, check the Don't Publish My Email Address check box. If you enter an e-mail address, you will always be able to recover a password if you forget it, as ICQ can send it to the address you enter.

▲ **Password:** Enter a password twice, once in the Password box and once in the Confirm Password box. Uncheck the Auto Save Password box if you want to enter your password each time you start ICQ for purposes of privacy.

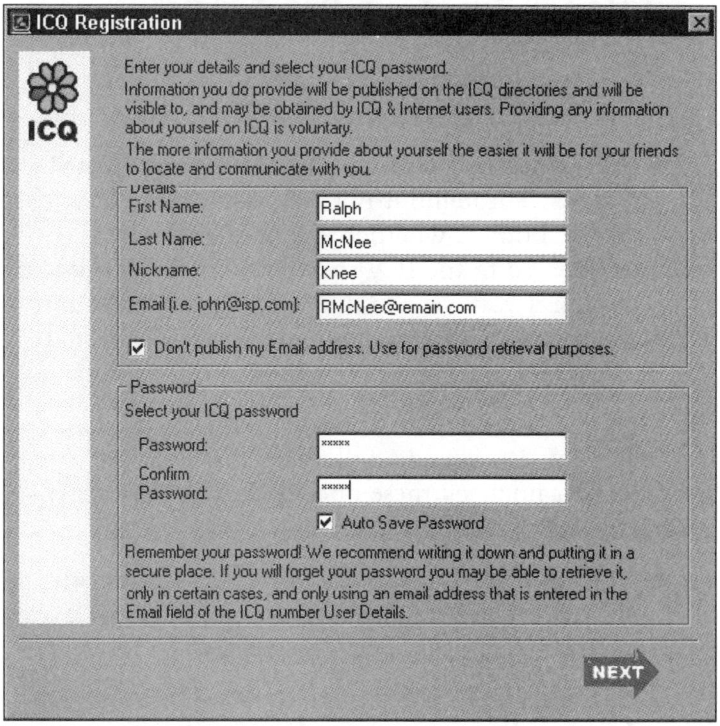

ICQ Registration

Enter your details and select your ICQ password.
Information you do provide will be published on the ICQ directories and will be visible to, and may be obtained by ICQ & Internet users. Providing any information about yourself on ICQ is voluntary.
The more information you provide about yourself the easier it will be for your friends to locate and communicate with you.

Details

First Name: `Ralph`

Last Name: `McNee`

Nickname: `Knee`

Email (i.e. john@isp.com): `RMcNee@remain.com`

☑ Don't publish my Email address. Use for password retrieval purposes.

Password
Select your ICQ password

Password: `xxxxx`

Confirm Password: `xxxxx`

☑ Auto Save Password

Remember your password! We recommend writing it down and putting it in a secure place. If you will forget your password you may be able to retrieve it, only in certain cases, and only using an email address that is entered in the Email field of the ICQ number User Details.

NEXT

Figure A-2. Registering with ICQ.

3. Click the Next button and describe yourself in further detail in the ICQ Reigistration dialog box. All the information you enter here is voluntary. You don't have to enter anything if you don't want to. Furthermore, you can change this information later.

4. Click the Next button. You see the number that ICQ assigns you.

5. Choose among these options under Privacy & Security:

▲ **All Users May Add Me to Their Contact List:** Choose this option to let others put your name on their Contact Lists without getting permission first.

Cross-Reference

Chapter 11 explains how to change the personal information you file with ICQ.

A

Installing and Registering with ICQ

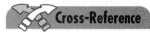

The names of your ICQ
friends go on the Contact
List. See Chapter 10 for a
detailed discussion of
whether to let others put
your name on their lists
automatically.

▲ **My Authorization Is Required Before
Users Add Me to Their Contact List:**
Choose this option to require others to get per-
mission to put your name on their Contact Lists.

▲ **Allow Others to View My Online/Offline
Status:** Throughout ICQ are status indicators
that tell others whether you or anyone else is
connected to the ICQ network. Uncheck this
option if you want to disable the status indicators
so that others can't tell when you are connected
to ICQ. See Chapter 10 for details.

6. Click the Next button. You see the ICQ Services
dialog box. It offers the following "Yes" options.
Check or uncheck these options to take the following actions when you start ICQ:

▲ **Search for My Friends Now:** Search the address books on your computer for people who
are also ICQ users. See Chapter 4.

▲ **Set the ICQ Homepage as My Default
Startup Page:** Go to the ICQ homepage
(www.icq.com) each time you open your
browser and connect to the Internet.

▲ **Make Myself Available for Chat:** Make
yourself available to other ICQ users who are
searching at random for someone to chat with.
See Chapter 6.

▲ **Send It to the E-Mail Address I Provided:**
Tell ICQ to send notices about new features and
services to the e-mail address you entered in
Step 2.

7. Click the Start button to start using ICQ.

Registering More than Once from the Same Computer

Sometimes people who share a computer all want to join ICQ. In that case, each person must register separately. To register another user on a computer on which the ICQ software has already been installed, follow these steps:

1. In Advanced mode, click the My ICQ button.

2. Choose Registration To ICQ⇨Register a New User. You see the ICQ Registration dialog box.

3. Follow the instructions under "Registering Yourself with ICQ" earlier in this chapter.

Cross-Reference

Chapter 2 explains how to switch between Advanced and Simple modes.

Registering Yourself on a Second Computer

Suppose you want to connect to ICQ in your office as well as home. In that case, you need to register yourself on a second computer. To do so, you need your ICQ number and password.

After you have installed ICQ on the second computer, you see the standard installation dialog boxes, including one that asks if you are already a user of ICQ. Choose the option that indicates you are already a user and take it from there.

If you have already registered under one name on your second computer, register again by clicking the My ICQ button and choosing Registration To ICQ⇨Register A New User. Then fill in the standard registration dialog boxes. See "Registering Yourself with ICQ" earlier in this chapter if you need help.

When Two ICQ Users Share a Computer

If you share your computer with another ICQ user, you
need to know how to run ICQ under your name. Follow
these steps to connect to the ICQ network under your
name:

1. Click the My ICQ button.

2. Choose Change User On This Computer⇨Change
   The Active User.

3. Choose your nickname on the submenu.

4. Click Yes in the Confirm Change User dialog box.

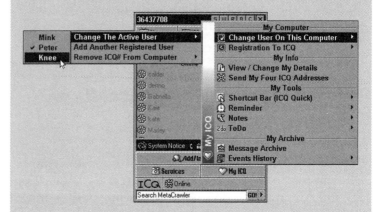

You might consider putting a password on ICQ if you
share your computer with others. That way, someone
with whom you share a computer cannot go on the network under your name. See "Clamping a Password on
ICQ" in Chapter 10 for more information.

Recovering a Lost Password

As long as you entered your e-mail address when you registered with ICQ or entered your e-mail address in the White Pages, you can recover a lost password. To recover it, go to this address in your browser: `www.icq.com/password`. Next, enter your ICQ number in the text box and click the Send button. ICQ will send the password to the e-mail address you entered. It goes without saying, but you can only recover your password if your current e-mail address is the same as the one you entered when you first registered.

Unregistering Your Membership in ICQ

To unregister your membership in ICQ or unregister from a single computer, you need to know your ICQ password. Follow these steps to unregister your membership in ICQ or unregister your membership on a single computer but retain your membership in the ICQ network:

1. In Advanced mode, click the My ICQ button.

2. Either unregister your membership in ICQ or unregister from a single computer:

  ▲ **Unregister your membership:** Choose Registration To ICQ⇨Unregister Existing User. You see the Unregister Existing User dialog box shown in the upper-left corner of Figure A-3. If necessary, choose a name from the ICQ# drop-down list and choose the name of the person you want to unregister. Then enter your password and click the Next button. Select the Yes option button and click Next. Then click Yes in the confirmation box that tells you that your ICQ membership will be permanently deleted.

▲ **Unregister only from the computer you are using:** Choose Change User on This Computer⇨ Remove ICQ# from Computer, and then the name of the person you want to unregister. You see the Remove User dialog box shown in the lower-left corner of Figure A-3. Enter your password and click the Next button. Then select the Yes option button again and click Next. Click Yes in the confirmation box that tells you the ICQ number will be removed from this computer only.

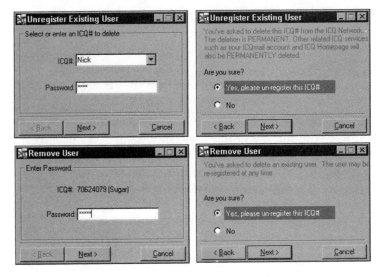

Figure A-3. Unregistering from ICQ altogether (top) and removing a user from a single computer (bottom).

Upgrading to the Newest Version of ICQ

From time to time, visit the Download ICQ Web page at this address: `www.icq.com/download/updates.html`. The Download ICQ page documents upgrades to ICQ. Now and then, ICQ upgrades to a newer version to repair bugs or to offer new features. As shown in Figure A-4, the Download ICQ page tells you when upgrades have been released, the version numbers of upgrades, and the build numbers of upgrades.

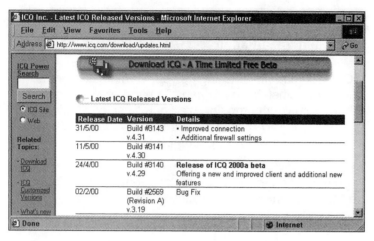

Figure A-4. The Download ICQ Web page tells you about upgrades to the ICQ software.

To find out if you have the most up-to-date version of ICQ, click the ICQ button and choose Help⇨About. The About ICQ dialog box appears. It tells you which version and build of ICQ is installed on your computer. If you don't have the latest version and build of ICQ, download and install the latest version of the program (see "Installing ICQ on Your Computer" earlier in this chapter).

You don't have to uninstall ICQ before you install the newest version of the program. And you don't have to re-register with ICQ, either.

Installing an ICQ Plug-In

Table A-1 lists the different ICQ plug-ins. A *plug-in* is an application that works in cahoots with ICQ to make ICQ more fun or more useful. Before you can use a plug-in, you have to download it from ICQ and install it on your computer.

In most cases, you can install a plug-in simply by trying to activate it. For example, if you click the My ICQ button and choose Message Archive and you haven't downloaded the Message Archive, you see a dialog box for doing so.

A

Installing and Registering with ICQ

Backing Up Your Contact List, Bookmarks, and More

ICQ recommends backing up your Contact List whenever you reinstall the program. To back up items, copy them from your computer to a floppy disk or zip disk. Later, if you have to restore items, copy them from the floppy or zip disk to your computer.

This list shows the default location of the ICQ items that you may need to back up. Restore items to the folders listed here when you are ready to restore items.

▼ Bookmarks: `C:\Program Files\Icq\Bookmark`

▼ Chats: `C:\Program Files\Icq\Chats`

▼ Contact List: `C:\ProgramFiles\Icq\DataFiles`

▼ Files: `C:\ProgramFiles\Icq\Received Files` or `C:\ProgramFiles\Icq\ReceivedFiles\Contact List Name`

▼ Pictures: `C:\Program Files\Icq\Pictures`

Table A-1. ICQ Plug-Ins

Plug-In	*Use*
Greeting Cards	For sending colorful communications to others. See Chapter 3.
Help program	For getting instructions for using ICQ.
ICQmail notification	For being notified when you receive e-mail in your ICQmail account. See Chapter 8.
IrCQ-Net Invitation	For sending invitations to join an IrCQ-Net chat room. See Chapter 5.
ICQphone	For chatting on the telephone with ICQphone. See Chapter 15.
ICQ Surf	For surfing the Internet along with other ICQ users. See Chapter 13.

Plug-In	Use
Message Archive	For storing and organizing chats, instant messages, and other events. See Chapter 12.
Voice-Messages	For sending voice-mail messages. See Chapter 3.

To install a plug-in, you download the plug-in program from ICQ. Then, after the program has been downloaded to your computer, you find the program in My Computer or Windows Explorer and double-click it. The program does the rest. It is installed on your computer so you can use it.

To download a plug-in, go to the ICQ Plug-In Center Web page on the Intenet in one of two ways:

▼ Go to this address in your browser: `www.icq.com/plugins`.

▼ Starting from the ICQ home page (`www.icq.com`), click the ICQ Plug-In Center hyperlink.

At the Plug-In Center Web page, choose the plug-in from the Quick Download drop-down menu. Then follow the directions for downloading and installing the plug-in.

Appendix B

PeopleSpace Directory General Areas and Subcategories

Table B-1 in this appendix lists the PeopleSpace Directory general areas and subcategories. Open your browser to this address to go to the PeopleSpace Directory: www.icq.com/people.

Table B-1. PeopleSpace General Areas and Subcategories

General Area	Subcategories
Age Groups	Age Groups; The College Age; The Rock Age; The Trance Age
Art	Animation; Art General; Artists Talk; Fine Arts; Humanities; Literature and Poetry; Museums; Opera; Other Art Organizations; Performing and Modern Arts; Theatres
Audio, Video, and Sound	Audio; Sound; Video
Away Off the Beaten Track	Away Off the Beaten Track; Unusual, Strange and Out of the Ordinary
Cars and Vehicles	Air Crafts; Cars; Marine Vehicles; Motorcycles; Other Vehicles; Space Vehicles
Computing	Computer Hardware Users; Computer Industry; Computer Related User to User Help and Q n' A; Computer Software Users; Other Computer Issues; Web Masters and Site Owners
Consumer and Shopping	Audio Video and Stereo; Automotive Supplies; Cellular Phones and Services; Computer Hardware; Computer Software; Consumer Electronics; Home Equipment; Other Consumer Subjects
Cultural and Spiritual	Buddhist Groups; Christian Groups; Cultures; Islamic Groups; Jewish Groups; Other Groups
Family	Friends and Family; Genealogy; Parenting; Pets
Games	Board Games; Card Games; Collecting, Trade and Exchange; Computer Games - A to Z; Computer Games - By Company; Console Games, Arcades and Emulations; Hard Core Gamers Section; The Toy Box

continued

Table B-1. PeopleSpace General Areas and Subcategories *continued*

General Area	*Subcategories*
Health and Medicine	Health and Medicine; Nutrition
Internet	Administrators - Newsgroups Networks; Apache Server; BBSs, Newsgroups and Usenet; GNU; IRC; ISP; Internet Organizations; Koko the Singing Gorilla; Linux; SendMail; Site Builders and Web Masters; Web Design and Graphics; Web Related Hardware; Web Related Software; Voice, Video, Data Conferencing and Collaboration
Internet Telephony Voice and Chat	CUseeME; Conferencing; IBM Internet Connection Phone; ICUII; Intel Internet Video Phone; Microsoft NetMeeting; Netscape CoolTalk; Other Voice, Video and Data; VDOLive VDOPhone; VocalTech InterPhone
Lifestyles	Gathering for Events; Leisure; Recreation and Hobbies; Lifestyles
Living Abroad	Countries; Lost Friends and Relatives
Local	By Cities and Towns; By Countries; By Languages; International
Money and Business	Agriculture; Banking; Business - Other; Community and Social Associations; Computers and Technology; Consumer Goods; Corporations A - Z; Creative Professionals; Economists; Engineers; Export, Import; Financial and Investment Services; Food; Government; Home-Based Businesses; Insurance; Labor Unions; Lawyers; Machinery and Equipment; Marketing; Medical Services; Military; Other Business Sectors and Professionals; Other Corporations; Professional Electronics; Public Sectors; Real Estate; Retail; Telecommunication Services and Professionals; Travel and Transportation Services
Movies and TV	Celebrities; Movies; TV Series
Music	60's music; 70's music; 80's music; Alternative Music; Avant-Garde, Underground; Blues and Soul; Boy Bands; Classical Music; Computer Music and Sounds; Country; Easy Listening; Eurovision; Fusion, Progressive Rock; General Music and Sounds; Girl Bands; Heavy Metal; Jazz; Marching Bands; Musicals; Musicians; New Age and Ambient; Radio; Rap, Hip-Hop, Reggae, R'n'B; Rock Pop, Punk; Techno, Breakbeat; Trance, House, Acid, Dance, Dream, Jungle; Trip-Hop, Drum 'n' Bass, Dub; Vocalists; Woodstock; World Music
Our Culture Heroes	Animation Cartoons and Comics Heroes; Fine Arts Heroes; Great Creators; Leaders; More Culture Heroes; Musicians, Actors, and Singers; Mythology; Our Childhood Heroes; Special Occasions and Holiday Heroes

General Area	Subcategories
Romance	Celestial Chat; Just Friends; Looking for Love; Other Chat Issues; Webcam Fun
Science and Technology	Nature and Environment; Science, Technology, and Research Networks; Space and Astronomical Events
Sports	Disabled Sports; Indoor; Other Sports; Outdoor; Professionals; Sports Officials; World Competitions
Students	Colleges and Universities; Education; Fraternities and Sororities; High Schools Alumni; Students by Field of Study
Travel	Commuter Request; Travel Agencies and Organizations; Travel Experiences and Advice; Travel Locations; Travel Mates
Volunteer and Community Services	Clubs; Community Services; Emergency, Rescue, and Law Enforcement; Social Organizations; Volunteer Groups
Women	Lifestyle; Marriage; Parenting Issues; Single Women; Women by Location; Women in Art and Music; Women in Business; Women's Organizations; Women's Rights

Glossary of ICQ Terminology

A

ActiveList
A list of people who share an interest in the same topic. ICQ users create and maintain ActiveLists. Being the member of an ActiveList puts you in touch with people who share your interests.

Address Book
A Message Archive folder where you find information about ICQ members who are on or were on your Contact List.

Advanced mode
One of two modes for operating ICQ. Advanced mode offers more commands and features than Simple mode. See also *Simple mode*.

Alert/Accept modes
Refers to a user's ability to give special consideraton to someone on his or her Contact List. Click a name on your Contact List and choose Alert/Accept Modes to determine how or whether you want to receive events from the person, as well as make other settings.

authorization
Refers to whether other ICQ users need permission to put your name on their Contact Lists.

C

channel
An area of the Internet that offers a unique insight into a certain topic. Click a button on the Channels bar to access a channel.

chat master
The person who creates and maintains a public chat room.

chat room
A Web page or communications channel where visitors can exchange messages with one another in real time. ICQ users can create their own chat rooms.

Communication Center
See *Personal Communication Center*.

Contact List
The list of your friends, family members, and colleagues who are ICQ users. You will find the list in the ICQ window.

D

database (db) converter
Software that updates your ICQ data — your Contact List and stored events — when you upgrade to a newer version of ICQ.

discussion
On the message board, messages that pertain to the same subject.

E

EmailExpress
E-mail that is sent to an ISP account and is then retreived by ICQ.

event
An incoming or outgoing instant message, chat request, or other communication that is sent from one ICQ user to another.

F

firewall
Hardware and software that serves as a gateway between a computer or network and the Internet. The firewall protects the computer from unauthorized access.

flower icon
The icon that appears in the tray when ICQ has been minimized. Double-click the flower icon to see the ICQ window.

G

greeting card
Colorful communications that ICQ users can send. After the greeting card arrives, you click a button in the Incoming dialog box and go to the Web page to view the greeting card.

groups
A means of organizing names on the Contact List in the ICQ window. ICQ offers four groups — General, Family, Friends, and Co-Workers — and you can create your own as well.

I

ICQ E-mail
A feature whereby ICQ users can send e-mail to or receive e-mail from others in the ICQ window. You have to be connected to ICQ to send and receive ICQ E-mail. You see the EmailExpress icon on your Contact List when someone sends you ICQ E-mail. See also *ICQmail*.

ICQ homepage
A Web page that ICQ offers its users for free. An ICQ homepage is hosted by computers at ICQ and is available to surfers at all times.

ICQ iT!
The name of the ICQ search engine at the bottom of the ICQ window. Type a keyword in the text box and click the Go button to search the Internet.

ICQ Surf
A feature for surfing the Internet along with other ICQ users. While you are visiting the same Web page or domain as other ICQ surfers, you can chat with them. ICQ Surf is also a neat way to meet ICQ users whose interests are the same as yours.

ICQ Web Front
A Web site, hosted from your computer, that others can visit while you are online and connected to ICQ. ICQ offers special tools for constructing an ICQ Web Front.

ICQ window

The ICQ "screen" where the Contact List and buttons appear. You can drag the ICQ window wherever you want, or position it on the top, bottom, right side, or left side of the screen.

ICQ.com

The ICQ Web site found at this address: www.icq.com. You can download the ICQ program from ICQ.com. The site is the community center for ICQ users.

ICQmail

A free, Web-based e-mail service that all ICQ users can subscribe to and use. See also *ICQ E-mail*.

ICQphone

A feature whereby ICQ users can have real-time telephone conversations. The conversations are carried over the Internet.

ICQuick shortcut bar

The shortcut bar along the right side of the ICQ window that consists of the ICQuick button and the smaller buttons below it that enables you to access ICQ functions quickly.

Ignore List

The list of ICQ users whose communications you want to ignore. Put someone's name on the Ignore List to keep from being bothered by that person.

interest goup

A list of people who share an interest in the same topic. ICQ users can find and join interest groups in the ICQ network. They can also create interest groups.

Invisible List

The list of ICQ users to whom you appear offline, even when you are connected to ICQ.

IrCQ-Net

A network of chat rooms that users and non-users of ICQ can visit. Chats take place in a special window, not in ICQ dialog boxes.

L

list master

A person who has created and maintains a user list.

M

Message Archive

Folders in ICQ where instant messages, chats, and other events are kept so you can retrieve them later. The Message Archive also includes an Address Book.

message board

Web pages, maintained by ICQ, where you can read and post messages in different categories.

N

NetDetect Agent
A feature whereby the ICQ starts whenever you connect to the Internet.

O

online status
Refers to status command users choose from the Status pop-up menu. Which online status you choose tells others whether you are online and whether you want to receive events.

online status indicator
An icon, found in various places in ICQ, that tells other people whether you are connected to ICQ. You can disable the online status indicator.

Owner Preferences
Refers to the settings in the Owner Preferences For dialog box that determine how you want to run ICQ. Click the ICQ button and choose Preferences to open the dialog box.

P

People Navigator
A means of searching by topic in the PeopleSpace Directory.

PeopleSpace Directory
The directory of general areas, categories, and subcategories by which ICQ organizes user lists, message boards entries, ActiveLists, chat rooms, interest groups, and other items.

Personal Communication Center
A Web page that people can visit to get in touch with an ICQ user. Each ICQ user has a Personal Communication Center page at this address: `wwp.icq.com/Your ICQ number`. Non-ICQ users can visit your Personal Communication Center.

plug-in
An application such as the Greeting Card application that works in cahoots with ICQ to send messages or make chatting possible.

public chat room
See *chat room*.

S

shortcut bar
See *ICQuick shortcut bar*.

Simple mode
The mode designed for new ICQ users that offers fewer options than Advanced mode. See also *Advanced mode*.

smiley
A bundle of punctuation marks or letters that form a picture. Smileys mimic facial expressions.

SMS (short messaging service) messages
Text messages that cellular phone users can send to and receive from one another. ICQ users can also send SMS messages.

status
See *online status*.

Status button
The flower button in the lower-right corner of the ICQ window that you click to display your status.

status indicator
See *online status indicator.*

Status menu
The menu on which you choose an option to declare your online status. See *online status.*

System message
A message from ICQ. You receive a system message when another user adds your name to his or her Contact List.

T

telephony
Refers to applications that you can use to make phone calls with your computer, engage in voice chats, and engage in video conferences.

tray
The area on the Windows taskbar, near the clock. The ICQ flower icon appears in the tray when ICQ is running.

U

User details
Refers to the information you give to ICQ. The information is stored in the White Pages. Click the ICQ button and choose View/Change My Details to enter your User details.

user list
A list of ICQ users who are interested in the same subject. ICQ users maintain user lists. They can submit the names of their user lists to ICQ, and ICQ puts the names in the PeopleSpace Directory.

V

voice-message
A recorded message or sound file sent through the ICQ network.

W

White Pages
The place in ICQ where information about all users is kept. You can search the White Pages and find someone with similar interests or an ICQ user whose name or number you know.

WWPager (WorldWide Pager)
Anyone who visits your Personal Communication Center can contact you by filling in the WWPager form. The message is delivered by ICQ as a WWPager message. See also *Personal Communication Center.*

Glossary of ICQ Terminology

Index

C

Notes

Notes

Notes

Notes

Notes

Notes

Notes